D1715138

ADOLESCENT GROUP PSYCHOTHERAPY

ADOLESCENT GROUP PSYCHOTHERAPY

edited by

FERN J. CRAMER AZIMA, Ph.D.

and

LEWIS H. RICHMOND, M.D.

Monograph 4

AMERICAN GROUP PSYCHOTHERAPY ASSOCIATION

MONOGRAPH SERIES

Series Consulting Editor:

Fern J. Cramer Azima, Ph.D.

INTERNATIONAL UNIVERSITIES PRESS, INC.

Madison Connecticut

Library of Congress Cataloging in Publication Data

Adolescent group psychotherapy / edited by Fern J. Cramer Azima and Lewis H. Richmond.
p. cm.—(Monograph series / American Group Psychotherapy Association ; monograph 4)
Includes bibliographies and indexes.
ISBN 0-8236-0082-3
1. Group psychotherapy for teenagers. I. Azima, Fern J. Cramer. II. Richmond, Lewis H. III. Series: Monograph series (American Group Psychotherapy Association) ; monograph 4.
[DNLM: 1. Psychotherapy, Group—in adolescence. W1 MO559PU monograph 4 / WM 430 A2385]
RJ505.G7A35 1989
616.89'152—dc19
DNLM/DLC
for Library of Congress 89-1972
CIP

Manufactured in the United States of America

Contents

Contributors

Fern J. Cramer Azima, Ph.D., is Associate Professor in the Department of Psychiatry at McGill University, Co-Director of the Therapy Day Centre for Emotionally Disturbed Children, and Director of the Adolescent Group Program of the Child and Adolescent Service of the Allan Memorial Institute, Montreal, Canada. She has served as consulting editor for the American Group Psychotherapy Association Monograph Series. Presently, she is President-Elect of the International Association of Group Psychotherapy.

Irving H. Berkovitz, M.D., is Clinical Professor, University of California at Los Angeles (UCLA), Former Senior Psychiatric Consultant for Schools in the Los Angeles County Department of Mental Health, and serves on the Faculty of the Southern California Psychoanalytic Institute, Beverly Hills, California.

Thomas Edward Bratter, Ph.D., is President and founder of the John Dewey Academy, Great Barrington, Massachusetts. Additionally, he is a well-known consultant to legal authorities pertaining to youth.

Judith Milner Coché, Ph.D., is Clinical Assistant Professor of Psychology in Psychiatry at the University of Pennsylvania, Clinical Assistant Professor of Mental Health Sciences, Hahnemann University, and also has a private practice.

Kathryn R. Dies, Ph.D., is Chairwoman of the Child and Adolescent Group Psychotherapy Subcommittee of the American Group Psychotherapy Association, and is in private practice, Fairfax, Virginia.

Rob Gordon, B.A. (Hons.), is Deputy Chief Psychologist and Coordinator of the Group Therapy Training Program in the

Department of Child and Family Psychiatry, Royal Children's Hospital, Melbourne, Australia.

James H. Fisher, M.Div., is Clinical Director of the Hilltop Preparatory School, Philadelphia, Pennsylvania.

Irvin A. Kraft, M.D., is Clinical Professor of Mental Health, University of Texas School of Public Health; Clinical Professor of Psychiatry, Baylor College of Medicine, and is affiliated with the Texas Children's and Methodist Hospitals in Houston, Texas.

Paul Kymissis, M.D., is Assistant Professor of Clinical Psychiatry Mount Sinai School of Medicine, Chief of the Child and Adolescent Mental Hygiene Clinic, and Director of the Group Therapy Program in the Division of Child and Adolescent Psychiatry, Mount Sinai Services, City Hospital Center, Elmhurst, New York.

Arnold William Rachman, Ph.D., is Senior Supervisor and Training Group Analyst, Postgraduate Center for Mental Health; a founding member and on the Board of Directors of the New York Institute for Psychoanalytic Self Psychology, Associate Professor in the Postdoctoral Program in Child and Adolescent Psychotherapy at Adelphia University, and maintains a private practice, all in New York.

Richard R. Raubolt, Ph.D., is adjunct Assistant Clinical Professor at Michigan State University Department of Psychiatry and is in private practice at the Center for Professional Psychology, Grand Rapids, Michigan.

Lewis H. Richmond, M.D., is Clinical Professor of Psychiatry at the University of Texas Health Science Center at San Antonio and is in private practice in San Antonio, Texas.

Michael D. Stein, Ph.D., is Chief Psychologist Mount Sinai Services at City Hospital Center, Elmhurst, an Assistant Professor of Clinical Psychiatry at Mount Sinai School of Medicine, and in private practice in Hartsdale, New York.

Foreword

This excellent volume is a most welcome, needed, and important addition to the theory and practice of group therapy with adolescents.

Adolescence is a time in our development when we especially value and are shaped by groups. As adolescents we use our peer groups to strengthen our identities and to assist in the difficult task of differentiating from families and forging autonomy. There is probably no time in human development when one uses groups in a more powerful way than during adolescence.

It is natural, therefore, that therapy groups are a powerful treatment modality for assisting adolescents in distress. Mental health professionals have long known that groups offer special treatment advantages with this population. Nonetheless, the available literature about group therapy with adolescents is unfortunately sparse, and this work fills that void. This practical and readable book is a necessary resource for those who work with adolescents in therapy groups. Furthermore, it should be of interest and value to any mental health professionals who work with adolescent patients.

Drs. Azima and Richmond are to be congratulated. They have thoughtfully organized this work into parts on theory, clinical applications in general and for special problems, and clinical research; and they successfully brought together an unusually talented band of contributors to write in each of those areas. This volume is a worthy addition to the excellent Monograph Series of the American Group Psychotherapy Association.

J. Scott Rutan, Ph.D.

Preface

There is little doubt that group psychotherapy is the treatment of choice for most adolescents who are in the process of separation from parents and who rely strongly on influential peers for identification and direction. The peer group is the natural developmental habitat in which the adolescent manifests his struggle for independence, a separate identity, and a transitional model for adulthood. The stimulation, activity, and self-disclosure provided by the group creates the therapeutic climate in which adolescents can come to grips with and work through their problems, angers, and frustrations in an acceptable, meaningful way.

This monograph is an attempt to present adolescent group psychotherapy in a contemporary light by blending traditional approaches with innovative variations in theory, research, and clinical applications. It is presented as a helpful manual for both the beginning therapist and the senior clinician who wishes to verify or modify theory, technique, and clinical research.

The contributors to this volume are a mixture of seasoned veterans and younger therapists, all of whom have worked intensively with adolescent groups. Their writings reflect a practical comprehension of the nature of leadership and the dynamics of the adolescent group. The book is divided into four parts, Theoretical Constructs, General Clinical Applications, Clinical Applications for Special Problems, and Clinical Research. In chapter 1, Fern Cramer Azima opens the section on theoretical constructs with a definition, comparison, and integration of the concepts of confrontation, empathy, and interpretation. This therapeutic triad is examined in the context of the first screening, the therapeutic contract, and alliance with the symptom; technique is demonstrated in two case vignettes.

Arnold Rachman, in chapter 2, offers an updated reformulation of his pioneer writings in the area of identity group psychotherapy with adolescents. By considering both the therapist and the peers, he offers a thorough and cogent discussion of the building of group identity, the techniques of working through identity issues, and, following their resolution, the continuation of the identity search.

In chapter 3, Rob Gordon proposes the use of the concept of symbiosis in the treatment of younger adolescents in group therapy. This author suggests that the symbiotic process provides a sense of predictability, belonging, and nurturing of a sense of identity. Additionally, the interpretive capacity of the therapist assists the younger adolescent in developing self and social awareness and a capacity to articulate needs and feelings.

Beginning the second part on general clinical applications, Irvin Kraft (chapter 4), presents an overview of a variety of traditional and more novel group approaches with the teenage group including activity, drama, and music therapies, the use of television playback, and group activities carried on outside of the actual psychotherapeutic modality.

In chapter 5, Michael Stein and Paul Kymissis review the sparse literature on inpatient group psychotherapy, then corroborate their own observations of the difficulties presented to this age group by the stigma of hospitalization, the involuntary confinement that lowers motivation, and the added stress of encountering new, powerful authority figures. They suggest the best treatment for severely impaired and psychotic inpatients is a combination of traditional psychotherapy, reeducation, and socialization groups.

In chapter 6, Lewis H. Richmond presents a case of a borderline adolescent, seen in long-term group psychotherapy while also involved in individual, parallel, and combined family therapy. Various approaches within peer group psychotherapy, including traditional psychodynamically oriented psychotherapy, role playing, Gestalt techniques, and the use of videotape, are involved. Therapeutically important contacts outside of the actual therapy situation, including those between therapist and family and between patient and peer group members, as well as the presence of peer guests during therapy sessions, illustrate the usefulness of network therapy.

Part III reviews clinical applications for special adolescent populations. Irving Berkovitz reviews the use of group therapy in secondary schools and draws special attention to the need to adapt the group program to the organizational context, mores, and expectations of each setting. He defines systematically the role and integration of the mental health consultant, the supervision of paraprofessionals within the school system, and the referral of significantly ill students to hospital and clinic treatment. This author emphasizes the role of preventive mental health care in the delivery of group therapies within the school system.

Judith Coché and James Fisher (chapter 8) focus on the group treatment of learning disabled adolescents in a residential setting. These authors review both the nature of learning disabilities and various therapeutic approaches. They propose a model of integrating reality therapy, group dynamics, child developmental theory, family systems, and educational therapy. The actual working model is carefully described for those clinicians who may wish to initiate therapeutic programs in this much neglected area.

Richard Raubolt (chapter 9) reviews the extensive literature related to the treatment of adolescents, including the permissive, directive, and psychoanalytic approaches. Recent advances include intensive work with parents, problem-oriented reality therapy, sequential confrontation, and written contracts.

Thomas Bratter, in chapter 10, gives a detailed review of his selected clinical and theoretical approaches that he integrates in the treatment of the addicted adolescent population. He concurs with Rachman and Raubolt that the therapist working with acting out adolescents must be willing to assume the "uncomfortable and awesome role of becoming the parent surrogate." Bratter underlines the curative contribution of the group therapist. With these adolescent populations, delinquency and addiction require toughness, confrontation, and a nonpossessive form of caring. The dual role of the leader as both therapist and prohibitor is fortunately addressed and protected by the rational, restraining force of the group members. Rachman, Raubolt, Bratter, and others propose that the group becomes a caring community that provides the corrective emotional experience. The need for innovativeness of the therapist is addressed by all of the authors of the monograph.

In Part IV, Clinical Research, Fern Cramer Azima and Kathryn Dies report on the limited number of significant research studies in the area of adolescent group psychotherapy. This chapter attempts to review methodologies useful to the clinician and proposes detailed guidelines for initiating research within the group psychotherapy context. The authors suggest that research, if presented properly to the adolescents, is well received and actually promotes the quality of the therapeutic experience, since they are appreciative of the intensity and commitment made by the clinical researcher.

Throughout this monograph, there is the integrated theme of the clinical application of the most appropriate forms of group psychotherapy for adolescents, and the added encouragement for clinicians to carry out research to validate the scientific importance of theory and technique.

As editors of this monograph, we would like to thank our contributors for their valued submissions. Additionally, we would like to acknowledge the support of the American Group Psychotherapy Association in accepting and pursuing the concept of the monograph series.

Fern J. Cramer Azima, Ph.D.
Lewis H. Richmond, M.D.

Part I

Theoretical Constructs

Chapter 1

Confrontation, Empathy, and Interpretation Issues in Adolescent Group Psychotherapy

FERN J. CRAMER AZIMA, PH.D.

INTRODUCTION

There is little doubt that group psychotherapy is considered by most clinicians to be the treatment of choice for adolescents. The psychotherapist working with adolescents must facilitate the formation of a meaningful and trusting relationship and combine this with the task of identifying and undoing long-held deviant emotional disorders. Central to this effort is the correct blend, timing, and sequencing of the therapeutic triad of confrontation, empathy, and interpretation, about which there has been considerable confusion. Outpatient adolescents, 15½ to 18 years of age, male and female, are seen once weekly for one and a half hours, in psychodynamic group therapy, for an average treatment duration of 18 months. The psychopathology of the adolescents ranges from personality disorder, anxiety, and depressive neurotic reactions, to the narcissistic and borderline. At least one-half of the group take various types of drugs and have severe behavior problems, and many are acutely depressed and suicidal. The therapist is faced with a group in transition to adulthood and sexual maturity. In the main, these adolescents are disenchanted with their relationships to their parents and the norms of the larger community. The spectrum ranges from young men and women who are acting out defiantly to those who are withdrawing into alienated depression. The challenge for the psychotherapist is how to respond to each member with the correct blend of confrontation and empathic feelings. For some developmentally arrested and borderline individuals, there must be a long period of nurturing, because too swift a confrontation causes panic and denial, while for others there is a need for limit setting and structure.

An unfortunate dichotomy has developed in the literature, though perhaps less so in clinical practice, between the theories and applications of confrontation and empathy. A clarification of these concepts and that of interpretation will be attempted in this paper, with examples of their use in selection, the therapeutic alliance, and in case vignettes.

It is my basic hypothesis that empathy and confrontation are intimately intertwined, and that they are the basic therapeutic pathways that must be established to provide exposure of problems, their gradual working through, and possible interpretation. The group is the context, par excellence, in which each member is a subsystem accentuating stronger or weaker components of confronting and empathic styles and in which, over time, there is a development of a cohesive matrix of social exchange. Although there are a variety of theoretical constructs available to group psychotherapists, the underlying communication involves emotional and cognitive systems, both verbal and nonverbal. Simplistically put, the group psychotherapist is challenged in terms of how to listen, relate compassionately, self-reflect, and mirror back to the group how he sees, hears, and comprehends the messages he is receiving in order to facilitate the beginning of an interchange. The therapist in the adolescent group is in a pivotal position to reengage the members in an empathic, confronting experience that provides some anchoring and it is hoped a healthier transition to adulthood. It is true that group therapists working with adolescents, as compared to adults, show greater activity, self-disclosure, and spontaneity, and that adolescents appear particularly receptive to empathic confrontations, which have been avoided most of their lives.

CONFRONTATION

The term "confrontation" in most instances conjures up negative, hostile, and often political connotations. It was defined in Webster's *Collegiate* as (1) to face, especially hostilely; (2) to cause to face or meet as to confront with proofs; (3) to set side by side for comparison. Greenson (1965) stated that one of the first steps in analyzing a psychic phenomenon is confrontation, and that the phenomenon in question has to be made evident and explicit to the patient's conscious ego. Cohen (1982) stated that it is the process anterior to interpretation, and that it is the "pivotal situation during the interactive process for without such recognition, treatment cannot progress" (p. 4). This author further elaborates that whenever the therapist intervenes, either by confrontation or interpretation, the patient is affected in some fashion and further that the confrontation is meant to alter and heighten purposefully the awareness of the patient. Since the confrontation is done in the here and now, it diminishes the possibility of denial, and we can add that since the statement is made before the total group, its impact and unavoidability is compounded not only for the member to whom the confrontation is made, but to every other resonating member.

Confrontation should be distinguished from casual observation and necessitates the overt articulation and description of the here and now ongoing events within the memory of the group. A confrontational statement should communicate how the therapist thinks and feels about the information he has accumulated.

It is clear that the therapist's confrontation must be reality based and not stem from a countertransference projection. As a therapeutic tool it is the point of engagement or focus that allows a shared discussion to begin. It is like a knock on a door that needs to be opened. Used negatively, confrontation can unleash irrational anger and lead to unjustified acting out, scapegoating, and defiance (Beck and Peters, 1981; Ormont, 1984). It is the fear of losing control over one's anger and the idealized wish to perform as the perfect therapist that often imposes the use of defenses, as for example, silence. There is little doubt that silence, according to its style of expression, can be interpreted as empathy, angry withholding, or as manipulation to force group members to talk. Silence is no less a confrontation than speech and may be perceived as empathic or as a thunderous rage.

From our perspective, further elucidation of the concept is necessary, including the various levels of confrontation, the subject and the object of the confrontations. Levels of confrontation include (1) the visible and audible verbal and non verbal behavior; (2) the underlying thoughts and feelings, denied expression by the speaker; and (3) the unconscious latent roots of the manifest behavior that are unknown to both the patient and the therapist.

To continue the paradigm, listening members may respond positively or negatively to a confrontation with realistic or transferential projections of their own. It is well known that even an "innocent" remark by the therapist or member may be seen by one member as suspicious and attacking, by a second as playful, and by a third as bland. Therefore, the externalization process by one member may trigger off various chain reactions in the group, which over time may be rendered to further elaboration. In terms of timing a confrontation, the skill of the leader involves being acutely attuned to both the content of the material of the session and the stage of the process. In the beginning stages, the therapist usually is more cautious and explicitly descriptive and over time collects the facts and intervenes when the occasion is "ripe." At times the adolescents in a playful or attacking mood similarly confront the therapist, and try to maneuver him into losing control. Ormont (1984) has written cogently: "to use my anger effectively, I must prepare mindfully. This means, above all, recognizing the anger, possessing it as a valid reaction to what is going on. To pretend to myself that I am not angry would only estrange me from any feelings. . . ." (p. 570). In this regard, I have previously noted (Azima, 1972) that: "therapists who have low frustration tolerance for anger, acting out, anxiety, fear and repressive behavior make poor candidates to work with adolescents" (p. 66).

Little is available in the literature regarding therapists' positive libidinal confrontations, such as praise of members' recall, identification of clues to problems, and ability to share intimate feelings. Recently, an adolescent remarked: "It all began to change when you smiled and said I agree with you, and that was very sensitive of you." These confrontations must not be used for manipulation, to enlist allies, and polarize the group into good and bad members, nor to encourage the therapist to develop a grandiose status for himself. On the other hand, it has been noted that the therapist working with adolescents, recognizing the danger of being perceived as a parent, takes a less scholarly, less controlling position than with adults (Azima, 1973, 1982).

Self-confrontation allows the therapist to deidealize himself, as, for example, by admitting error, or by pointing out that he is not a miracle worker, or admitting (openly or silently) his hopelessness and despair. Those self-disclosures are used at times to make the adolescents recognize the therapist's humanity and to encourage action by the group. On the other hand, the adolescents, although resenting the authority, become confused and frustrated when they realize there is no omnipotent, all-powerful protector who will solve all of their problems. It is only after this initial period that the transference–countertransference clash becomes open, and if not resolved, usually leads to a crisis or fragmentation of the group (Azima, 1972). This stage is similar to that of the collapse of utopian fantasies described by Gibbard and Hartman (1973) in which the ideal, all-perfect mother group gives way to feelings of engulfment, malevolence, and loss of boundaries. This is the critical stage in the development of the group process that allows the group members to "face" (confront) their primitive rage and dissatisfaction and to experience that others do listen with understanding and feeling. In this way, the first wedge is made into the beginning of the working-through process.

The value of the confrontational process allows the therapist and members to focus and delineate the problem, and to seek clarification without undue delay, with the appropriate degree of empathic understanding and acceptance. For adolescents, confrontations are, more often than not, made in a playful, joking fashion. The joke brilliantly illuminates and unmasks the taboo subject of sexuality, ridicule of parental power, and primitive envy. Probably no other age group jokes as much to express their true feelings and to get the message across. Similarly, the therapist working with adolescents must be able to take and make a joke without always interpreting it as resistance. Nicknames within the group and for the therapist often are the confronting communications that mirror how the group members see each other; for example, the wealthy dude, the bully, the know-it-all, the king. The jokester in the group is often used to emote for the group, the most attractive young woman or man are used to evoke libidinal confrontations, while the "bad guy" ridicules and denigrates everybody.

EMPATHY

In 1905 Freud utilized the concept of empathy precisely in his treatise on jokes and the unconscious and remarked that "we take the producing person's psychical state into consideration, put ourselves into it and try to understand it by comparing it with our own. It is these processes of empathy and comparison that result in the economy in expenditure which we discharge by laughing" (p. 186).

Greenson (1967) suggested that the therapist's empathy and intuition may facilitate therapy, whereas sympathy, which contains elements of condolence, agreement, or pity, may impair it. Kohut

(1977) described empathy as vicarious introspection and used it as a cornerstone of his therapeutic self psychology approach. The nurturing, noninterpretative approach was independently heralded by the nondirective Rogerian therapy, and the research of Truax and Carkhuff (1967) identified empathy and unconditional positive regard as the major therapeutic agents. Stone and Whitman (1980) defined intuition as the immediate perception of ideas, and empathy was postulated as a broader process that embraces feelings in addition to thoughts. They also differentiated empathy from identification. The latter is unconscious and relatively ongoing in a relationship (thus an aspect of countertransference), while empathy is conscious or preconscious and is in response to the more immediate interaction.

My working definition of empathy is of a process in which the therapist puts himself into the same experiential mode as the individual evoking the response. Next, he compares these responses with his own thoughts and feelings, and finally he assesses the degree of empathy toward other members in the group. The variation in the degree of empathy within the group allows the therapist to be aware of the feelings and thoughts of any member, the reciprocal responses of others, and his own self-reflection. These constant empathic shifts monitor and broaden the therapist's appreciation, but may also realistically dilute the empathy to any one member. Because of the primitive, directly incorporative nature of empathy, the therapist is put in jeopardy for unconscious countertransference reactions.

There is considerable overlap between the concepts of empathy and confrontation and when examined closely, I regard them as stemming from one common source. Statements such as "I feel for you," "I understand you," may be construed as equally empathic and confrontational. A smile or a frown may both be simultaneously empathic and confrontational. For the sake of distinction, I would limit the definition of empathy by the therapist to when he puts himself into the same experiential mode, demonstrates or mirrors the essence of the patient's feelings and thoughts here and now, with no intentional elaboration to clarify, to understand, or to change the speaker. It is also clear that empathy, although appearing more subtle, is as powerful a therapeutic tool as confrontation. On the other hand, confrontation is a more forceful articulation. This statement differs from casual observation in that it communicates how the therapist is thinking and feeling, based on the information from the present or past memories gathered within the group. The purpose of the empathy is to build caring, trust, and compassion, while confrontation carries these attitudes further and is meant to model how the therapist listens, stores memories, generalizes, and brings to conscious awareness factors that should not be forgotten and need further clarification. This mode of reflection is encouraged for the membership. For adolescents, specifically, the two tiers of empathic and confrontational engagement are used judiciously to cause ruptures in ongoing maladaptive, homeostatic states. The value of this approach is to make a positive, informed action that calls for further working through. In essence, the process of empathic confrontation may prove to be one of the most therapeutic forms of communication.

INTERPRETATION

The act of interpretation occurs at the point in the therapeutic process when there has been sufficient empathic confrontation and clarification to decode and give meaning to the underlying unconscious conflicts that have been repeatedly identified in the ongoing transferences of the individual. The group members respond differentially to emotional and cognitive significances that are projections of their own vulnerability. The task of the therapist is to be an integrator of the empathy and confrontations and to time his interpretations judiciously that they may be "heard" and responded to in the here-and-now context. The art of timing and delivery of the interpretive confrontation still remains a cornerstone of intensive reparative treatment. For adolescents who are in the process of new separations from parents, too scholarly an interpretation is likely to be felt as an accusation and may be denied, while an over close, intrusive, emotional approach may even be more feared.

The therapeutic skill is for the group leader to allow the interpretation to unfold gradually in the working through and for the individual and the group to be in synchrony in reaching these understandings. A brilliant interpretation may be gratifying to the therapist's grandiosity but may distance him from the adolescents. A correct, well-timed interpretation generally should lead to understanding and change.

It is apparent that there has been an increasing focus on noninterpretative techniques that has resulted from the lack of statistical support for interpretation as a leading curative agent (Lieberman, Yalom, and Miles, 1973; Yalom, 1975; and Corder, Whiteside, and

Haizlip, 1981). The nondirective approaches, as well as that of self psychology, demoted interpretation in favor of empathy, caring, and support. Finally, the current stress on short-term therapies has set limited goals, often short of the interpretive stage. Reviewing my own work with adolescents who stay in group therapy on the average of two years, interpretation is still felt to be a powerful therapeutic agent for many youngsters who are searching for understanding and change in their lives. They themselves mock the superficial attitude that "everything will turn out for the better," and want a serious dialogue about the nature of their private and interpersonal worlds. A certain number of teenagers, however, do profit from a supportive, nurturant, accepting environment in which they become more comfortable and, in turn, become less defensive. A frequent remark is: "It's nice to feel nice, but we want some ways to guarantee we understand what happens to us when we are not and how we can independently solve our own problems."

Of paramount importance for the young adolescent is how he learns to conceptualize and problem solve so that he separates from a dependent, angry relationship with authority. Therapists can only encourage him to think, not what to think.

Both therapist and group members may make interpretations. Initially it is the therapist who demonstrates the interpretive style. An interpretation can be made to a specific individual, to the group as a whole, or about the self. There is still considerable controversy as to what approach is more meaningful. In my own work (Azima, 1970), a group-as-a-whole address or interpretation is not made until there is a consensus for the majority of the group. In work with adolescents, it is especially necessary to work on individuation as well as group conformity, and the I and We need to be distinguished for this peer group.

Members may make interpretations about each other and the therapist. With sufficient time spent in the group, they may make a group interpretation and risk an interpretation about themselves. The latter is usually a descriptive generalization (e.g., "all kids feel angry at their parents"). Adolescents, more than adults, often risk hasty interpretations and show less dependence on the group leader. Therapists used to working with older age groups often diminish their interpretive style in adolescent groups. It is an ingenious therapist who can demonstrate how to reason and encourage teenagers to make interpretive comments about themselves, each other, and the group leader.

The therapist, in most cases, must be responsible for handling the more serious deviant personality disorders, including the demanding narcissist and the borderline (Azima, 1983). In my experience, it is the peers, not the therapist, who quickly confront and interpret the behavior of the acting out members, especially once the group has developed some loyalty and cohesion.

Rutan and Stone (1984) draw attention to the recent advances in utilizing interpretation in the framework of self psychology with, for example, narcissistic disorders. They remark that "when interpretations by the therapist are directed to other individuals, or even to the group-as-a-whole, some members feel injured, as if they have received major blows to their self-esteem" (p. 70). The therapist has to decide whether to focus on a specific patient or to give a group-as-a-whole interpretation, and, in a fraction of a second, to evaluate how to formulate the level of the interpretation. This latter decision will likely depend on the maturity of the group process and the personal style of the therapist.

The use and integration of the elements of confrontation, empathy, and interpretation will be illustrated in the areas of (1) initial screening and therapeutic contracting; (2) therapeutic alliance; (3) alliance with the symptom; (4) two case vignettes.

INITIAL SCREENING AND THERAPEUTIC CONTRACT

Adolescents from the ages of 15 to 18 are screened to judge their ability to function in an intensive, psychodynamic group model. The goals of the therapist in this initial meeting are to judge the ego strength, psychological mindedness, motivation, intelligence, empathy, and frustration tolerance of the patient. In this modality, the operating rules of the therapeutic contract are clearly outlined, including the time, place, and exclusion of the parents in the therapy proper. Younger adolescents who come with their parents are seen together for approximately 15 minutes, at which time the style of the group, its rules, and goals are discussed. During the joint session, it is made clear that the adolescent has the responsibility for acceptance or rejection of this approach, and that if there is an emergency and the parents need to call, the adolescent must be informed in advance of the reason for the call. It is explained that to protect and promote confidentiality, trust, and responsibility for both the adolescent and parent, the same rules apply to all members. It is further stated that should the parent call, without their son's or daughter's knowledge, and insist that it is an emergency, the therapist will accept the call with the understanding that at the next session the fact of the phone call will be reported. Parents may be seen at the end of the therapy year only with their teenager's consent and only together with them. The relative exclusion of the parents in this approach fosters confidentiality and sets the goals for independence and responsibility for the adolescent's own personal change.

This therapy approach is not appropriate for inpatient settings where confidentiality must be shared with the team and parents. It is geared to promote individuation and autonomy for adolescents who function poorly in individual and family-oriented approaches. It has been my experience that both the adolescent and the parent are grateful when these rules are clarified and that the goal for change is the adolescent's responsibility.

A brief case history is taken, if it has not already been taken by the clinic, but the patient is told that he must share this material, and in much greater depth, with the group. The nature of the one-way screen setting is described and a consent form must be signed by the adolescent.* They are told that audiovisual techniques are used, that observers are professionals being trained in group psychotherapy, and that from time to time they may be asked to fill out some evaluation forms (in the event that there is ongoing research).

During the interview, the therapist tests out his own rapport with the candidate, and makes a judgment as to whether this person's specific personality structure will blend in with the existing membership. Most adolescents are usually more motivated for group than individual or family therapies and are very pleased with the prospect of working independently. It is also clearly pointed out to the members that many sessions may be anxiety provoking and frustrating as more hidden feelings and thoughts are expressed, but that this is essential for working through their problems with a group of peers who equally will share their experiences.

The style of the selection process models clearly for teenagers the components of confrontation, empathy, and interpretation, and focuses on their need to seek solutions to their problems.

*By Canadian law, parental consent is not necessary over the age of 16, and may differ from American state laws.

The open-ended ongoing group consists of six to eight adolescents of both sexes, aged 15 ½ to 18, with varying diagnoses. At the end of each year decisions are made within the group as to who will continue for the second year and who is ready to leave.

THE THERAPEUTIC WORKING ALLIANCE

Following the notions of Greenson (1965) and Glatzer (1978), I have elaborated this concept of the therapeutic alliance to refer to the construction of a positive, collaborative, realistic endeavor that must be established, both between the patient and the therapist, and between the patients themselves, to genuinely search for solutions to emotional disorders (Azima, 1983, 1986). For adolescents in particular, a genuine, more outgoing working relationship is necessary. The therapist's activity and self-disclosure are increased and include appropriate use of humor and more direct confrontation.

In addition to the establishment of the working norms of time, place, and duration of treatment, I believe it is essential to identify the therapeutic norms of self-reflection, empathic, confrontional, and interpretive styles. In the very earliest stages of the group, I describe the various components and levels of communication, noting those feelings and thoughts that are openly discussed, others that the individual knows of but withholds, and finally deeper, unconscious conflicts hidden by defenses. I use such statements as, "Our therapeutic goal is to say what we feel and think, to gradually admit more of our thoughts, which are currently censored, and to search for clarification of our hidden internal worlds. Working together, we will mutually explore, clarify, and understand the nature of our problems as we search for better solutions."

The definition of the working alliance is essential to impart the true therapeutic nature of the treatment approach. The concepts of confrontation, empathy, interpretation, defense, resistance, and transference become the therapeutic instruments that promote understanding and change in the group.

THE ALLIANCE WITH THE SYMPTOM

My approach is to identify a problem whether it be a symptom, an acting out, or a resistance, to befriend it, to become its ally, and to demonstrate the willingness to accept and contain it, with no immediate goal to change it. The following example will outline the technique. Mary, a 16-year-old, explained many times that she could not stop biting her nails. Many of the group members started to give her suggestions as to how she might stop (i.e., paint them, put a bad-tasting liquid on them, or wear gloves). When it was my turn, I asked to see her hands and, after examining them closely, remarked casually: "You do not bite them down far enough to bleed." General laughter ensued and there was agreement that the nails were not so bad. The strategy here was in the form of a paradox, and also framed so as not to make an accusation prohibiting the nail biting. The surprise of the "reframing" of the therapist's response adds an important confirmation. Similarly, with cases of drug taking, phobia, or psychosomatic symptoms, the therapist does not attempt to disqualify their existence. The strategy is one of empathic acceptance and confrontation that the distorted behavior is only a reflection of a disguised problem. Too fast a superego sanction evokes a rebellious reaction. In the case of drug taking, I have remarked: "I am sure that the pleasure you get from the drugs is better than anything else you have at the moment, and until you have other pleasures and rewards, it is not likely that you will be able to surrender your habit."

The therapist's early alliance with the symptom, acting out, or resistance demonstrates his empathic acceptance of the deviant patterns (at the present time) and enforces that he will not act in a judgmental, parental fashion. In a way, the defense and underlying conflict are confronted in a supportive, tolerant way that does not threaten the individual or the group with the expected ridicule and chastisement. The stage is then set for collaborative interpretative working through, which if successful, leads to the surrender of entrenched defective personality patterns.

CASE ILLUSTRATIONS

The following two cases will illustrate the relative uses of empathy, confrontation, and interpretation.

Case Example 1

Joseph was a very shy, withdrawn 16-year-old, an extremely orthodox Jew who had been diagnosed as a borderline with some evidence of intermittent paranoid reactions. For the first four months of the group, he sat at the extreme outer edge of the half-circle, kept his black coat and hat on, and rocked on his chair, keeping his head bowed, and reading from a small bible. He never talked and looked up only occasionally. The therapist made no attempt to engage him in conversation. Each week he was greeted warmly, with a smile, first by the therapist and then gradually every member. He was accepted as a member of the group and his presence was always acknowledged. I would look at him when he raised his head, and at times, I would openly include him in the survey of the group process. Slowly, he settled into the group and took off his hat and coat, only to reveal his skullcap, and his prayer shawl under his jacket. His rocking diminished and this was noticed by everyone, who now greeted him in a very friendly, kind way. This initial phase stressed a strong empathic approach. Confrontation was rarely articulated until there was sufficient evidence that he was paying attention and that his agitation had decreased.

At the beginning of a session in the fifth month, a young man who had been reading *Playboy* magazine slipped it into his pocket, but not before acknowledging to Joseph that he had noted his keen interest in it. He jokingly said that he believed that Joseph did not only read his bible, and in a sudden confrontation he asked him: "Where do you hide your girly books?" to which Joseph replied with a deeply flushed face, "under my mattress." All of the members of the group recognized that this was the first time Joseph had talked. Peter, who had started the confrontation, continued with great tenderness and said in a serious, nonjoking way: "Joseph, now that you know us so well, and we have told you so much about ourselves, and our secrets, won't you tell us why you have come to group and how we can help you?" Joseph slowly began by stating that he had been picked up by the police. When asked for the reason, he responded in a halting, confused fashion: "Well, every day I walk home from school through the alley . . . (member inquiry) to see a dog who lives in a basement apartment." The group members responded with surprise and started to question more actively. I asked about the dog and whether it was only the dog he wanted to see. He replied that there was a young, pretty girl who played with the dog, and he liked to watch this scene. One of the male members smiled and in a teasing way, said: "Joseph, I am sure you didn't get picked up for looking in the window at the dog, and I bet you were having fun with your hands." The group laughed in an understanding way and Joseph admitted that he was caught for being a Peeping Tom and exhibiting himself.

After this session, the way to more direct confrontation and clarification was opened. Soon he was able to tell the group that his own playmate had been a dog as a child, and that in the last year he would catch a dog, explore its genitals and gradually become both excited and enraged to the point where he would injure the animal. Even with these bizarre disclosures, the group did not recoil or reject him, and with the therapist's help identified an interpretive way to understand the reason for Joseph's emotional problems. The use of interpretation was minimal in this case and the focus was mainly to supply the missing love and attention this patient needed and could only express to animals. Over a two-year period there was a significant decline in the sadistic treatment of animals, his voyeurism was kept to socially accepted areas and was gratified by his looking at the girls in the group. At the close of the second year when the members were shaking my hand, giving me a kiss on the cheek, Joseph blew me a kiss, whispering "you know I can't touch a woman" (acknowledging his religious prohibitions).

Case Example 2

The second case illustrates a more confrontational, interpretive approach. Cicely was a 15-year-old, very pretty, somewhat overweight teenager who came from a broken home and lived with her father and 20-year-old brother. She did not speak to her mother, who routinely attacked her physically when she was upset. When she started in the group, she was somewhat histrionic, talkative, and controlling. She gave the above details with little affect, but while doing so, she began to scratch her left arm, which looked as if she had drawn X's and O's on it. As the scratching continued, I asked her if she had an allergy. She smiled and said: "Yes, to cutting myself up. I wasn't going to tell you, you are smart to have noticed my arm." Very quickly, the extent of her suicidal gestures became known as well as the fact that she was fascinated with watching blood drip. She said she had no pain, and in fact, her major emotion was exhilaration. In this case it was important, I felt, to confront the patient with understanding, but also to convey to her her grave danger. She continued to cut herself for six months and then was able to stop this behavior. She was well able to interpret her rage which could only be vented against herself and her marked depression that she tried to hide. She is presently in her second year of group, has shown no suicidal impulses, passed school with high grades, and did well in a summer job. She is preparing to do a course in forensic psychology. Laughingly, she said: "If anybody can understand delinquents, it's me because to tell you the truth, in thinking about them, I'm thinking about me." This patient is now able to speak to her mother, but is still involved in physical brawls with her brother. Her sexual identity is not clarified and she says she has to be careful not to become a lesbian.

CONCLUSION

This paper has outlined the therapeutic interventions of empathy, confrontation, and interpretation. There is a strong overlap between the concepts of confrontation and empathy, and the likelihood is that both elements must be judiciously blended for an adequate therapeutic intervention. This blend and sequencing appears to depend on the degree of ego strength, the severity of the deprivation, intelligence, and the nature of the disorder. The length of empathic incubation and the decision to confront and interpret will depend on the underlying dynamics of each member. The demanding, narcissistic, histrionic, acting out adolescent, although demanding confrontation, may be better served by empathic interventions, while the fragile, shy, depressed teenager may be better served by more active confrontation than the usual soothing empathic reactions they crave. In essence, the task of the therapist is to make an adequate juxtaposition of empathy and confrontation, followed by interpretation when appropriate. It is the hypothesis of this paper that intensive psychodynamic group psychotherapy is the treatment par excellence for outpatient adolescents who are in the process of individuation and have the potential for self-reflection. The promotion of a working alliance and the cultivation of therapeutic norms offer both the therapist and this age group collaborative, realistic ways of communicating with each other. A knowledge of the specificities of the therapeutic triad of confrontation, empathy, and interpretation can offer clinical tools as well as a nonpartisan common theoretical framework.

REFERENCES

Azima, F.J. Cramer (1970), *A Multi-Levelled Explication of Projective Group Therapy*. Unpublished doctoral dissertation. University of Montreal, Canada.

———(1972), Transference–countertransference issues in group psychotherapy for adolescents. *Internat. J. Child Psychother.*, 4:51–70.

———(1973), Transference–countertransference in adolescent group psychotherapy. In: *Group Therapy for the Adolescent*, eds. N.S. Brandes & M.L. Gardner. New York: Jason Aronson, pp. 101–126.

———(1982), Communication in adolescent group psychotherapy. In: *The Individual and the Group, Boundaries and Interrelations*, Vol. 2, eds. M. Pines & L. Rafelson. New York: Plenum, pp. 133–145.

———(1983), Group psychotherapy with personality disorders. In: *Comprehensive Group Psychotherapy*, 2nd ed., eds. H.I. Kaplan & B.J. Sadock. Baltimore: Williams & Wilkins, pp. 262–269.

———(1986), Countertransference: In and beyond child group psychotherapy. In: *Child Group Psychotherapy: Future Tense*, eds. A. Riester & I. Kraft. Madison, CT: International Universities Press, pp. 139–155.

Beck, A.P., & Peters, L. (1981), The research evidence for distributed leadership in therapy groups. *Internat. J. Group Psychother.*, 31:43–73.

Cohen, A. I. (1982), *Confrontation Analysis: Theory and Practice*. New York: Grune & Stratton.

Corder, B. F., Whiteside, R., & Haizlip, T. (1981), A study of curative factors in group psychotherapy with adolescents. *Internat. J. Group Psychother.*, 31:345–354.

Freud, S. (1905), Jokes and their relation to the unconscious. *Standard Edition*, 8. London: Hogarth Press, 1960.

Gibbard, G.S. & Hartman, J.J. (1973), The oedipal paradigm in group development: A clinical and empirical study. *Small Group Behav.*, 4:305–354.

Glatzer, H. (1978), The working alliance in analytic group psychotherapy, *Internat. J. Group Psychother.*, 28:147–167.

Greenson, R.R. (1965), The working alliance and the transference neurosis. *Psychoanal. Quart.*, 34:155–181.

———(1967), *The Technique and Practice of Psychoanalysis*. New York: International Universities Press.

Kohut, H. (1977), *The Restoration of Self*. New York: International Universities Press.

——— Wolf, E.S. (1978), The disorders of the self and their treatment: An outline. *Internat. J. Psychoanal.*, 59:413–425.

Lieberman, M.A., Yalom, I.D., & Miles M.B (1973), *Encounter Groups: First Facts*. New York: Basic Books.

Ormont, L.R. (1984), The leader's role in dealing with aggression in groups. *Internat. J. Group Psychother.*, 34:553–572.

Rutan, J.S., & Stone, W.N. (1984), *Psychodynamic Group Psychotherapy*. Lexington, MA: Collamore Press.

Stone, W.N., & Whitman, R.N. (1977), Contributions of the psychology of the self to group process and group therapy. *Internat. J. Group Psychother.*, 27:343–359.

———(1980), Observations on empathy in group psychotherapy. In: *Group and Family Therapy*. eds. L.R. Wolberg & N.L Aronson. New York: Brunner/Mazel, pp. 102–117.

Truax, C.B., & Carkhuff, E. (1967), *Toward Effective Counselling and Psychotherapy*. New York: Aldine Publishing.

Yalom, I.D., (1975), *The Theory and Practice of Group Psychotherapy*, 2nd ed. New York: Basic Books.

Chapter 2

*Identity Group Psychotherapy with Adolescents: A Reformulation**

ARNOLD WM. RACHMAN, PH.D., F.A.G.P.A.

In the early 1970s, I first presented a theory of adolescent group psychotherapy (Rachman, 1972b, 1975; Rachman and Heller, 1974). An earlier article had discussed these ideas in embryonic fashion (Rachman, 1969), and this in turn became an expanded version of the case study that illustrated the theory (Rachman, 1975, pp. 30–45). I thought then, as I do now, that the greatest shortcoming in the field of adolescent group psychotherapy is the absence of coherent theoretical frameworks.

Application of the theoretical concepts and clinical techniques first described in identity group psychotherapy have withstood the test of the present decade. Continued application of these ideas and methods by other clinicians have verified their significance, and broadened their application (Rachman and Heller, 1974, 1976; Raubolt, 1982, 1983; Sabusky and Kymissis, 1983).

A meaningful and relevant theory is indispensable to, and cannot be divorced from, meaningful and relevant clinical practice. In fact, without such an underpinning, clinical practice with adolescents can be a haphazard, disorganized, difficult, and confusing enterprise. The practitioner of adolescent psychotherapy has a particular mandate to be organized, consistent, and clear in his method, technique, and mode of therapeutic intervention. Adolescents need direction, organization, consistency, and clarity in their attempts at identity crisis resolution.

*I am very grateful to Monica Moser, Dipl. Psych. BDP, for her time, encouragement, and expertise in preparing this manuscript. In addition, a word of gratitude to Drs. Richard Raubolt and Saul Scheidlinger for their critical reading of the material.

THE ADOLESCENT IDENTITY CRISIS: EGO IDENTITY

The major theoretical construct in this frame of reference is the concept of ego identity described by Erikson (1950, 1959, 1968). Ego identity has three distinct aspects: an intrapsychic or personal identity, interpersonal or group identity, and an ideological or philosophical identity.

Personal Identity

The intrapsychic aspects of ego identity refer to an adequate sense of oneself as a separate, functioning, positive person with a sense of destiny and goal directedness. Colloquially speaking, ego identity is when: You know who you are; where you want to go and how you're going to get there. And, somewhere in the middle of you, you have a good feeling about yourself, and no one can take it away from you.

Identity formation is the process of discovering who one is as a separate, distinct person; to be aware, accept, and value one's distinct assets as well as shortcomings. This identity search can be exemplified in a creative period of self-discovery, as in George Bernard Shaw's withdrawal from society as a young adult (Erikson, 1959), or in a protracted, severe identity crisis exemplified by Martin Luther's agonizing young adulthood (Erikson, 1958). Adolescent therapists are also susceptible to identity crises (Coles, 1970; Rachman, 1977).

Individuals need to have a period of creative retreat in the service of self-exploration. As social structures that reinforce withdrawal and introspection in our culture change, opportunities for "retreats of self-actualization" become scarcer for youth. Psychotherapy can become a significant social structure in which young people can have an opportunity for creative withdrawal in the service of personal identity formation.

Philosophical Identity

Identity formation has the implicit notion of self-actualization, that is, the individual's capacity and motivation for becoming fully what he is as a person. "The end point of this stage is a development of fidelity as a virtue. That is, a developing capacity to be faithful to some ideological view. Without the development of a capacity for fidelity the individual will either have what we call a weak ego, or look for a deviant group to be faithful to" (Erikson, 1968, pp. 133–134).

Without a philosophy of life—a cause for which we exist—to

provide overall meaning to our existence, we feel ourselves to be in an existential vacuum. Identity formation helps define the meaning of one's existence, creating new value and direction.

Fidelity can also refer to valuing oneself, being secure in knowing who one is, and being faithful to this sameness. It is a feeling that one will be the same person tomorrow that one is today, a kind of psychic balance and predictability. This is the stage in human development beyond object constancy. The individual develops a sense of himself as a constant object, allowing himself to be less dependent on another.

A sense of sameness does not refer to a rigid, inflexible, compulsively oriented intrapsychic and interpersonal stance. The sameness is experienced as a good feeling, one knows who one is and what one is becoming.

Adults need to provide adolescents with meaningful, positive ideologies with which to identify. A psychotherapist needs to have a meaningful, positive, consistent, personal, and professional frame of reference with which adolescents can identify. A psychotherapist working with adolescents must stand for something and make his stand known.

Group Identity

The process of identity formation is also an interpersonal one. It occurs not only within the individual but also between the individual and a group: "Identity expresses a mutual relation in that it connotes both a persistent sameness within oneself (self sameness) and a persistent sharing of some kind of essential character with others" (Erikson, 1968, p. 139).

Adolescence is also characterized by the psychosocial mandate to form positive, meaningful peer relationships. An individual's history throughout childhood in peer group experience aids the capacity as an adolescent for group identity resolution. Identity formation is not complete without such an encounter.

At all stages of the life cycle, ego identity "transcends mere 'personal' identity; this is the knowledge of who you are" (Evans, 1969). Peer group affiliation is a psychosocial need of man: "Personality, therefore, can be said to develop according to steps predetermined in the human organism's readiness to be driven toward , to be aware of, and to interact with a widening radius of significant individuals and institutions" (Erikson, 1968, p. 106). Such a view recognizes man's inherent social nature. An individual's growth and development is directly related to the interaction with significant others throughout the life cycle (Mead, 1934). The most pathologic identity problems occur when individuals have been seriously deprived of meaningful human contact; for example, so-called "feral children" reared in isolation without human contact (Bettleheim, 1954; Rachman, 1983a, b; R. Rachman, 1983).

PATHOLOGY OF ADOLESCENCE: IDENTITY CONFUSION

The psychological danger of the adolescent stage of development is identity confusion, the negative stage of the identity crisis:

> You are not sure you are a man or woman, that you will ever grow together again and be attractive, that you will be able to master your drives, that you really know who you are, that you know what you want to be, that you know what you look like to others, and that you will know how to make the right decisions without, once and for all, committing yourself to the wrong friend, sexual partner, leader or career [Erikson, 1959, p. 89].

Identity confusion, although the negative stage of the identity crisis, can be normative. All adolescents pass through a period when feelings of confusion, disorganization, impulsiveness, lack of commitment, and inconsistency predominate their thinking and behaving. Therefore, adolescent confusion is not an affliction or disease, but a "normal phase of increased conflict characterized by a seeming fluctuation in ego strength as well as by a high growth potential" (Erikson, 1968, pp. 163–164).

It must be emphasized, however, that such a normative crisis has the inherent potential for psychopathology as well as for self-actualization. Which direction the adolescent takes depends on his previous personality development (perhaps especially the development of ego strength) as well as his interaction with adults and society.

Besides personal pathology, social conditions can lead to identity confusion, a lack of positive and meaningful adult leadership, absence of meaningful ideologies with which to identify, little or no opportunity for free role experimentation.

It is when identity confusion predominates and continues that psychotherapeutic intervention is crucial.

CONTEMPORARY ADOLESCENT IDENTITY PROBLEMS

The psychosocial context is crucial for ego identity formation. There are many serious social problems in our time that present a negative psychosocial context for identity formation. Several kinds of evidence suggest this trend. A significant number of contemporary adolescents and young adults feel alienated, confused, and disoriented. They do not really know where they are going, what to believe in, or whom to follow. They are suffering from a protracted crisis. Clinicians report a significant increase in the incidence of severe personality disturbance in youth (Masterson, 1968). Substance abuse in youth has reached epidemic proportions (Casriel, 1973). The third highest cause of death in adolescence is now suicide (Giovacchini, 1981; Kolodny, Kolodny, Bratter, and Deep, 1984).

There are several psychosocial forces in our culture that contribute to the protracted identity problems for our contemporary youth. Our contemporary technocratic society has so interfered with family relations that it has encouraged father-absent families. Both business and government have encouraged heads of households to be physically absent from their families over long periods of time in order to fulfill their job requirements. Such families develop a father-absent frame of reference, where emotional adaptations are made to father-absence. The children of such families often develop identity confusion symptoms: a sense of alienation, feelings of uprootedness, and a lack of direction (Kelman, 1960; Lesse, 1969). Perhaps this is an explanation for the attraction of adolescents to cults. They are attracted to an alternate family with a strong father, e.g., the "Moonies."

Family instability is clear from the high divorce rate (about 50 percent nationally, with some counties in California reaching 70 percent). Extended family ties have also been eroded by geographic mobility of grandparents, as well as children, large-scale unemployment among those formerly employed in the steel and related industries, life-styles, demands by business and the military to relocate, and the need to move to different parts of the country in search of work (e.g., population movement from the Northeast and the Midwest to the Southwest). Grandparents are not as available to provide continuity, wisdom, emotional support, and actual help as they were a generation ago.

Parents and grandparents are also having difficulty setting limits on adolescent behavior and providing strong role models. This has become "the age of indulgence." Parents need to practice "benign deprivation." They should allow their children to struggle toward goals, and be responsible for a reciprocal relationship with their parents rather than being indulged by them.

Ongoing problems of an economic, racial, and political nature have encouraged the development of inadequately socialized children. Children in urban ghettos have grown up without positive parental contact or family life. Unsocialized street children inhabit our cities and behave in an antisocial, dehumanized, "feral-like" fashion (Rachman, 1983a,b; R. Rachman, 1983).

Substance abuse has reached epidemic proportions among our youth. Adolescents and young adults have turned to drugs to medicate themselves from the pain of family and personal disturbance. Drug abuse among ghetto youth has demonstrated that an artificial, euphoric, semiconscious fantasy state is preferable to the dehumanizing reality of the ghetto. Middle-class youngsters also share a similarly negative view of their families and their environment, even though they have every material comfort.

We are beginning to confront the psychological effects of the Holocaust on Jewish survivors and their children. These kind of parental traumas have created identity difficulties for children of survivors (Prince, 1985a,b).

The above-mentioned symptoms of the identity crisis of the family and the negative psychosocial forces in our culture, have encouraged identity confusion, emotional disturbance, and acting out behavior in contemporary adolescents. Our mandate is to explore group psychotherapy as a therapeutic intervention, which both attract adolescent participation and relate to their need for identity crisis resolution.

GROUP MILIEU AND EGO IDENTITY

The most basic implication of the concept of ego identity for group psychotherapy with adolescents is that adolescents must develop peer group affiliation to gain a sense of ego identity. As a defense against identity confusion, adolescents are emotionally drawn toward peer group membership. Group membership, then, represents a "life-saving device," or the necessary and sufficient conditions for identity formation in adolescence. Adolescents can enhance their self-esteem only by their own action in the culture of a peer group that is positive, meaningful, and continuous. The psychological context for identity formation acknowledges the social imperative of man.

Ego identity is an integration of intrapsychic and interpersonal functioning. The person and the group are interwoven in a social, cultural, and historical matrix. The relationship is mutual and reciprocal. An individual gives meaning, significance, direction, and support to a group. The group serves similar functions for the individual. We are then led to reorient our thinking regarding anxiety in the interaction between personal and group identity. We can conclude there is no individual anxiety (intrapsychic anxiety) which does not reflect a latent concern common to an immediate and extended group. Individual anxiety (e.g., neurosis) is of concern and affects others in a given social group. Group therapy and family therapy acknowledges this concept as an essential ingredient for the diagnosis of pathologic interaction.

The concept of ego identity offers one of the most meaningful and basic rationales for including an individual in a group therapy experience. A primary contribution of group psychotherapy is to foster separateness and independence from infantile dependence on parental figures, while fostering relatedness to peers (Wolf and Schwartz, 1962).

The development of group identity moves the adolescent toward adulthood with the capacity to hear and respond to the *voice of the group* and away from the neurotic bind of hearing only the *voice of the parent.* Many clinicians are faced with adults who are only cordial to the voice of a parent, usually the mother. The adult so neurotically bound is not free to hear and respond to a peer, because he searches for the surrogate parent to finally fulfill unresolved infantile needs.

Adolescents need to confront a meaningful authority figure in a therapeutic or corrective emotional climate to provide the bridge for separation from infantile ties with parents while moving toward peer relationships. They gain a greater sense of independence, a feeling of ego strength, and a sense of mastery by such a meaningful confrontation. A therapy group of peers provides that adolescent with the necessary emotional support and courage to confront an adult authority figure. There is greater risk of losing the favor of the parental figure in individual therapy: "The therapist will not like me if I tell him off; I have to be a good guy with him." A fellow group member, confronting the therapist, can introduce a new way of being. Initially, the adolescent merely observes, risking nothing. Gradually, silent confrontation develops. With the encouragement of the therapist and the group, the adolescent risks a direct confrontation opening up a new way of being in the group.

In an adolescent group therapy setting, authority is vested in the group that can explore, interpret, and develop insight into a member's identity problem. An adolescent does not have to listen only to the voice of the adult authority, the therapist; he can listen and respond to the voice of the group.

The group can become the surrogate family, providing a corrective emotional experience that can lead to new meaning and new ways of being for the adolescent. Children and adolescents can cope with their negative experiences within their original family milieu by creating in fantasy imaginary siblings and parents (Rapaport, 1941; Burlingham, 1954; Bender and Vogel, 1954; Rachman,1967; Epstein, 1967).

In group therapy setting, adolescents can perceive and support each other in their common struggle to discover who they are as individuals and to whom they belong. They can perceive the same ego struggle within each other, feeling more aware and comfortable with their own struggle. By identification with the significant others of a therapeutic peer group, the prototypical defensiveness and psychological myopia ascribed to adolescents can be converted into psychological awareness and insight.

THE STRUCTURE AND PROCESS OF AN ADOLESCENT PSYCHOTHERAPY GROUP

There is a technology that aids identity crisis resolution, namely, blend of active psychodynamic and humanistic psychotherapies. The humanistic dimensions particularly relate to the establishment and maintenance of a positive, real relationship in the here and now of the therapy experience. The active dimensions allow a more immediate and intense stimulation of the uncovering process as well as a translation of insight into action within the context of the therapy experience.

The structures established to aid an adolescent psychotherapy group develop the necessary emotional and psychosocial climate follow the process of identity crisis resolution (Rachman, 1975).

This process in an adolescent group is conceptualized to occur in five phases: (1) establishment of a group identity, (2) the identity search, (3) working on and through identity issues, (4) resolution of identity conflicts, and (5) leaving group to continue the identity search.

The basic aim in the technique of group psychotherapy with adolescents is to establish and maintain structures and functions within the group process that foster identity crisis resolution.

The present orientation for the clinical practice of group psychotherapy with adolescents incorporates contemporary developments in active techniques within a humanistic psychoanalytic frame of reference (Rachman, 1969, 1971, 1972b, 1974, 1975; Rachman and Heller, 1974). Active techniques provide the opportunity to foster the crucial activities of free role experimentation, psychosocial play, and free elaboration of fantasy and dream material, which are necessary for the *identity search*.

The identity search aimed toward resolving the identity crisis occurs in the following process.

1. The group therapist brings the identity crisis into the group's conscious awareness. The three spheres of identity formation are considered for ego examination by asking the four basic identity questions: Who am I? With whom do I identify? What do I believe in? Where am I going?
2. Individual identity problems are identified by focusing on identity conflict areas particular to group members. They are asked to describe their identity conflicts and feelings. Feelings are sorted out. By sorting and identifying feelings as one's own, one deals with identity confusion and disorganization.
3. The group therapist provides the encouragement and impetus for the identity search. Through free role experimentation, psychosocial play, exploration of fantasies, dreams, early recollections, transference reactions, and group interaction, adolescents are encouraged to experiment with a variety of different roles to become aware of alternate ways of being in the world, and to become cordial to the alienated portions of their identity.
4. The therapist encourages group members to make decisions,

develop choices, and take a stand in their developing identity. He helps them to translate their identity stance into overt behavior, functioning both within and outside the group.

5. The role of activity and action takes on special significance in adolescent groups that focus on identity crisis resolution.

There are three basic ingredients of identity crisis resolution that need to be blended into a whole. These are the individual adolescent, the group experience, and the interaction of the group leader. In previous discussions I have focused on the experience of the adolescent, as well as the contribution of the group experience (Rachman, 1972b, 1974, 1975; Rachman and Raubolt, 1984b). We will now turn our attention to the specific contribution the leader makes in this process:

THE ROLE OF THE LEADER IN ADOLESCENT GROUPS

Adolescents need compassionate, demonstrative, and active involvement by the therapist. Naturally, nondirectiveness, "strict objectivity," or the role of the expert observer are rigidly defined therapeutic roles that encourage emotional distance, negative transference, and a pseudotherapeutic relationship.

The group therapist's capacity to enter into an active humanistic relationship with adolescents enhances the therapeutic exploration of identity conflicts. Adolescents will not unfold themselves to a passive, indirect, neutral, or inhibited authority figure. Also they do not want to be in the presence of an "expert" who is treating them as if they were clinical cases.

Five parameters within the active dimension help identity conflict exploration and resolution: (1) the adolescent alliance, (2) the empathic dialogue, (3) active analysis, (4) compassionate confrontation, (5) judicious self-disclosure. Employment of these parameters is also an attempt to intensify the group process by responding to an adolescent's natural psychosocial need for active involvement. The leader's capacity to develop and employ these parameters enhances the ability to successfully treat the identity issues of youth.

The Adolescent Alliance

Adolescents need to experience a special kind of relationship with an adult authority figure. They need to develop the feeling that the adult has an especially positive bond with them. Adolescents want and need to experience directly the leader's concern, interest, liking for, and dedication to youth. Ideally, they want to be considered a favorite group of people. This should be conveyed openly and directly, but not for manipulative purposes. Leaders of adolescent groups must be especially wary of brainwashing or using their charismatic personal qualities to influence an adolescent group seriously so that the members' sense of ego identity is compromised. Because adolescents need adults to lead them and to identify with, it becomes a special "identity trust." The psychotherapist employs his natural liking, concern, and dedication to help an adolescent crystallize his own identity needs, *but not the needs of the leader.*

The alliance or special bond is related to the issue of confidentiality. Confidentiality favors the adolescent. Any information the adolescent reveals will not be conveyed to the parents. This "golden rule" can be broken when the adolescent wishes material to be revealed or when the therapist feels there is a self-destructive emergency developing. Conversely, everything the parents tell the group leader will be conveyed to the adolescent (with the exception of parental confidences that could disturb the alliance).

Advocacy on behalf of the adolescent members also establishes and maintains the alliance. There are many instances in dealing with teachers, parents, courts, institutions, and the adult world where adolescents need both support, advice, and direct intervention by the group leaders to negotiate through the system. The range of advocacy behavior can vary from letter writing to accompanying a teenager to court. For a fuller discussion of this active technique see Bratter (1972, 1973). In all instances the psychotherapist's interventions are predicated on an adolescent's need for extraordinary help in resolving an issue, and not on the therapist's need for manipulation, control, power, dominance, love, or adulation.

The Empathic Dialogue

This refers to the ongoing struggle of the group psychotherapist to understand the adolescent's thinking, feeling, and behavior from the internal frame of reference of the adolescent. It is an ongoing hovering attention to the perceived felt state of the adolescent. We attempt to enter the adolescent's inner world, as an "empathic visitor," to linger long enough to begin to see, feel, and think as they do.

Active Analysis

The integration of activity as viewed in traditional therapy and contemporary action techniques within a psychodynamic framework allows for an active analysis (Rachman, 1979, 1980, 1981, 1988; Rachman and Raubolt, 1984b; Papiasvili, Rachman, and Papiasvili, 1982). An adolescent group is a natural psychosocial environment for an active approach. (1) The adolescent ego is in an evolutionary stage and maintains a capacity for dramatic shifts in functioning. (2) Id impulsivity is close to the intrapsychic surface; intense and primal feelings are available for expression. (3) Physical growth spurts, increased metabolism, and chemical changes produce a need for physical activity. (4) Three issues in identity formation, for example, a psychosocial moratorium, psychosocial play, and free role experimentation, encourage "an ethos of action."

Psychosocial Play. In adolescent therapy there is a general issue of concern regarding the tendency for acting out behavior. Their constant activity, "provocative playfulness," impulsivity, experimentation in the areas of sexuality, aggression, and antisocial behavior, and their tolerance for the bizarre, unusual, and peculiar actions of others encourages a general taboo against action. There are several basic problems inherent in this potentially "repressive stance" for an adolescent group. The group therapist interprets the action as a hostile acting out in the transference; the action is a negative activity by the group against the therapist. It is assumed that the action is detrimental to the mental health and emotional growth of the patient. An assumption is also made that verbal interaction is either the primary or most meaningful mode of therapeutic activity. This "repressive" orientation is being characterized as inappropriate with adolescent groups, and is, in itself, a countertransference reaction. What is more, it belies a lack of understanding of adolescent psychology and of the identity search. The potential countertransference problem facing the group therapist in this instance would be the desire to take a repressive stance toward an adolescent group's need to be active and experiment with a variety of roles or ways of being in the world in order to have opportunities for the identity search.

As has been mentioned, adolescents need a "psychosocial moratorium," a temporary delay in assuming adult commitments. This moratorium should be a period characterized by a "selective permissiveness" on the part of the leader, and of "provocative playfulness" on the part of youth. If the group climate provides such periods of psychosocial moratoria, adolescents will have the appropriate context for ego identity formation. They need opportunities, "to try on for size" various roles, feelings, actions, and philosophies, in order to find their own identity, role, and meaning in life. The concept of "psychosocial play" should replace the concept of acting out.

Group therapists need to provide the appropriate psychosocial context for ego identity formation in adolescents. The adolescents in a therapy group should be given encouragement, support, and opportunities for psychosocial play and free role experimentation. Within the therapy group adolescents are encouraged to experiment with a variety of roles through the use of active techniques that enhance the identity search (Rachman, 1971, 1972b). In addition, there are structures within the group process that the group therapist can institute to aid in a therapeutic expression and management of action and physical interaction (Rachman, 1972b).

Fostering Free Role Experimentation. In order to aid the adolescent ego in synthesizing the collective elements in a sense of ego identity, judicious opportunities to experience, experiment, and reject alternatives in thinking, feeling, and behavior are necessary.

> But it is important to emphasize that the diffused and vulnerable, aloof and uncommitted, yet demanding and opinionated personality of the not-too-neurotic adolescent contains many necessary elements of a semi-deliberate role experimentation of the "I dare you" and "I dare myself" variety [Erikson, 1964, p. 102].

As has been discussed, role confusion limits the individual's psychological freedom, sense of choice, and ability to contemplate alternative modes of functioning. What is more, role confusion can drive an adolescent to decide on a fixed role identity. Premature, limited, narrow, or neurotic adaptations occur in order to relieve the intense anxiety of role confusion. Such negative choices retard the development of ego identity. Free role experimentation provides the necessary psychosocial experience to prevent premature or fixed role identity.

Free role experimentation is also used as a designation for a process occurring throughout the course of adolescent group psychotherapy. The process is akin to the working through process described in adult psychotherapy. First, the stage is set for an attitude change and a new cordiality to freedom in functioning. Freedom to experiment becomes an acceptable and desired therapeutic event, a group credo. Such freedom allows an awareness of alternatives to neurotic or role fixated behavior.

After the process of group identity has been firmly established, the process of free role experimentation pervades the general functioning of an adolescent group. Group behavior is characterized by a flexibility, a looseness, "comfortable uncertainty," and an air of excitement and anticipation regarding role experimentation.

A moratorium is placed on choice of permanent roles or adaptations. The focus is rather on becoming aware of alternative ways of being in the world through the temporary experience of being that new or different way. The savoring of the new self-definition, where the change is allowed to permeate the individual's thinking, feeling, and behaving is a significant aspect of the experience. Premature decisions, judgments, and adaptations preclude this process of assimilation.

The basic technology of free role experimentation involves: (1) creative introspection and free thought, (2) verbal and fantasy experimentation, and (3) active techniques.

Creative Introspection and Free Thought

Adolescents are encouraged to disclose their innermost thoughts to their peers. They are shown how sharing the burden of the identity crisis allows for psychological relief and creates a positive excitement of mutual discovery. "Thinking out loud" replaces self-absorption and withdrawal from others.

Verbal and Fantasy Experimentation

Free role experimentation is aided by the personal freedom to contemplate, explore, and own any thought or feeling regardless of the social taboos associated with it, so that "Nothing human is alien to me."

Active Interventions

Active techniques explored within a psychodynamic framework provide the potential for heightening emotional interaction between therapist and patient, and patient and patient. The adolescent group can be more attentive and emotionally related in active situations. Rather than attending to a group member "talking about" a feeling, they can experience and share the feeling. Experiencing and sharing feelings has the potentiality for increased group interaction and dynamic exploration of feelings, thoughts, and behaviors.

The judicious employment of action techniques such as role playing, encounter experiences, psychodrama, active dream interpretation, direct interpretations, confrontation, judicious self-disclosure, and specially devised scenarios is used to aid adolescent group members in their struggle for self-determination (Rachman, 1971, 1972b, 1975; Rachman and Raubolt, 1984b).

The Compassionate Confrontation

A basic humanistic consideration that underlies the employment of confrontation is the preference to challenge certain resistances directly rather than to remain neutral, detached, clinical, or wait for the unfolding process. The analogy that best fits this situation is the role or responsibility of "good parenting." A responsible parent judiciously intervenes in a child's life in order to encourage the growth process and curtail any obstacles to ongoing development. Such intervention can take the form of encouraging abstinence, setting limits, prohibiting behavior, or forcing a confrontation. If one does not intervene, sometimes dramatically at crucial moments in a child's life, it can be viewed as neglect. A concerned group psychotherapist takes a stand, risks a negative reaction and some possible temporary erosion of the relationship in order to persuade, exhort, pressure, demand, and even plead with the youth to face the conflict anxiety or crisis. In essence, the therapist asks the youth to change.

Confrontation with adolescents mandates that the psychotherapist use this technique in a compassionate, empathic, caring manner. In the present orientation, compassionate confrontation is seen as a special form of empathy. For example, in the instance of severe substance abuse, confrontation is used as the leader's expression of concern for their welfare and survival to force the member or group to face their self-destructive behavior (Rachman and Heller, 1974; Rachman, 1975, 1976; Rachman and Heller, 1976; Rachman and Raubolt, 1984a).

In instances where confrontation takes the form of "attack therapy," the leader is using the group to vent anger, hostility, frustration, or act out some unresolved conflict with a member or the group. Such behavior is antitherapeutic and a countertransference reaction. It needs to be examined rather than continued.

Judicious Self-Disclosure

Adolescents need and want to be in significant emotional contact with significant others who are open, authentic, and direct. Identity concerns mean they need adults who stand for something, who communicate a sense of values, philosophy, and a belief system. By "bouncing themselves off" adults, adolescents struggle to define their own emerging values, beliefs, and philosophies. Personally, revealing who the leader is and had been in the past allows adolescents to accomplish this necessary ego development. Among some of the judicious considerations in such disclosure are these.

1. Sharing for the purpose of enhancing the group's functioning.
2. Sharing should come from an area of personal functioning where the therapist has worked through or is in the process of successfully resolving an issue.
3. Sharing can be offered voluntarily or in response to a request. Requests for self-disclosure are not seen as inherent resistance, but as a dimension of the identity search.
4. The therapist can set limits on the amount, content, and frequency of self-disclosure, so as to protect a sense of privacy.
5. Self-disclosure is limited to appropriate material, that is, issues, conflicts, feelings that are part of the expressed interest of the group (not a preoccupation of the therapist).
6. It is not necessary to reveal all the minute details, or "all the gory details" in an area of functioning.

THE IDENTITY OF THE ADOLESCENT GROUP PSYCHOTHERAPIST

Identity group psychotherapy also focuses on the concept of ego identity in regard to the functioning of the group therapist. In order to aid in an adolescent's ego identity formation, the group therapist needs to emphasize several aspects of his functioning: (1) the identity search of the therapist; (2) identity role modeling; (3) identity countertransference; and (4) self-actualization of the therapist.

The adolescent group therapist needs to establish his own identity search in the areas of personality functioning relevant to an emotional encounter with adolescents. The analysis of unresolved identity conflicts in the areas of authority, dependency, aggression, sexuality, and affection becomes part of the therapeutic work. The therapist's ongoing identity search will encourage empathy and enhance his capacity to offer himself as an "ego identity role model" to the adolescent group.

Identity group psychotherapy relies heavily on the capacity of the group therapist to offer himself as a role model. Identity role modeling is the adolescent's temporary borrowing of a portion of the therapist's ego to aid in the identity search. By emulating and patterning themselves after significant adults in their life, they hope to gain a sense of ego mastery and organization and temporary relief from identity confusion. Drug rehabilitation programs have intuitively sensed the dynamic significance of identity role modeling, and rely on it to help adolescent drug abusers (Rachman and Heller, 1974).

The components of identity role modeling are

1. The therapist is an adult authority with a positive sense of himself and the direction in which he is going. He is someone who is working on his own identity.
2. The therapist is caring, warm, understanding, and compassionate, yet firm, assertive, and direct in his interaction with the group. The leader can be both "tough and tender" with the group.
3. The therapist is willing to risk himself in the relationship and to share his own feelings, thoughts, and behaviors. He develops a humanistic, person-to-person relationship. Yet the therapist is always an authority in the group.
4. The therapist takes definite stands in the relationship, expressing and sharing his values, ideas, and beliefs in a compassionate, nonauthoritarian, humanistic fashion. He offers these as hypotheses for the group to accept or reject; he allows them the psychological room to breathe.
5. The therapist encourages the adolescent to have a meaningful dialogue with him and the group members, emphasizing empathic understanding and creating meaning, rather than judging or prohibiting feelings, thoughts, or behavior. The group ethos is that since we are all brothers in the human

community, there are no alien feelings, thoughts, or behaviors.

Identity countertransference is the crucial sphere which helps the group therapist to become aware of, own, and resolve his identity conflicts. Adolescent groups stimulate the greatest variety and intensity of countertransference reactions in the therapist (Rachman, 1972a, 1977). An ongoing program of analyzing the group therapist's countertransference, therefore, contributes toward the necessary and sufficient conditions for adolescent group psychotherapy. The program contributes the following ingredients to the success of the therapy:

1. It enhances the therapist as an ego identity model.
2. It provides the group with a heightened sense of emotional encounter with the group therapist and with each other.
3. It allows the group therapist to develop a humanistic rather than a defensive stance.
4. It enhances the group therapist's sense of "being alive" in the relationship; provides new vistas for emotional experiencing and understanding.
5. It provides the therapist with opportunities for self-actualization and ensures a sense of flexibility in personality functioning.
6. It reduces the therapist's need for acting out identity conflicts with the group.

Adolescent group psychotherapy provides inherent opportunities for personal growth and personality changes for the therapist if there is a direct encounter with identity conflicts stimulated by group interactions. The act of giving or sharing oneself with a group is a significant opportunity to understand oneself more fully. The therapist can analyze what he has given to others (or has not been capable of giving).

Since adolescent groups stimulate intense feelings in a therapist, that is expose "weak points," it demands a willingness to sustain a certain amount of personal vulnerability, to have "personal wounds" opened up from time to time. If a group therapist is not open to experiencing and dealing with intense feelings, one could expect limited success with adolescent groups. If, however, one is open to an ongoing program of becoming aware, experiencing, and analyzing identity conflicts, eventually "the sweat" is taken out of working with adolescent groups. Then, working with adolescents in groups becomes a joyful, exhilarating, and lusty experience.

REFERENCES

Bender, L., & Vogel, F. (1954), Imaginary companions of children. *Amer. J. Orthopsychiat.,* 11:56–66.

Bettleheim, B. (1954), Feral children and autistic children. *Amer. J. Soc.,* 64: 455–467.

Bratter, T.E. (1972), Group therapy with affluent, alienated adolescent drug abusers: A reality therapy and confrontation approach. *Psychother.: Theor., Res. & Pract.,* 9:308–313.

——— (1973), Treating alienated unmotivated, drug abusing adolescents. *Amer. J. Psychother.,* 27:589–596.

Burlingham, D.T. (1945), The fantasy of having a twin. *The Psychoanalytic Study of the Child,* 1:205–210. New York: International Universities Press.

Casriel, D. (1973), The acting out neurosis of our times. In: *The Neurosis of Our Times: Acting Out,* eds. D. S. Millman & G. Goldman. Springfield, IL: Charles C Thomas.

Coles, R. (1970), *Erik H. Erikson: The Growth of His Work.* Boston: Little, Brown.

Epstein, N. (1967), A comparison in observation and techniques in group therapy with male adolescent character disorders from varying socioeconomic backgrounds. Paper presented at the American Group Psychotherapy Association Conference. Chicago, IL.

Erikson, E.H. (1950), *Childhood and Society.* New York: W. W. Norton.

——— (1958), *Young Man Luther: A Study in Psychoanalysis and History.* New York: W. W. Norton.

——— (1959), Identity and the Life Cycle. *Psychological Issues,* 1/1. New York: International Universities Press.

——— (1964), *Insight and Responsibility.* New York: W. W. Norton.

——— (1968), *Identity: Youth and Crisis.* New York: W. W. Norton.

Evans, R.I. (1969), *Dialogue with Erik Erikson.* New York: Dutton.

Giovacchini, P. (1981), *The Urge to Die—Why Young People Commit Suicide.* New York: Macmillan.

Kelman, N. (1960), Social and psychoanalytic reflections on the father. *Amer. Scholar.,* 29:335–358.

Lesse, S. (1969), Obsolescence in psychotherapy. A psychological view. *Amer. J. Psychother.,* 13:381–398.

Kolodny, R.C., Kolodny, N.J., Bratter, T., & Deep, C. (1984), *How to Survive Your Adolescent's Adolescence.* Boston: Little Brown.

Masterson. J.F. (1968), The psychiatric significance of adolescent turmoil. *Amer. J. Psychiat.,* 124:1549–1554.

Mead, G.H. (1934), *Mind, Self and Society,* ed. C. W. Morris. Chicago: University of Chicago Press.

Papiasvili, Eva, Rachman, A.W., & Papiasvili, A. (1982), Action techniques in residential therapeutic communities for neurotics. *Internat. J. Therapeut. Commun.,* 2:102–112.

Prince, R.M. (1985a), *Legacy of the Holocaust.* Ann Arbor, MI: WMI Research Press.

——— (1985b), Second generational effects of historical trauma. *Psychiat. Rev.*, (in press).

Rachman, A.W. (1967), A life saving fantasy. Lecture presented at the Postgraduate Center for General Health, New York City.

——— (1969), Talking it out rather than fighting it out: Prevention of a delinquent gang war by group therapy intervention. *Internat. J. Group Psychother.*, 19:518–521.

——— (1971), Encounter techniques in analytic group psychotherapy with adolescents. *Internat. J. Group Psychother.*, 21:319–329.

——— (1972), Countertransference: The forgotten encounter. Paper presented at the American Group Psychotherapy Association Conference. New York City, February.

——— (1972b), Group psychotherapy in treating the adolescent identity crisis. *Internat. J. Child Psychother.*, 1: 97–119.

——— (1974), Identity group psychotherapy. In: *New Directions in Clinical Child Psychology,* eds. S., Gordon, & G. Williams. New York: Human Science Press.

——— (1975), *Identity Group Psychotherapy with Adolescents.* Springfield, IL.: Charles C Thomas.

——— (1977), Identity conflicts of adolescent psychotherapists. Paper presented at the American Psychological Association Conference. New Orleans, LA, August.

——— (1979), Active psychoanalysis and the group encounter. *Group Therapy 1979: An Overview,* eds. L.R. Wohlberg & M. Aronson. New York: Stratton Intercontinental Medical Book Corp.

——— (1980), The role of "activity" in psychodynamic psychotherapy. Distinguished Lecture Series, Pine Rest Christian Hospital, Grand Rapids, MI, March.

——— (1981), Humanistic analysis in groups. *Psychother.: Theor., Res., & Pract.,* 18:457–477.

——— (1983a), Feral behavior in neurotic and borderline adolescents and adults. Unpublished manuscript.

——— (1983b), Modern feral children: The savage skulls of the South Bronx. Unpublished manuscript.

——— (1988), Liberating the creative self through active combined psychotherapy. In: *Borderline and Narcissistic Patients in Therapy,* ed. N. Slavinska-Holy. Madison, CT: International Universities Press, pp. 309–340.

——— Heller, M.E. (1974), Anti-therapeutic factors in therapeutic communities for drug rehabilitation. *J. Drug Issues,* 4:393–403.

——— ——— (1976), Peer group psychotherapy with adolescent drug abusers. *Internat. J. Group Psychother.*, 26:373–384.

——— Raubolt, R.R. (1984a), The pioneers of adolescent group psychotherapy *Internat. J. Group Psychother.*, 34:106–136.

——— ——— (1984b), The clinical practice of group psychotherapy with adolescent substance abusers. In: *Current Treatment of Substance Abuse and Alcoholism,* eds. T.E. Bratter & G.C. Forrest. New York: The Fress Press.

Rachman, R.B. (1983), The feral child syndrome: Some contemporary issues. *Junior Essay.* Friend's Seminary, New York City, June.

Rapaport, J. (1941), Fantasy objects in children. *Psychoanal. Rev.,* 31: 316–321.

Raubolt, R.R. (1982), Short-term adolescent therapy group. In: *Varieties of Short-term Therapy Groups,* ed. M. Rosenbaum. New York: McGraw-Hill.
——— (1983), Brief, problem focused group psychotherapy with adolescents. *Amer. J. Orthopsychiat.*, 53:157–166.
Sabusky, G.S., & Kymissis, P. (1983), Identity group therapy: A transitional group for hospitalized adolescents. *Internat. J. Group Psychother.*, 33: 99–109.
Wolf, A., & Schwartz E.K. (1962), *Psychoanalysis in Groups.* New York: Grune & Stratton.

Chapter 3

Symbiosis in the Group: Group Therapy for Younger Adolescents

ROB GORDON, B.A. (HONS.)

A therapy group for adolescent boys has been part of the Group Training Programme in Australia for twelve years. It is an open group in which the average length of stay is about two years. The members range in age from 12 to 15 years and have tended to be boys who, for a number of reasons, were felt unsuitable or unavailable for individual therapy. Some have been constricted and unable to talk to a therapist; others were aggressive, defensive, and unable to accept insight; still others have had difficulties in peer relationships. The problems represented have been varied.

It is our experience that group therapy has been able to help these quite disturbed boys in a way that did not seem possible with individual therapy (Gordon, 1983). Hence, group therapy deserves to be recognized as a powerful technique that has its action in a domain distinct from that of individual therapy. However, to make full use of group therapy, a theory is necessary to define that domain and conceptualize its functions, and, it may be hoped, be adequate to grasp those phenomena peculiar to the group and on which its therapeutic power rests. As Freud (1921) observed, in "Group Psychology and the Analysis of the Ego," the group precedes the individual. This is evident both historically and in the development of a child. It is not that the group ceases to be important, but rather the individual is at first an undifferentiated part of a group and only gradually emerges from it as an individual. He can then take up a stance in relation to the group. Nor does he leave the group behind, for it still exists for him even when he has left it; it is there as a necessary mark of his identity, and to an extent, it forms the structure of that identity (Gordon, 1985).

It is the function of the group in providing a milieu for the development of individuality that gives rise to its therapeutic power; and the events of group life that mobilize these forces are best understood, not by attempting to analyze what happens within individuals as they interact in the group, but in terms of what Maurice Merleau-Ponty (1962) calls "intersubjectivity." This refers to the existence of what lies *between* individuals as distinct from what lies *within* them. Group and family phenomena bring home to us the inadequacy of confining psychic events to the boundaries of the bodies of those involved, and intersubjectivity provides a notion that allows us to conceptualize psychic activity that is not private and confined to one individual. In other words, it enables us to get beyond seeing a group as a collection of subjectivities.

The child, as Merleau-Ponty describes, takes the intersubjective world as a self-evident fact. He never doubts his capacity to see into those around him, or the reality of what he sees. In the same way he feels able to reveal his own inner experiences. This consciousness evolves out of his awareness of the body of the other, its similarity, and when he knows it, its identity with his own. For the young child the body is not a barrier, it is a window. Have we not all experienced the penetrating, revealing look or words of a child?

As the child grows toward adulthood, the intersubjective dimension becomes overlaid; it seems less conscious but remains as a powerful unconscious factor binding together the members of a group. It becomes no longer in keeping with the nature of group phenomena to speak of the inner experience of one individual interacting with that of others, but experience of groups persuades us that there is a body of unconscious, shared experience that occurs at the level of the primary process and shows itself in the manifest behavior and speech of the group. Interactions between individuals certainly occur, but they are based on the unconscious, mutual regard of feelings, thoughts, and impulses that belong to the group as a whole. The intersubjective experience exerts a strong binding force that can be helpfully understood in terms of Margaret Mahler's notion of the symbiotic unit (Mahler, Pine, and Bergman, 1975). She describes the establishment of a symbiotic union between mother and infant that effectively makes them one. Gradually, in a number of identifiable stages the child emerges from this union. At first he begins to differentiate himself from mother, then he enters a stage of practicing at moving away from her while returning to "refuel." Mother is then rediscovered as a loved other, in the stage of "rapprochement"; and with added confidence the child consolidates himself as a separate entity. Mahler uses the image of the child hatching from a psychic membrane at the age of three years.

Blomfield (1972, 1982) points to the parallel between this membrane enclosing mother and child and the unifying effect of the intersubjective realm in a group. As a group establishes itself and the members identify themselves as "belonging" together, a symbiotic situation asserts itself. The group ceases to consist of individuals but functions as a unit. Sudden, spontaneous changes of affect, unconsciously coordinated behavioral events, or the repetition of the same themes in apparently unconnected utterances by members, point to this integrity of the group. Anxieties and defenses also manifest themselves, leading to splitting and other processes, which may activate struggles on the part of members to resist incorporation into the symbiosis. Individuals may fear being engulfed by the group and remain aloof or attack the group.

In this way the group reconstitutes the situation in which some of the most primitive and fundamental processes of personality development take place. The fear of engulfment, the security and dependence of the symbiotic union, and the practicing and rapprochement of individuation are all available. Problems in these areas can be repeated and reworked with the help of therapists, as well as providing opportunities for dealing with more current problems. Our function as therapists has been to bring to consciousness the state of the group and articulate and interpret the group's anxieties as they arise. Wherever possible we have kept interpretations at a group level, relating behavior or verbal themes to the status of the group. Where individual material is taken up and interpreted, it is regarded as symptomatic of the group and its difficulties. Group members' individual problems are not taken up by the therapists, and if raised are again related back to the group.

Before making a few more comments about technique, I would like to give some results from our work with the adolescent group. In general, the referrals have been boys who were by no means functioning at an adolescent level. Common adolescent themes were replaced by more immature play. From time to time the membership of the group would change but a pattern was discernible. Early sessions tended to be disorganized. Some members would be silent, keeping themselves aloof and defending against the group. Then there would be moments where they would come together, but soon be frightened or hurt and the tentative unity would dissolve. At first, this took the form of a game or activity, later it took the form of conversation. We would interpret both the development and subsequent loss of the symbiosis and put into words the feelings and anxieties that seemed to be involved.

Gradually, as the boys felt able to enter more fully into the group, they would value it more, even wanting to continue during vacation times. We found then that conversation about work, girls, and independence would replace paper darts, jokes, and comic books. One or two group members left because they felt that they had outgrown the group, and this was in fact true—new members were still at a much earlier stage; while the longer term members wanted to talk, the others only wanted to play.

Fred, a depressed, isolated, persecuted boy who was so distrustful he could not allow himself to be medically examined, was 13 when he entered the group. During the assessment he was unable to talk about his problems. He was constantly in fights at school, and often attacked his mother when his sailor father was away from home. He began his 18 months in the group as a silent, withdrawn boy, playing with toy cars and jigsaw puzzles. Then he began to play in parallel with the others and then to interact. He would withdraw from conversations when they were established by other members. In spite of fluctuations, however, he slowly began to talk and tease the others. His mother reported steady and sustained improvement in behavior at home and at school and the ability to show his feelings more appropriately. Just before he left, he was able to bring his problems at school into the group, he also talked of his father's lack of support and acknowledged the importance the group had for him in the face of his loneliness. Shortly after this he obtained an apprenticeship and has done well. When seen several months later he asked eagerly about the group and said wistfully that it was impossible for him to come. At no stage did we focus directly on his problems or attempt to interpret his behavior to him. Fred is typical of the type of boys treated in the group.

This leads back to the consideration of technique. In individual psychotherapy the act of interpretation is to make conscious the latent or unconscious content that lies behind what the patient says. Its function is to bring him into a relationship with his own unconscious thoughts and impulses. In group therapy the interpretation can provide a description of the strengths and deficiencies of the symbiosis in a way that allows individual members to *locate* themselves in relation to it.

One sometimes reads that a characteristic of adolescent groups is their complete disregard of interpretations. But it has become increasingly clear that a properly constructed and timed interpretation of the intersubjective state of the group almost always has an effect. But the sort of effect is different from what one may expect from a good interpretation in individual therapy, namely, a response from the patient that embodies his recognition and feeling for what has been said and for the therapist who said it. What is different in the group is that the interpretation is received with almost no overt recognition of the words of the therapist. There may be just a slight pause in the group process apparently coincidental with the delivery of the interpretation. By all the usual modes of observation, it has not been heard by anyone but the cotherapist. But after a short latency period, it becomes clear that the interpretation effects a change in the way the group is functioning. Often it is not apparent at first that what follows is a result of the interpretation, but experience gives more and more confidence that an interpretation of the intersubjective state of the group is almost always taken up. For example, in a group where the members had been together for only a few sessions and had not yet formed any relationships of consequence, there had been a long silence followed by each boy making his own paper planes. Although they were functioning separately, the boys expressed their unconscious group affiliation by doing the same thing. A therapist interpreted this by saying to the group as a whole that they were able to do something together now by all engaging in the same activity of making planes even though they were not yet ready to communicate directly with each other. The function of such an interpretation is to highlight the common intersubjective experience, which when acknowledged provides the basis for the development of the group symbiosis. The interpretation then should enable each individual to recognize this commonality with the others and allow him to determine his own response to it.

In this instance, the interpretation was followed by the boys continuing their activity uninterruptedly as though nothing had been said. However, after a few minutes in a perfectly natural and seemingly spontaneous manner, one boy spoke a few words to another about his plane. The other replied, and they began a conversation about their activity. Their interaction encouraged the others and over the next ten minutes the group separated into several subgroups that engaged in lively conversations.

Although this would have appeared a natural and unremarkable transition to a casual observer, it was, in fact, the first time these boys had been able to achieve such a level of group interaction. Experience shows too that such individual parallel activity can continue without change for many sessions if appropriate interventions are not made. A single interpretation does not have the power to constitute a group, but by enabling the members to define their common bond, they can take the next step toward the formation of an effective symbiotic group structure.

Where there is really no effect from an interpretation, it is probably due to the fact that it has not been a good one; that is, it has not brought into words a current intersubjective reality for the group. Perhaps it focuses too much on an individual, or simply misses the real issue, or is not timed properly.

Proper interpretation seems to promote the member's entry into the symbiotic state of the group by verbalizing the anxieties and defenses it evokes. Instead of leading them into relationship with their own unconscious, group interpretation leads them into the tension between symbiotic union and differentiation, between dependence and what Blomfield called "centricity"—the capacity to be centered in oneself. Interpretations provide words by which members may grasp their intersubjective experience and work their way toward a relationship to the others—of which they are a part.

This differentiation and individuation process seems to make available new resources, which come partly from within the individual himself but also become available from the others who can be approached and drawn out when the fears of engulfment or loss are manageable. Although the individual's specific problems may not have been touched directly, he has achieved a maturity, and most importantly, a capacity to put his experience into words. In almost every case the development of the therapy could be measured in terms of the function of language and culminated in the member's wish to speak about himself, which marks the experience of individuality and the entrance to a new stage of development.

Because of the disorganized and poorly motivated families from which these boys come, follow-up is difficult. However, interviews on discharge indicate fairly consistent improvement in most boys along a number of parameters. They included greater social sensitivity, readiness to help and cooperate in the family, improved peer relations, establishment of more stable friendships, greater ability to identify and articulate feelings, better personal emotional control, greater all-round maturity as indicated by more age-appropriate activity and interests, and more satisfying family relationships.

The group helped to maintain some boys in school for their final year or two when they were under threat of exclusion because of bad behavior. Attendance in the group was accepted by teachers as a condition of remaining in school. In most cases consistent attendance in the group was associated with significantly reduced behavior problems, and this sometimes led to the school and parents then applying pressure to terminate because of concern at the time spent away from school in the group.

Termination occurred for many boys when they found jobs, changed school in the process of finding more appropriate educational programs for their needs or career plans, or because presenting problems had been resolved. In most cases termination was on the initiative of the boys and would be worked through with the group and in interviews with the cotherapists.

Longer term follow-up has not been systematic; however, some boys have been encountered up to six years following termination. Such a case was Fred, who stopped me in a hospital corridor recently, where he was waiting to visit his girl friend's younger brother. He was eager to know if the group was still in existence and if my cotherapist was still there. His history since termination had been checkered. He had held a number of jobs but was now apprenticed as an upholsterer. He had a steady relationship with his girl friend, but had had a number of encounters with the law because of his aggressive tendencies. More recently he had come to recognize that he still had a psychological problem and had consulted a psychiatrist and was about to enter an adult therapy group.

He spoke of the group as a turning point in his life, which he often thought about. He said wistfully that, "You should have made us talk more about our problems, we wasted so much time—but then I suppose if you'd have put pressure on us we wouldn't have come." Similar comments have been made by other boys looking back on their group experience. It seems to pinpoint the development of an ability to confront their needs in retrospect with an insight of which there was no indication prior to their group experience. The poignant sense of having wasted a valuable opportunity for growth suggests the possibility of the group experience continuing to be active as an incitement to capitalize on growth opportunities for the future, even if, as in the case with Fred, initially he has to confront his problems in other ways.

In other cases, referring workers have provided follow-up information indicating that since the termination of the group, their patients have continued, though not always uneventfully, on the course set when they terminated. This characteristic of consistency is usually absent from the pretreatment histories of these boys; and it usually becomes apparent in their behavior and general functioning when they have allowed themselves to become part of the symbiotic unit of the group. Often it is only achieved by very determined efforts from the cotherapists to follow up nonattendance, keep contact with unmotivated parents, pacify anxious parents, and placate angry and frustrated school staff and other workers. Not all outcomes are successful, however, and some boys leave the group when the process triggers unmanageable anxieties or when an external event in their lives upsets the tenuous balance that keeps them in the group.

With the group providing a slowly developing centerpoint of predictability and belonging, most boys seem able to bring a new element of control into their lives. While the experience of entering a symbiosis, and individuating within it, nurtures their sense of identity, the interpretive activity of the therapists seems to assist them to develop social and self-awareness, and a capacity to articulate needs and feelings. These characteristics are evidence that the therapeutic effect of the group is to help the boys gain entry to adolescence proper and begin work on its tasks—with all the hazards that this new phase of life involves.

REFERENCES

Blomfield, O.H.D. (1972), Group: The more primitive psychology—A review of some paradigms in group dynamics. *Austral. N. Z. J. Psychiat.* 6: 238.

——— (1982), "I am given to myself—from a dark and doubtful presentiment"—The symbiotic phase of development and group process. *Austral. J. Psychother.* 1(1):1–15.

Freud, S. (1921), Group psychology and the analysis of the ego. *Standard Edition,* 18: 69–144. London: Hogarth Press, 1955.

Gordon, R. (1983), Group therapy with adolescents. *Austral. J. Psychother.*, 2(1): 18–28.

——— (1985), Group psychotherapy and the primal horde. In: *Festschrift for Winston S. Rickards.* Melbourne: Royal Children's Hospital, pp. 62–69.
Mahler, M., Pine, F., & Bergman, A. (1975), *The Psychological Birth of the Human Infant, Symbiosis and Individuation.* New York: Basic Books.
Merleau-Ponty, M. (1962), *Phenomenology of Perception.* Toronto: Methuen Publications.

Part II

General Clinical Applications

Chapter 4

A Selective Overview

IRVIN A. KRAFT, M.D.

As in most areas of medicine and the behavioral sciences, emphasis and interests change with time. In the early years of work in adolescent group psychotherapy the literature reflected a major concern for the treatment of delinquents (Kraft, 1961). Few articles, for example, described the intricacies and vicissitudes of adolescent group psychotherapy in private practice settings with adolescents demonstrating symptomatology primarily of adjustment reactions. Why variations in themes and subjects occur remains unknown.

A paucity of training programs or opportunities existed in the early 1950s, especially in university-based psychiatric residencies or in field placements for schools of social work. Ackerman (1955) broke ground in this field in his work with mixed gender adolescent groups, which, interestingly, covered an age range from 16 to 22. Others who described their work with this age group in the early and midfifties included Schulman (1956), with a spurt in the 1970s (Brandes, 1971; Berkowitz, 1972; and Sugar, 1975).

As the American economy expanded in the 1960s and 1970s and rapid urbanization took place, concomitant economic factors, such as the increase in major medical insurance for outpatient psychiatric care, enhanced treatment resources. Adolescence itself became lengthened as more youths completed high school and went on to higher education rather than entering the work force. During the 1960s' counterculture greening of society, one of many forces it represented was that of the adolescent vigorously pushing for his individuation.

Counseling, therapy, treatment, "being shrunk," getting your head straight," and "getting your stuff together"—these and other terms reflected a growing concern about social and psychological deviancies, which were now eligible for professional examination and care. Parents realized that their adolescent offspring might not just grow out of those behaviors but rather grow to become further troubled as time went by. The drug scene in the mid-1960s impinged on behaviors and family dynamics to an extent that could no longer be ignored, and this continues even more so in the 1980s.

In previous overview articles (Kraft, 1961, 1968), the literature reflected basic concerns for adolescent group psychotherapy to be recognized as a viable and valuable treatment modality. In the mid-1980s group therapy for adolescents seems fully accepted as a treatment option, and the emphasis is on developing basic approaches to learning it, standardizing training requirements, describing its own technical characteristics and uniquenesses, and in the ways in which theory relating to group therapy for adolescents might differ from theory regarding other age groups undertaking group therapy. A key element that pervades reports is the development of the adolescent and how adolescent group psychotherapy aids, abets, and anneals those intrinsic processes.

As more information accumulates about the "normal" adolescent in our culture, emphasis on development grows apace (Offer, 1973). This raises the question of diagnosis, symptom relief, and the goals of adolescent group psychotherapy. Where this technique alters and reduces behavior, which we call signs and symptoms of developmental distress and deviance, are we also significantly affecting basic psychodynamic, adaptational, developmental processes of identity formation, healthy disentanglement from parents, further nondestructive individuation, more secure sexuality, and really acute thinking processes?

The number of reports dealing with adolescent group psychotherapy in private outpatient settings (Brandes, 1973; Richmond, 1974) has increased. The quantity of patient flow, in contrast to clinics and inpatient services, mostly acts counter to having enough adolescent patients at any one time to start a closed group. Thus, the groups tend to be open ended and fluctuating in numbers, age, and gender distribution. The leaders find enough patients who form a core aggregation that persists not only through the school year but through the summer as well. With devotion to the action of adolescent group therapy, a dauntless leader may establish a group that creates a basic core identity lasting over many years (Richmond, 1974).

The drop-out rate in group psychotherapy generally runs from 20 to 40 percent (Holmes, 1983). Adolescent group therapy can, if the group anneals early, maintain a steady membership for at least six to nine months, sometimes as long as 12 to 18 months. Exceptions exist, of course (Richmond, 1978). Departures may represent a positive growth spurt of the family system, as when a youth gains sufficent ego strength and integration to leave his current mother-headed family to live with a father from whom he had previously been estranged. Over and over again, though, a major threat to continuity in the group emerges from the patient's family system as he no longer plays his assigned roles, and his parents then find reasons (excuses) for him not to continue his treatment.

One set of investigators tested the influence of parental participation on adolescent attendance (Richmond and Gaines, 1979) and found that the teenagers attended more regularly and longer when their parents were involved. Others (Corder, Whiteside, Koehne, and Hortman, 1981) used structured techniques for the problem of leavings and additions in a hospital setting. Another technique, brief, problem-focused group psychotherapy, responds to attendance difficulties as well as promoting emotional catharsis and group cohesion (Raubolt, 1983).

This illustrates the inherent conundrums in treatment goals for the adolescent in that they may conflict with the unstated purposes of the family system. Another way to picture it would be to use Offer's (1973) findings of male adolescents falling into roughly four groups: continuous (23 percent), urgent (35 percent), tumultuous growth patterns (21 percent), and 21 percent with mixed features. Following that schema, we could suggest adolescent group psychotherapy being of value primarily for the tumultuous categories with some value for those in the urgent group, if the parents had become concerned enough to seek professional consultation. Improvement by the patient might be judged by Offer's criteria: in effect moving from the tumultuous to the urgent or even to the continuous growth group.

We assume that intergenerational transmission of basic interpersonal phenomena emphasizes those problematic themes the family has not solved satisfactorily. All families deal with power, dependency, money, anger, sex, losses, love, and other human concerns, and some bungle one or more of these as they struggle on and on without resolution.

The adolescent patient in his group psychotherapy compares his family's procedures and techniques with those of his group mates, often achieving some newer perspective. He can go on to include what he observes in other peers at school and elsewhere. These perspectives become sharply focused at times when his family of origin encounters those crises indigenous to family life and its development.

Adolescents in cultures subjected to high-energy mass communications receive superabundant information input of all kinds, with the emphasis on what is new. One wonders how the teenager finds opportunities for adequate contemplating, reflective, and associative time as part of learning purposive decision making. Sadly, as Gibson (1973) points out, "we have arrived at the stage where the time required to make decisions (i.e., assemble and examine all necessary information), even simple ones by human beings, is considerably longer than the time required to transmit the information over a communication system." Both valid and invalid information flows with equal ease. How to acquire methods for securing accurate information, whether cultural, interpersonal, or intrapsychic, becomes a group therapy issue when reality-oriented decision making proves necessary.

Adolescents in their group psychotherapy mode find a setting and techniques through which they glimpse at varying levels of abstraction the roles of their family in its functioning as a message center and information processor. In the group process, a teenager obtains a sense of inherent systems of negotiation in his family rather than seeing only individual quirks and psychopathology. In group interaction, evidence mounts that the patient demonstrates the schisms, secret alliances, and power plays of his family of origin (Melville, 1973). The adolescent's capacity for identification, both with his group peers and with the leader, as a built-in feature from birth, combats this trend (Bandura, 1969; Grunebaum and Solomon, 1980).

Peer-focused group therapy emphasizes the recapitulation of the latency and adolescent peer group more than the reliving of the family group (Hogan, 1980). Adolescent peer group emphasis helps to initiate separation from the family and to further identity formation. Adolescents and their parents frequently feel buffeted by their lack of time and facility to monitor and to filter the bombardment of overt and covert stimuli. These include information for rational decision making as well as subliminal messages designed not to inform but to influence. The group may aid the teenager and his family in providing emotional support and in training the patient in competency (age and gender-adequate control of his body and his symbolic environment). Megamachine living, a product of this century (Mumford, 1972), strongly affects these functions, more frequently than not in a negative fashion. Faulty communications within the family result from its increased tensions and decreased control, as in interpersonal areas, and from the familial disorganization so prevalent, which we see reflected in divorces, single parent families, and blended families. Survival under such circumstances, however, may not be equivalent to health.

As he inevitably views his family through his particular and customary perceptual screen, in his group therapy interactions the adolescent receives input from his group mates for comparison. He may have blocked out positive facets of his own family, and these come through the din of group discussions as assets worth recognizing, despite his contentiousness in the home itself. Likewise, he garners insight into how to handle his family differently, and, it is hoped, more constructively.

Concurrently, group members encounter at some level of awareness their fantasies about family, the opposite sex, peers, goals, themselves, and other objects. Since these phenomena, at both unconscious and conscious levels, serve as drives for behaviors (Stoller and Herdt, 1985), behavioral changes consequent to the group experience of exposing and even examining certain fantasies might well be accentuated or accelerated. No doubt some, if not many, fantasies get displayed, shared, compared, reworked, and possibly discarded. Sexuality, for example, resides constantly in these groups, an ever present companion in overt discussion and in the group's vocabulary for anger, dissent, and prowess. Sexual and gender identity, sex-role fit, and how to go about interacting with the opposite gender comprise sexuality in the group. In mixed gender adolescent therapy groups, while never entirely absent, these factors can assume major proportions. Again, fantasies about sexuality, once verbalized, become open to realistic, factual correction of distortions, to comparison of "weirdness" and immorality, and to the ways they push these youths to behaviors that can be self-punitive.

Fantasies about alcohol-drinking behaviors emerge as the participants describe in the group their social subgroups, which may have contrasting or hostile values, attitudes, and leisuretime patterns (Riester and Zucker, 1968). Clothing patterns, activities, auto availability, drugs, and so on—all of these get examined and discussed in the group. Not infrequently one member points out the "macho" notions imbedded in what the other does. Thus, as Brandes and Moosbrugger (1985) point out, the group experience serves as an "ideological simplification of the universe," so needed by the adolescent ego in organizing experience. As they deal with alcohol, drugs, sexuality, hostility to adults, parental vagaries, and other themes, they learn to share emotions and to support each other, a phenomenon not usually so available in individual therapy or in their life realities (Brandes and Moosbrugger, 1985).

At some points integral to the group's function and to the participation of the members, yet often termed adjunctive, the leaders may use techniques that differ from stereotypes of adolescent groups, as a group of six to eight adolescents sitting in a circle with one or two therapists and having quite an intense discussion of their problems. Alternative techniques include movement, art, psychodrama, Gestalt, encounter, minithons, games, music, and videotaping. Art, mainly as drawing or painting, finds adjunctive use primarily to "loosen up" the group members. Brandes and Moosbrugger (1985) describe art's catalytic value on an occasional basis with those adolescents who just will not interact readily or communicate verbally. After drawing and painting, the members discussed each other's productions, and this opened up even very taciturn patients. They could present their conflicts, worries, and concerns to the more verbal members and get reactions from them. Enhanced vocal involvement followed. Sometimes a group drawing (Lubell, 1983) works very well. The patients respond vigorously and even enthusiastically to "putting my stuff right out there with the others," especially when any anatomical detail and/or verbal expression can be put on the paper with impunity.

Another challenging form of art group therapy utilizes it and associated techniques throughout the duration of the group, which can be time-limited. Carozza and Heirsteiner (1982) describe a 22-week group therapy in a community agency setting for adolescent incest victims. Interestingly, they included prepubescent girls in the groups with adolescents up to age 17 in order to influence modeling by the youngsters. As with other time-limited groups, a sequence of gathering, self-disclosure, regression, reconstruction, and ending occurred. Throughout sessions, while verbalization is encouraged, art projects flow constantly; these can be structured or nonstructured. After showing a film on incest, the discussion by the group occurs while art media, specifically clay, offer opportunities to express the feelings stimulated by the film. A high emphasis is placed on furnishing information, such as birth control and sexual anatomy. Insight into how one is viewed by others results from constructing collages of the group as a whole.

Because music occupies so important a role in adolescence, some therapists play and discuss current popular records in the groups. Not uncommonly, one or more of the group will bring a portable radio–cassette player and, by coming early to the session, have a round of music in the waiting room before discussing or playing his favorite rock band in the group session. Frances and Schiff (1976) point out that the emotions stirred by the music become socially acceptable to the group more often than by verbalizations alone. They believe teenagers experience group cohesion and intimacy in a musical environment, so they can enter the group more willingly and drop out less frequently. Using metaphors, allusions, and symbols in songs leads to greater understanding of themselves in their own behavioral and verbal metaphors. Frances and Schiff (1976) use a reentry period at the end of each meeting to resolve and to interpret feeling and behavioral options.

A modification of music therapy in adolescent groups emerges in the work of Wells and Stevens (1984), who use music to stimulate creative story writing solely on a rotational basis, each member writing a part of the story as the music changes. They classify their technique as a projective diagnostic instrument in their inpatient settings and as a means to promote group cohesion and interactions.

As Corder, Whiteside, McNeil, Brown, and Corder (1981) demonstrate, structured, brief videotape feedback sessions, compared with control group sessions, produce significant differences in content intimacy levels and the frequency of verbal feedback among inpatient group members. They suggest this helps the group members handle the high anxiety levels engendered by intrinsic insight-oriented therapy (Kraft, 1961). They structured the 15 minutes of alternate sessions in which a videotape of a previous session was shown, by reviewing group goals, showing two-minute segments, and asking for feedback, for example, on how someone is shown working on goals, obeying or violating the group's rules for behavior, and so on.

As to techniques and skills, anyone interested in using videotape can consult numerous sources about equipment, where to place the camera and how to use its versatile capabilities, and the numerous ways the leader may make use of the taping itself, as well as the videotape product (Berger, 1970). We have videotaped an initial portion of a session, asking for dreams, negative and positive reports about daily life, and for anyone who wants to act out a scene from family or school. We station the video equipment in the same room, presenting no hindrance to the group processes. Either then or later in the session the group reviews segments of the tape, commenting with hoots, hollers, giggles, upsets, and denials that such events really happened and serious discussion of the psychodynamics in evidence.

A less developed form of group therapy is dance or movement therapy. "Movement encompasses the world of physical motion, whereas dance is a specific creative act within that world" (Klein, 1983). Some of this work with adolescents indicates that small groups (six to eight) function better; however, the question remains about mixing boys and girls in the same movement group. The warm-up period becomes crucial to overcoming the feelings of strangeness and awkwardness, and then the skilled dance therapist gets the group into using the body to portray fantasy, tightness, anger, sadness, and other expressions of emotion adolescents may have difficulty with. Verbalizations may be encouraged during or even at breaks in the flow of the sessions. If one could somehow get an ongoing verbalizing adolescent group to utilize movement therapies at intervals, as an alternative to regular sessions, this might prove highly productive, especially if a videotape of it could be played in the regularly scheduled meetings.

Psychodrama embodies ideas and techniques that make certain assumptions about time, space, and reality as it constructs a therapeutic setting using life as a model (Moreno, 1983). Several investigators in the 1960s utilized this with adolescents (Lebovici, 1961; Head, 1962; Boulanger, 1965; Pate, 1966) both by itself and in conjunction with other therapies. Since the here and now of daily living preoccupies many adolescent patients, psychodrama, interpolated into the more traditional group psychotherapy, adds a strong element of "show-and-tell" in the group, almost akin to videotaping. The leader who knows therapeutic soliloquy, self-presentation, self-realization, role playing, future projection, and other productive techniques of psychodrama utilizes these to lead the patient into another phase of safe self-recognition (Holmes, 1983).

Another view of man's perceptions of his cosmos and himself rests in a Gestalt or a patterning to achieve unity, continuity, and organization. In the United States certain therapists (Perls, Simkins) have become almost synonymous with these techniques, which emphasize the practical and the here and now (Kepner, 1980; Roth, 1983). We have used the "hot-seat" with adolescents, and they really get involved in the dialogue with a parent, a school principal, or even a girl friend as they portray the persons responding to each other. As with the other ploys, staleness creeps in if the leader persists in doing this throughout most of the group session, rather than inserting it at propitious moments.

One study (Ibanez, 1984) examined the effects of a Gestalt-oriented group approach on the development of self-actualization in 44 high school juniors and seniors, randomly assigned to experimental and control groups, in language art classes. None of the hypotheses for the Gestalt growth group emerged a winner, but its members believed this experience enhanced their abilities to be self-supportive and independent.

Dream work, using a group modification of a Gestalt technique, goes well. We obtain a dream from one of the patients by asking him to relate in the present tense, and then we turn to the group asking if anyone wishes to comment about the dream. Some remarks ensue, and then we return to the presenter, using Gestalt devices: "Be the train in the dream. What are you feeling, train, as you speed through the crossings? Train, where are you going?" and so on. Then we ask for a volunteer or choose a member to be the train. They tend to get into the fantasies of the dreams readily, and, of course, reveal themselves in the process. More traditional dream work can be utilized also.

Among other innovations in psychotherapy, the previous decade produced the encounter group. Here the leader emphasizes intense activity, utilizing psychodrama, role play, and other more active forms of interaction (Osorio, 1970; Rachman, 1971; Olsson and Myers, 1972; Kraft and Vick, 1973; Vick and Kraft, 1973). The group uncovers materials that afford opportunities from which insight develops, and the group becomes the apparatus for heightened emotional interaction between therapist and patient and between patient and patient. Group members learn to experience and to share the feelings of others as they become evident. "Free role experimentation" facilitates the resolution of the adolescent ego identity crisis by allowing the adolescent to experiment with a wide variety of feelings, thoughts, and behaviors in the group. These experiences and others tend to foster group cohesion, especially when the group undergoes common emotional experiences, as in sharing field trips.

A specialized field trip involved attending a rock concert as a group. We discussed at length the special subculture of rock concerts, including the rituals of buying titled T-shirts, eating certain foods, dressing correctly, using marijuana, responding to the musicians, and even those about safety from muggers. We agreed on rules for getting to the concert and staying together as a group once there, and we furnished the tickets, one to each member of the group at a session prior to the concert. Obviously, at the next group session after the adventure we had loads of material for group discussion, both from our own observations and from those of the patients.

A different orientation of sharing involves therapeutic games for structuring and facilitating group performance. One such device has been described by Corder, Whiteside, and Vogel (1977), which she calls "The Learning Life Game." It consists of a colorful gameboard, bordered with squares labeled to correspond with the item categories. These fall into "Knowing Yourself," "Understanding Each Other," and "Problem Solving," along with room for "Learning Cards," which deal with transactional analysis (TA) concepts. The patients take turns rolling dice, which places a gamepiece on a square, which in turn requires the patient to turn to a task from the top card of the designated stack. Variations on the game itself (when to use it, how to interweave the TA cards, participation by the leader in the game, and how to let spirited discussion grow) produce interactions suitable to the group's special characteristics. The inventors believe their work stimulates gains in modeling and training in verbalization of feelings, focusing on the development of techniques for impulse control, appropriate lowering of intense anxiety levels, and increased opportunities for identification with appropriate role models. The game materials proved very useful in facilitating interaction and communication in short-term treatment groups, especially with resistive youngsters possessing limited communication skills.

Still another phase of adolescent group psychotherapy lies in its combination with psychopharmacotherapy. Both treatment modalities can aid each other in certain patients. The deeply depressed adolescent, the severely borderline teenager, the anxiety- and panic-ridden youth, and the patient with severe maturational brain dysfunction usually need medication to aid their involvement and responsiveness to the group processes. Other sources (Sussman, 1983;

Davis, 1985) detail the complexities of what agent to use for which disorders and their signs and symptoms. How a patient reacts to a drug may be influenced by his group peers. For example, Charles, a quite bright, solitary 15-year-old, solidly tied in with his divorced, obese mother, claimed he was severely depressed. Imipramine in adequate dosage failed to aid him, for he portrayed at home and in the group the forlorn, beleaguered, pitiful, lost youth. The therapist brought this up to the group, and they let him know he overdid it, that they were also depressed at times, and why didn't he get off his center of gravity to do more with them? By this time he wanted to be an important member of the group, so their chiding reached him. Subsequently he responded to the medication and the group, several weeks later reporting he felt good enough to handle an after-school and weekend job.

So, in using medication with the knowledge of the group members, the leader finds an emphasis on traditional reactions: transference, countertransference, resistance, and identification (Sussman, 1983). Openness of the group enables the leader to know how the patient utilizes his medication from his internalization of the drug's meaning to him. The patient can downgrade its value and deny he needs it, but the group may well reach a different consensus. Usually someone in the group queries whether the medicine acts like a street drug, grass, or even LSD, and the patient then faces either describing it realistically, or how he wants it to be in order to enhance his status with the group. In effect, he becomes more realistic about his expectations and magical beliefs, easing up on his negative transference to the leader and on his own dependency through the medication on a medical authority figure.

Statistics grimly confront us with the fact that suicide in this age group comprises an ever present possibility for the individual patient, and there is in addition the so-called epidemic of serial suicides where in a small community as many as five or six teenagers kill themselves in a brief span of time. This topic should be quite openly discussed in the group; for example, when a member has a peer at school or otherwise who committed suicide. The revelations of how many have flirted with the notion, of those who chose to get stoned and then drive a car or motorcycle, and of those engaged in activities (glue-sniffing or tailpipe-inhaling) they know to be injurious or death dealing: these come forth and receive serious, thoughtful treatment beneath the jests, crudities of speech, and seeming lack of concern of the group. The group will mostly respond supportively in the long run.

Adolescent group psychotherapy challenges its practitioners as much as its patients. Leadership qualities (Hurst and Gladieux, 1980) differ from those necessary for adult group leaders, and therapists operate in a highly charged atmosphere where peer relationships dominate. So often in psychotherapy for adults, both individual and group, we feel time is on our side, while in adolescent work we have a sense of lack of time, which lends urgency to our efforts.

REFERENCES

Ackerman, N. W. (1955), Group psychotherapy with a mixed group of adolescents. *Internat. J. Group Psychother.*, 5:249–260.

Bandura, A. (1969), Modeling and vicarious processes. *Principles of Behavior Modification*, New York: Holt, Rinehart & Winston.

Berger, M.M. (1970), *Videotape Techniques in Psychiatric Training and Treatment.* New York: Brunner/Mazel.

Berkowitz, I.H. (1972), On growing a group: Some thoughts on structure, process, and setting. In: *Adolescents Grow in Groups*, ed. I.H. Berkowitz. New York: Brunner/Mazel, p. 60.

Boulanger, J.B. (1965), Group analytic psychodrama in child psychiatry. *Canadian Psychiat. Assn. J.*, 10:427–431.

Brandes, N.S. (1971), Group psychotherapy for the adolescent. *Curr. Psychiat. Ther.*, 11:18–23.

——— (1973), Outpatients. In: *Group Therapy for the Adolescent*, eds. N.S. Brandes & M.L. Gardner. New York: Jason Aronson, p. 71.

——— Moosbrugger, L. (1985), A 15-year clinical review of combined adolescent/young adult group therapy. *Internat. J. Group Psychother.*, 35:95– 107.

Carozza, P.M., & Heirsteiner, C.L. (1982), Young IMS in treatment: Stages of growth/ A group art therapy model. *Clin. Soc. Work J.*, 10(3):165–175.

Corder, B.F., Whiteside, R. Koehne, P., & Hortman, R. (1981), Structured techniques for handling loss and addition of members in adolescent psychotherapy groups. J. Early Adol., 1(4):413–421.

——— ——— McNeil, M., Brown, B., & Corder, R.F. (1981), An experimental study of the effect of structured videotape feedback on adolescent group psychotherapy process. *J. Youth & Adol.*, 10(4):225–262.

——— ——— Vogel, M. (1977), A therapeutic game for structuring and facilitating group psychotherapy. *Adol.*, 12:261–268.

Davis, J.M. (1985), Antipsychotic drugs. In: *Comprehensive Textbook of Psychiatry/IV*, Vol. 2, 4th ed., eds. H.I. Kaplan & B.J. Sadock. Baltimore: Williams & Wilkins, pp. 1481–1558.

Frances, A., & Schiff, M. (1976), Popular music as a catalyst in the induction of therapy groups for teenagers. *Internat. J. Group Psychother.*, 26: 393–398.

Gibson, R.E. (1973), The ambassador and the system. *Johns Hopkins Mag.*, 24:2–8.

Grunebaum, H., & Solomon, L. (1980), Toward peer theory of group psychotherapy. I. On the developmental significance of peers and play. *Internat. J. Group Psychother.*, 30:23–49.

Head, W.A. (1962), Sociodrama and group discussion with institutionalized delinquent adolescents. *Men. Hygiene*, 46:127–135.

Hogan, R.A. (1980), Introduction. *Group Psychotherapy*. New York: Holt, Rinehart & Winston, pp. 2–3.

Holmes, P. (1983), "Dropping out" from an adolescent therapeutic group: A study of factors in the patients and their parents which may influence this process. *J. Adol.*, 6:333–346.

Hurst, A.G., & Gladieux, J.D. (1980), Guidelines for leading an adolescent therapy group. In: *Group and Family Therapy*, eds. L.R. Wolberg & M.L. Aronson. New York: Brunner/Mazel.

Ibanez, P. (1984), The Effects of the Gestalt Oriented Group Approach on the Development of Self-actualization in an Adolescent Population. Unpublished doctoral dissertation. United States International University, San Diego, CA.

Kepner, E. (1980), Gestalt group process. In: *Beyond the Hot Seat: Gestalt Approaches to Group*, eds. B. Feder & R. Ronall. New York: Brunner/Mazel, pp. 5–24.

Klein, V. (1983), Dance therapy. In: *Comprehensive Group Psychotherapy*, eds. H.I. Kaplan & B.J. Sadock. Baltimore: Williams & Williams, pp. 184–188.

Kraft, I.A. (1961), Some special considerations in adolescent group psychotherapy. *Internat. J. Group Psychother.*, 11:196–203.

——— (1968), An overview of group therapy with adolescents. *Internat. J. Group Psychother.*, 18:461–480.

——— (1983), Child and adolescent group psychotherapy. In: *Comprehensive Group Psychotherapy*, 2nd ed., eds. H.I. Kaplan & B.J. Sadock. Baltimore: Williams & Wilkins, pp. 184–188.

——— Vick, J.W. (1973), Flexibility and variability of group psychotherapy with adolescent girls. In: *Group Therapy: An Overview*, eds. E. Schwartz & L. Wolberg. New York: Intercontinental Medical Book Corp.

Lebovici, S. (1961), Psychodrama as applied to adolescents. *J. Child Psychol. Psychiat.*, 1:298–303.

Lubell, D.J. (1983), Art therapy in groups. In: *Comprehensive Group Therapy*, 2nd ed., eds. H.I. Kaplan & B.J. Sadock. Baltimore: Williams & Wilkins, pp. 177–183.

Melville, K. (1973), Changing the family game. *Sciences* 13:17–18.

Moreno, Z.T. (1983), Psychodrama. In: *Comprehensive Group Psychotherapy*, 2nd ed., eds. H.I. Kaplan & B.J. Sadock. Baltimore: Williams & Wilkins, pp. 158–166.

Mumford, L. (1972), *Pyramids of Power*. New York: Harcourt, Brace, & Jovanovich.

Offer, D. (1973), *The Psychological World of the Teenager*. New York: Basic Books.

——— (1980), Normal adolescent development. In: *Comprehensive Textbook of Psychiatry*, 3rd ed., eds. H.I. Kaplan, A.M. Freedman, & B.J. Sadock. Baltimore: Williams & Wilkins.

Olsson, P.A. & Myers, I. (1972), Nonverbal techniques in an adolescent group. *Internat. J. Group Psychother.*, 22:186–191.

Osorio, L.C. (1970), Milieu therapy for child psychosis. *Amer. J. Orthopsychiat.*, 40: 121– 129.

Pate, J.D. (1966), Psychodrama for disturbed children. *Hosp. Comm. Psychiat.*, 17:26–27.

Rachman, A.W. (1971), Encounter techniques in analytic group psychotherapy with adolescents. *Internat. J. Group Psychother.*, 21:319–329.

Raubolt, R.R. (1983), Brief, problem-focused group psychotherapy with adolescents. *Amer. J. Orthopsychiat.*, 53(1):157–165.

Richmond, L.H. (1974), Observations on private practice and community clinic adolescent psychotherapy groups. *Group Process* 6:57–62.

——— (1978), Some further observations on private practice and community clinic adolescent psychotherapy groups. *Correc. & Soc. Psych. & J. Behav. Technol.*, 24(2):57–61.

——— Gaines, T., (1979), Factors influencing attendance in group psychotherapy with adolescents. *Adol.*, 14:715–720.

Riester, A.E. & Zucker, R.A. (1968), Adolescent social structure and drinking behavior. *Pers. & Guid. J.*, 47:304–312.

Roth, B.E. (1983), Gestalt and other types of group psychotherapy. In: *Comprehensive Group Psychotherapy*, 2nd ed., eds. H.I. Kaplan & B.J. Sadock. Baltimore: Williams & Wilkins, pp. 210–214.

Schulman, I. (1956), Delinquents. In: *The Fields of Group Psychotherapy*, ed. S.R. Slavson. New York: International Universities Press.

Stoller, R.J., & Herdt, G.H. (1985), Theories of origins of male homosexuality: A cross-cultural look. *Arch Gen. Psychiat.*, 42:399–404.

Sugar, M. (1975), The structure and setting of adolescent therapy groups. In: *The Adolescent in Group and Family Therapy*, ed. M. Sugar. New York: Brunner/Mazel.

Sussman, N. (1983), Psychopharmacology and group psychotherapy. In: *Comprehensive Group Psychotherapy*, 2nd ed., eds. H.I. Kaplan & B.J. Sadock. Baltimore: Williams & Wilkins, pp. 195–209.

Vick, J., & Kraft, I.A. (1973), Creative activities. In: *Group Therapy for the Adolescent*, ed. N.S. Brandes. New York: Jason Aronson.

Wells, N.F., & Stevens, T. (1984), Music as a stimulus for creative fantasy in group psychotherapy with young adolescents. *Arts in Psychother.*, 11: 71–76.

Chapter 5

Adolescent Inpatient Group Psychotherapy

MICHAEL D. STEIN, PH.D.
PAUL KYMISSIS, M.D.

A search of the professional literature reveals a broad range of articles reflecting diverse approaches to group psychotherapy in the psychiatric hospital treatment of adolescents; however, we have not noted any prior comprehensive review of this specific topic. This may be due in part to the fact that the number of articles reporting on this specific subject was surprisingly small. This was unexpected, considering the general acceptance of the importance of group effects on teenagers. It would be unthinkable to have an adolescent program without a group treatment component, yet this aspect of hospital treatment for youngsters has clearly been insufficiently studied. Our survey describes the development of group-based programs for adolescents and the current differentiation of group efforts. One aim of this review is to show the considerable need for additional attention to this topic for training as well as treatment purposes.

DEFINITION OF TERMS

The criteria for inclusion of articles were defined by four terms: "inpatient," "adolescent," "group," and "psychotherapy." Inpatient treatment is the area of greatest concern to the authors because of our activity at a municipal receiving hospital. However, it must be noted that credit for the pioneering efforts in this field is generally awarded to Aichorn (1925), whose exemplary work was in a residential treatment setting. Many of the points discussed here may still be applicable to group therapy in residential treatment (Evans, 1965) and those increasingly rare long-term hospital programs. Modern hospital services, with significantly shorter average stays, are more crisis-oriented in approach and must accept more modest goals as treatment targets. The task for group therapists is to redefine the group approach for use with this reduced time frame (Yalom, 1983).

For many years the standard practice in hospitalizing adolescents in freestanding and general hospital psychiatry units has been to include them among the adults. Adults represent the bulk of psychiatry admissions, and for years special units for teenagers, particularly in acute-care hospitals, seemed unnecessary, expensive, or both. In recent years the argument for all-adolescent programs has been advanced (Sands, 1953; Gralnick, 1969).

The inpatient short-term adolescent psychiatric unit is a relatively new development. Such settings are still not widespread, and the treatment of adolescents in such units has not been extensively studied. An all-adolescent treatment unit may be established, changed, or disbanded on grounds of treatment philosophy, for practical or structural reasons having to do with the existing architecture of the hospital, or because the current treatment programs were developed, guided, and understood by a program director who has since departed.

Elizur, Gaoni, and Davidson (1981), in discussing their establishment of an all-adolescent unit, described several disadvantages of mixing adults and adolescents on a single ward. First, the impact of their acute problems presented special difficulties for the staff. For example, the adolescents' needs for attention were frequently expressed in unacceptable behavior toward adult patients and in manipulation of the staff. Second, dealing with these problems actually resulted in less staff time spent with the adolescents, who thus had less of the necessary staff contact when they actually needed more. Third, a mixed ward inhibited a teen-centered social framework that might encourage peer relationships. Fourth, the study of family pathology, not always a required focus for adults, is essential in the treatment of adolescents. This represents considerable training and effort and requires still more time. The staff had difficulty in the task of focusing on the teenagers' families' problems that added to those of the hospitalized patient. During hospitalization, family dynamics must be carefully monitored for several purposes, including minimizing splitting and manipulation of the situation by the patient or the family.

While the group therapy literature is immense, there are comparatively few reports on use of this modality on inpatient adolescent units, and it is even harder to find evaluation studies of the effectiveness of this and other forms of treatment in such milieus. Yalom (1983) has discussed the considerable impediments to rigorous evaluation studies of the contribution of group therapy to treatment programs.

The inpatient adolescent unit is a highly complex milieu. Many disciplines participate in the evaluation and treatment of the patients: psychiatry, psychology, social work, nursing, rehabilitation services, and so on. Besides the psychotherapeutic interventions, the biological treatments, especially chemotherapy, play a very important role.

Adolescence has traditionally been defined as beginning at about 12, and it is rare to find use of the term referring to anyone older than 18 or 19. Because people change so much during this period, the demarcations of early, middle, and late adolescence have generally been accepted. The need for consideration of differing treatments partly based on age has been acknowledged (Stein and Davis, 1982). For example, we have observed that age is a frequent segregating factor in group activities. Early adolescents often have difficulty on a ward when, as sometimes happens, they are almost alone in a group of older, more socially active teens, where the interactions are often tinged with sexual overtones. Instances such as this illustrate why the adolescent is best conceptualized as other than a small adult. He or she is in one of a series of transitional stages, struggling to establish an effective identity, find a meaning in his life, and plan for the future. Program planning for adolescents must take these multistage developmental tasks into account.

Peer pressure and peer support exert an exceptionally important influence during adolescence. The fact that youngsters tend to be more socially sensitive during this period of life means that group therapy is potentially an especially powerful therapeutic tool. The hospitalized adolescent tends to view himself in a dislocated position, disconnected from the usual relations that contribute to his usual self-image. He feels deprived of his freedom, often sees hospitalization as punishment for his actions, and shows little trust in the "adults" who are "trying to help." Interpretations, confrontations, and help may be more easily accepted from his peers, in addition to orientation to the ward and to reality, and translations of the treatment professionals' remarks.

DEFINING THE GROUP

The majority of articles located in our search do not devote space to consideration of what constitutes a group. This seems to reflect the fact that the number of adolescents, their ages, diagnostic groupings, and their dispersion within the hospital has been predetermined. Additionally, professionals in hospitals frequently confront a preexisting setting, where structural considerations such as ward size and architectural design make it hard to deal with clinical issues such as patient selection or the optimum number of group members.

The theoretical bases for group work with adolescents support treatment methods ranging from traditional psychoanalytic interpretations (Westman, 1960) to behavior modification programs aimed at specific identified weaknesses (Hauserman, Zweback, and Plotkin, 1972). In the papers examined, the recommended focus for the therapist ranges from examination of the group as a whole process, following Bion (1961), to the reward characteristics of the controlling ward environment. The influences of peer interaction and pressure, guided interchanges, transference problems, and recommended therapist behaviors and attitudes have also been discussed.

EARLY APPROACHES

Papers by Powles (1959a,b) and Westman (1960) describe a type of program with goals and an evolving process that is rare in this age of short-term hospitalization. Their groups lasted at least a year with largely constant membership, and they were able to identify stages of group development that do not emerge in short-term groups with rapid turnover of members (and sometimes staff). The reasons for forming groups are worth noting, for they retain their validity today.

Powles saw the groups as essential for management of adolescents who were distributed in wards throughout the hospital. A decision had previously been taken not to have a comprehensive adolescent program centered around a single ward. Acknowledging the early contributions of Aichorn, Redl, and Bettelheim, among others, the authors viewed the use of groups as providing the opportunity to engage in adolescent community activity.

A male psychiatrist began the group, with a female social worker joining within a month. In addition to her experience with social interaction techniques, the female therapist provided a comparatively more nurturing role, in distinction to the male, who tended to carry more of the weight of the authority role. This separation of roles, while somewhat variable, evolved deliberately and provided for a great range of adolescents' responses to adult figures.

One of the inevitable features of the ongoing inpatient group is the ever-changing proportions of certain diagnostic groups on the ward. The diagnostic mix is an important contributor to the group's functioning. Powles (1959a) reported an impression that a mixture of diagnoses made for a good group, but if "behavior disorders" were too high a proportion, tension and acting out increased, impairing group performance. Psychotics, especially those whose behavior was particularly bizarre, did more poorly and the group had difficulty with them.

Westman (1960) reported on a program for hospitalized delinquents, based on psychoanalytic concepts. In this year-long program, initial emphasis was placed on direct control, use of arbitrary rules to target the problem of impulse control, and provision of a model for identification (the therapist) who consistently and ably responded to adolescent provocation. Such rapid responding was deemed essential in order to gain members' respect. It was less necessary after a while, since within a month peer pressure emerged as an aid to members' self-control, supplanting staff control in some areas. Westman enhanced the value of the group by creating a waiting list, running alternative disliked activities simultaneously (which nonmembers had to attend), and providing refreshments, among other steps.

The long-term group described by Elizur et al. (1981) allowed for development of themes beyond the primary and frequent one of patient and staff struggle for leadership and role identification in the group. The program goals included teaching of behavior boundaries, emotional and behavior reeducation, and improved socialization. Group building was fostered by a variety of scheduled activities that included all adolescents. Initial group therapy sessions featured monologues and little meaningful interaction. As signs of the feeling of belonging to the group and the setting appeared, group members began to listen better to each other. Role assignments were further evidence of the group's development. Special use of words, songs, and nicknames reflected members' involvement with the group. Entrance of new members and departure of others were among the chief reasons for the frequent fluctuations in the group's emotional level.

Membership in adolescent inpatient groups is significantly

shorter today than in the groups described by Powles (1959a,b), Westman (1960), and Elizur et al. (1981). The challenge for today's group therapists is to foster meaningful commitment by the individual to the group process during the briefer period of hospitalization prevalent in almost all hospital programs. More frequent groups may be one answer, more active guidance by the therapists may be another. A third source of help to the group may be the articulation of clear goals for the group, and the development of techniques to assist in achieving them.

PROBLEM-FOCUSED GROUPS

Early writers such as Westman and Powles described problems and offered solutions in areas such as staff roles, dealing with membership, and resistance issues, and the need for limits and boundaries, which have applicability in a wide range of adolescent groups. What has almost disappeared from the literature is examination of psychosexual or stages of development of the inpatient group (Powles, 1959b; Elizur et al., 1981). These are rarely seen in short-term groups with constantly changing membership. Instead the characteristics of the formative group phase, often interpreted as concerned with preoedipal or oral issues (Glatzer, 1959; Kymissis, 1978), predominate. These themes, coupled with basic problems of limit-setting, fluctuate in intensity while remaining ever present.

The stress of the group provokes an upsurge of irrational feelings, including the wish for protection and nurturance by the good object. Oral themes are sometimes exhibited in extended discussion of the effects of medication (Kymissis, 1978). Glatzer (1959) identifies preoedipal themes of preoccupation with both the good and the bad mother. Noting that themes of orientation to good mother figures (wish for feeding, insatiability) are more easily observed, she stresses the equally necessary task of identifying and interpreting behavior that ties patients to the bad mother object. A common example of this is the provocative patient who seems to seek reactions that can be interpreted as punitive, unfair, and a justification of oneself as mistreated. Should they neglect the oral nature of the group, staff will be repeatedly surprised by changes in the group's level of demands and shifting ability to examine itself. It is as if the primitive, constantly changing group has no memory of its own characteristics or its relation to its leaders. Members do not retain the impression of being nourished or controlled. We suggest that the prime task of therapists working with adolescents in this short-term group modality is to formulate with utmost clarity a series of goals for the group. These goals should explicitly differ from long-term treatment goals. These short-term goals, which require frequent representing to members, are more modest, less intrapsychically focused, and capable of being seriously explored if not always reached in a brief hospital stay.

An example of focused, goal-oriented group treatment is the "Positive Group" (Rogeness and Stewart, 1978; Rosenstock and McLaughlin, 1982). Its primary feature is that the staff allows only positive comments to be made. Rogeness and Stewart reported that this group evolved from a dull, end-of-week meeting held to review patients' progress. It was decided to include patients and encourage their involvement. Banning negative remarks about oneself or others led to a focus on progress. This rule allowed members to request or return positive remarks. The unusual focus directed attention toward the adolescent's positive resources, an area often neglected by the youngster and his or her family. This procedure, which sharply alters the proportion of positive and negative remarks, offers a guided experience in noticing the effects one has on others.

Sometimes, however, the salient problem is an almost complete lack of verbalization. This becomes the primary consideration, even in a group designed for another purpose. An example of this occurred in a project by Hauserman et al. (1972). A group therapy program and a token economy were already in place at this state hospital; however, the results were observed to be poor due to the patients' minimal verbalization. When tokens were awarded for initiation of verbal interchanges (without any explanation being given), the increase in verbal behavior was clear enough to result in this pilot project's incorporation as a permanent part of the hospital's treatment program. The potential positive effects of modeling as an additional factor were acknowledged as well. Also mentioned as effective were shaping behavior, such as reinforcement for answering, for unusually silent members, and peer reinforcement. The effectiveness of peer reinforcement was noteworthy in the support of relevant responses, while also discouraging foolish or immature verbalizations.

Use of technological innovations has not been sufficiently exploited in treatment programs. For example, videotape can be used in a variety of ways to alter interaction patterns of adolescents. Corder,

Whiteside, McNeill, Brown, and Corder (1981) offer an example of this, using a structured feedback method with adolescents at a state hospital. Each session of this open-ended therapy group was videotaped. On alternate sessions, preselected parts of the preceding session were shown, with a guided discussion. Group goals, which were repeated at the start of the review period, were handling and talking about feelings, giving and receiving opinions and feedback, and learning to understand oneself. Corder et al. (1981) found that the viewing and discussion segments significantly affected behavior during the rest of the session. Interestingly, as group cohesion appeared to develop, the differences between "viewing" and "nonviewing" sessions became less pronounced, suggesting that some changes in behavior were taking more permanent hold.

The preceding several articles (Hauserman et al., 1972; Rogeness and Stewart, 1978; Corder et al., 1981; Rosenstock and McLaughlin, 1982) were primarily aimed at the patients' verbal and social interactions with each other. Another problem that can be addressed by a specific procedure is denial of and resistance to the hospital experience. This is manifested in such acts as lateness and nonparticipation in school and hospital program activities, feigned drowsiness, as well as other passive-aggressive responses. To respond to this, Rosenstock, Galle, and Levy have developed "Early A.M. Group Therapy" (1978). This event, held every three to four weeks, is called when the level of resistance in the group is perceived to be at a generally high level. One hundred percent attendance is expected, and the group is not held if this does not happen. The group meets at 6:00 A.M. for 75 minutes, with the staff purchasing refreshments (this led to the meeting's becoming known as the "donut group"). The group, according to the authors, represents a challenge to the members' behavior, and a sign that the staff care enough to make this effort at such an early hour. Night staff, traditionally rarely included in therapeutic events, felt more involved. The suggestion is offered that this activity helps new members join the milieu, and restimulates involvement in the program, supplying the ward's sporadic need for a change of pace.

Zabusky and Kymissis (1983), discussing the use of groups as crucial to strengthening the adolescent's positive ego identity, describe a group aimed at youngsters awaiting discharge. Adolescents at this point of hospitalization have special difficulty with the fact of having "no place to go." Fears of future placement and tolerance of the sad fact of leaving newly made friends are frequent themes.

MANAGEMENT OF DISRUPTIVE BEHAVIOR

No treatment program for adolescents can claim to have a comprehensive approach if provisions for dealing with limits testing or acting out are omitted. Strictly speaking, this is perhaps not a goal of therapy but rather a requirement of any successful program if it is to survive (Straight and Werkman, 1958). Staff rules, consequences for infractions, and the development of predictable responses are required. Westman (1960), as mentioned above, described the inclusion of arbitrary rules (e.g., everyone must sit around the table) as a procedure to evoke and clarify the presence of the leader's authority. This was employed with delinquent hospitalized adolescents. In our view this approach would not be as necessary (although it could be reserved as an option) where the majority of patients are psychotic, as opposed to character disorders.

Crabtree (1982) describes acting out problems and their resolution on a ward of up to 20 adolescents. "Cycles of tension," which underlie individual or group eruptions, are to be expected and are best understood as a group-as-a-whole phenomenon (Bion, 1961). Rapid staff response to behavior eruptions is advisable, but as experience attests, hard to implement. Early and rapid feedback is needed most at the earlier stage of hospitalization. Crabtree describes one way of providing these requirements, using a "level system."

To be effective the employment of a level system requires frequent evaluation of observable behavior. At the orientation or entry level, this is accomplished by daily opportunities to earn tokens, which are spent that day. Each day's failures are erased the next morning. The opportunity to succeed is thus presented daily, maximizing the possibility for success.

Advancement to the next step, working level, requires demonstration of ability to work with decreased supervision. Crabtree notes that sociopathic youngsters frequently meet with failure at this point. They require special attention to their deficits in internalizing codes of behavior.

Crabtree also discusses the problem of the antisocial "outlaw leader," who often evokes difficult feelings in staff. They represent a threat to the therapeutic environment. Staff often feel themselves to be losing control of the treatment. Techniques for responding therapeutically to such provocation include the repeated delineation of the individual's responsibility for his or her decisions. Also discussed is a four-stage process of "therapeutic dismissal" from the program, with repeated clarification of the tasks required, education of the family, and time deadlines that are enforced. The treatment of antisocial adolescents requires clearly stressful procedures such as these. Directors of such programs and therapeutic staff should be prepared to deal factually and consistently with frequent disbelief by the sociopathic patient as denied consequences, including expulsion, become reality. Program heads may also have to allow for expressions of sadness on the part of the staff. Their emotions may reflect a mixture of reactions, including concern for the future of the youngster, a sense of professional failure, or narcissistic injury stemming from the disappointment of unrealistic estimation of the unit's ability to help the extremely antisocial youth.

INVOLVEMENT OF THE FAMILY

Multiple family therapy (Laqueur, LaBurt, and Morong, 1964; Laqueur, 1972) has been employed in efforts to engage the patient's family more actively and directly in treatment. Multiple family therapy can be considered as an aid in reengaging the help of families of patients, including the families of patients who may have been deemed chronic and unlikely to return to the community. Chronic patients' relations with their families can be poor both in quality of relations and in minimal frequency of contact. This large-group forum involves parents in the hospital treatment program, with the aim of helping them understand the treatment process, minimize the "splitting" process that often hinders collaboration between parents and staff, and forging an effective alliance.

McClendon (1976) emphasizes the reengagement function of family groups, reporting on a group of inner-city teenagers who were placed 50 miles away from their parents in a state hospital. A weekly bus trip was arranged, with the youngsters traveling to the city for a two-hour session with their parents. McClendon found the parents, who had been labeled as resistive and hostile, to be generally responsive to the program, attending regularly, dealing with here-and-now situations, and sharing others' concerns.

Elizur et al. (1981) used a families' group as part of their comprehensive treatment program. They observed that the families' participation was a clear demonstration to the hospitalized adolescent of their parents' desire to help. In some instances this collaboration led to separate therapy sessions for an individual family.

Shapiro and Kolb (1979) arranged multiple family therapy meetings for a milieu-based ten-bed adolescent unit. A 75-minute meeting included all family members and broad representation from staff, not just therapeutic personnel. A group-interactive, nondirective procedure was employed. The process was conceptualized using Bion's (1961) "basic assumption" descriptions of group life. The use of multiple family therapy was a response to the perception that the hospitalization signaled a "shared family regression." This meeting permitted observation of and response to poorly controlled and projected hostility and the shared regression.

GROUP LEADERSHIP ROLE AND TASKS

The special difficulties of the leadership role have only been briefly considered in previous articles on adolescent inpatient groups. This is a regrettable deficiency, as the problems of the therapists are multiplied by the severity of the adolescent patients' pathology and their levels of resistance to treatment and to the (usual) fact of involuntary hospitalization.

A major point upon which there is emphatic mention by several authors (Powles, 1959a; Westman, 1960; Fisher, 1976) is the clear public definition, whether in word or act, of the therapist's role and authority. The use of this authority as a method to explore and encourage change in adolescents' distorted responses to major authority figures is perhaps the primary task of dynamically oriented group psychotherapy. Bion's (1961) description of the tasks of the leader are of striking relevance. The leader must be able to define the common enemy (mental illness) and be unafraid in addressing the task of confronting this difficulty. The behavior of the therapist thus exercises an enormous effect on the group's willingness or anxiety in tackling its problems. Evans (1965) provides an illustration of this process when applied in a group-as-a-whole approach.

Fisher (1976) presents the traditional viewpoint in describing her "credo" for conducting group therapy. She stresses the fact that she is an adult, and does not try to "join" their group by dressing down or talking like an age-peer (although one should be familiar with current adolescent slang terms). The therapist must continually provide standards, judgments, clarifications, close attention without the pretence of instant intimacy (a favorite illusion of this age group), and humor. Experienced therapists will note that this by no means exhausts the list of skills and behaviors required for this frequently exhausting activity.

In setting up adolescent treatment programs, special consideration should be paid to the training of group therapists to work with hospitalized adolescents in this special setting. Training and support are essential for group staff to function effectively in this highly stressful task. Too often, formal supervision of the treating staff's group work is neglected as other clinical questions and crises arise, as they so often do. Group therapy supervision is a special activity that deserves its protected time in the training process.

Another activity that is often lost due to time pressures and reestablished only with difficulty is the staff postgroup meeting, which should be held right after the therapy group. The exchange of impressions, as staff share their perspectives on the special aspect of the group that drew their attention, provides a unique learning forum and helps to keep a unit team in practice in communicating their own differences across personal and professional lines. The importance of this time must be stressed to our students. Without such meetings the information learned in group therapy is often lost, and group therapy may become viewed as an activity unconnected to the rest of the therapeutic effort.

The implicit role of the therapist, and the explicit goals of treatment in adolescent inpatient groups, must be clarified as early as possible for incoming patients. This may be done before the group, in ward orientation meetings, and it may often be repeated at the start of each session in which a new member is introduced.

CONCLUSIONS

It is a common observation that adolescents present special treatment problems for mental health professionals. Their developmentally based attempts at separation and individuation, combined with their rapidly shifting emotional state, causes difficulties even for experienced therapists. Treating adolescents in a group poses additional difficulties—if any were needed. One has to diagnose and respond effectively to group resistances. These often appear as notoriously contagious and short-lived phenomena, while the more difficult aspects of both the individual and group resistances tend to remain hidden from view. Enormous amounts of patient (and, it must be admitted, staff) anxiety are apparent, related in part to the problems of being in a group. This often emerges in attempts at confrontation with the leader. Another frequently reported activity is observation of others' problems in control of behavior and feelings. This is a finding that may have opposite results in two different youngsters. One may be reassured by seeing that his problems are not unique, while another may be extremely unsettled by seeing another teenager losing his self-control. The group leader's active intervention is especially important at this point. When psychotic adolescents form a significant part of the group, the failure of the impaired ego to manage these tasks becomes even more threatening to group members. The difficult task we all must manage, maintenance of ego boundaries and a sense of self in the pressure of a group setting, is incomparably more difficult for these severely impaired youngsters.

In a hospital setting, the additional pressures on the adolescent group come from the perceived stigma of hospitalization and the involuntary aspect of the treatment. This brings yet another order of difficulty to the problem of carrying out adolescent group psychotherapy. Perhaps this is why, despite the vast literature on group psychotherapy, the number of articles we were able to locate, using both computer and hand searches, focusing on the use of this modality with inpatient adolescents, barely reached two dozen.

The existing literature does, however, clearly show that this technique has evolved over the last few decades to meet the changing conditions of shorter hospitalizations and more specifically defined treatment needs. Inpatient group psychotherapy is a viable treatment procedure for brief-stay patients (Sadock and Gould, 1964; Yalom, 1983). A group environment is seen as providing fewer management problems (Powles, 1959a) and a broad range of activities with therapeutic impact (Chiles and Sanger, 1977; Elizur et al., 1981). The traditional group psychotherapy is one of a broad range of treatment activities aimed at providing the patient with increased coping skills.

There are a number of different methods and techniques even at this early point in the evolution of the adolescent milieu. Criteria for evaluation of the usefulness of these procedures have largely been confined to subjective impressions of therapist or patients. Yalom (1983) has noted the considerable obstacles to rigorous and highly controlled research to evaluate the contributions of this procedure. He nevertheless concludes with emphasis that group therapy makes a valuable contribution to the overall treatment effort. With respect to adolescents, we suggest that they can benefit from a therapeutic environment where social, limit-setting, educational, and confrontational events can occur.

Despite the diversity of viewpoints and methods, we believe there is more to be gained by attending to the similarities in these articles than to the differences. This is so for several reasons: First, there are parameters common to all of the settings described. These include a meaningful number of emotionally disturbed adolescents, usually meeting for the first time in the hospital; a mildly to severely confining environment with sharply reduced self-determination and autonomy; a sense of estrangement from parents; sudden encounter with a number of unfamiliar personnel (such as physicians, nurses, and other therapeutic staff), some possessing and exercising authority over them, some with offers of help for problems the patients may not acknowledge. Even allowing for variations in the programmatic emphasis, consideration of the role of each factor was beyond the scope of all the papers located.

Second, following closely on this point, the limited space and focus of professional papers requires attention to distinctive elements of the selected topic. We found no paper attempting an overview of the problems of conducting adolescent group psychotherapy. However, the common elements described in the preceding program may exist in many programs, with mention being omitted due to publication-related considerations. Terminology may be more different than methodology in other cases. We suspect that, with appropriate translations of terms, authors focusing on guided interaction procedures, for example, would not strongly disagree with, say, many of Fisher's (1976) convictions.

Some multigroup programs may offer such a diversity of group activities that staff may decide to dispense with traditional group psychotherapy, which is probably one of the groups that makes the most demands on staff. We suggest that to omit traditional therapy groups is a mistake. While the reeducative and socialization goals of activity groups is useful, we feel the time has not come to do away with therapies that deal directly rather than indirectly with the feelings and fantasies that pose such threats to teenagers. The skills that have evolved in the history of this treatment modality should not be taken so lightly by those who have learned it with difficulty.

A final point is the suggestion that more of the work we believe is currently being done should be made available through presentations and publication. It is our impression that work on adolescent inpatient group therapy is significantly underreported, relative to the amount of group therapy being practiced. More exchange of techniques and ideas and discussion of common problems is highly desirable. An expanded discussion of the problems of inpatient adolescent group therapy should include consideration of the need for special training of therapists to work in this especially challenging treatment setting. It is our hope that this review will stimulate presentations and publications, leading to further development of what we believe should be a vital part of any adolescent treatment program.

REFERENCES

Aichhorn, A. (1925), *Wayward Youth.* New York: Viking, 1935.

Bion, W.R. (1961), *Experiences in Groups.* New York: Basic Books.

Chiles, J.A. & Sanger, E. (1977), The use of groups in brief inpatient treatment of adolescents. *Hosp. & Commun. Psychiat.,* 28(6):443–445.

Corder, B.F., Whiteside, R., McNeill, M., Brown, T., & Corder, R.F (1981), An experimental study of the effect of structured videotape feedback on adolescent group psychotherapy process. *J. Youth & Adol.,* 10(4):255–262.

Crabtree, L. (1982), Hospitalized adolescents who act out: A treatment approach. *Psychiat.,* 45:147–158.

Elizur, A., Gaoni, B., & Davidson, S. (1981), The treatment of adolescents and their parents in group settings in a psychiatric hospital. *Internat. J. Soc. Psychiat.,* 27(2):83–92.

Evans, J. (1965), Analytic group therapy with delinquents. *Adol.,* 1:180–196.

Fisher, H. (1976), A credo for responsible group therapy with hospitalized adolescents. *Clin. Soc. Work J.,* 4(2):121–126.

Glatzer, H.T. (1959), Clinical aspects of adult therapy. I. Notes on the preoedipal phantasy. *Amer. J. Orthopsychiat.,* 29:383–390.

Gralnick, A., ed. (1969), *Collected Papers of High Point Hospital.* New York: Brunner/Mazel.

Hauserman, N., Zweback, S., & Plotkin, A. (1972), Use of concrete reinforcement to facilitate verbal initiations in adolescent group psychotherapy. *J. Consult. & Clin. Psychol.,* 38(1):90–96.

Kymissis, P. (1978), Pharmacotherapy combined with analytically oriented group therapy. In: *Group Therapy 1978,* eds. L. Wolberg & J. Aronson. New York: Stratton International.

Laqueur, H.P. (1972), Mechanisms of change in multiple family therapy. In: *Progress in Group and Family Therapy,* eds. C. Sager & H.S. Kaplan. New York: Brunner/Mazel.

——— LaBurt, H.A., & Morong, E. (1964), Multiple family therapy. In: *Current Psychiatric Therapies,* Vol. 4, ed. J.H. Masserman. New York: Grune & Stratton.

McClendon, R. (1976) Multiple family group therapy with adolescents in a state hospital. *Clin. Soc. Work J.*, 4:14–24.

Powles, W.E (1959a), Group management of emotionally ill adolescents in a Canadian mental hospital. *Can. Psychiat. Assn. J.*, 4(2):77–89.

——— (1959b), Psychosexual maturity in a therapy group of disturbed adolescents. *Internat. J. Group Psychother.*, 9:429–441.

Rogeness, G., & Stewart, J.T. (1978), The positive group: A therapeutic technique in the hospital treatment of adolescents. *Hosp. & Commun. Psychiat.*, 29 (8):520–522.

Rosenstock, H.A., Galle, M., & Levy, H.J. (1978), Early A.M. group therapy. *J. Nat. Assn. Priv. Psychiat. Hosp.*, 9(2):37–38.

———McLaughlin, M. (1982), Positive group efficacy in adolescent treatment. *J. Clin. Psychiat.*, 43 (2):58–61.

Sadock, B., & Gould, R.E. (1964), Preliminary report on short-term group psychotherapy on an acute adolescent male service. *Internat. J. Group Psychother.*, 14:465–473.

Sands, D.E. (1953), A special mental hospital unit for the treatment of psychosis and neurosis in juveniles. *J. Ment. Sci.*, 99:123–129.

Shapiro, E.R., & Kolb, J.E. (1979), Engaging the family of the hospitalized adolescent: The multiple family meeting. *Adol. Psychiat.*, 7:322–342.

Stein, M.D., & Davis, J.K. (1982), *Therapies for Adolescents.* San Francisco: Jossey-Bass.

Straight, B., & Werkman, S. (1958), Control problems in group therapy with aggressive adolescent boys in a mental hospital. *Amer. J. Psychiat.*, 114:998–1001.

Westman, J.C. (1960), Group therapy with hospitalized delinquent adolescents. *Internat. J. Group Psychother.*, 11:410–418.

Yalom, I.D. (1983), *Inpatient Group Therapy.* New York: Basic Books.

Zabusky, G., & Kymissis, P. (1983), Identity group therapy: A transitional group for hospitalized adolescents. *Internat. J. Group Psychother.*, 33 (1):99–109.

Chapter 6

A Case Presentation of a Borderline Adolescent in Long-Term Group Psychotherapy

LEWIS H. RICHMOND, M.D.

This chapter presents adolescent peer group psychotherapy as the primary treatment mode of a borderline patient, but also utilized are counseling with parents, parallel parent group, and multiple family therapy. Various approaches within peer group psychotherapy include traditional psychodynamically oriented psychotherapy, role playing including family sculpting, Gestalt techniques, introduction of peer guests, and the use of videotape. Contacts, outside the actual therapy situation, were also felt to be of therapeutic importance and included those between therapist and family and between patient and peer group members.

CASE EXAMPLE

G. was a 15-year-old sophomore, who was referred because of marked decrease in grades over the past two years; inability to form meaningful peer relationships; and acting out behavior, including poor school attendance and performance and shoplifting. He lived with his Hispanic father, a construction supervisor; his British mother, a housewife with a limited education; and his 27-year-old brother, a student. Completing the family was a 23-year-old sister who was married and living in another city.

During the evaluation, G. appeared as a friendly, obese male, who was moderately anxious and mildly depressed. He related coherently and relevantly. He described much chaos within the family constellation, with mother being emotionally volatile and father withdrawing when angry. Both parents were described as overprotective. He indicated that he had difficulty with any type of social relationship, especially with females, and stated that he had frequently been the butt of jokes by classmates. He described some suspiciousness of peers' intentions and difficulty with trusting others. He appeared quite bright, but described difficulty with school performance because of boredom. This resulted in his being talkative in class and rude toward teachers. He indicated he had talent as a musician and his future plan was to pursue a career in music. Although he denied overt depressive symptoms and aggressive fantasies, he described emotional lability and gave evidence of chronic low self-esteem and unexpressed anger. He seemed uncertain as to appropriate ways of expressing underlying feelings. Initial clinical impression was that G. was experiencing both intrapsychic and interpersonal conflicts. These problems related to his separation–individuation difficulties, and resulted in identity distortions, both in how he viewed himself and how he felt others saw him. As a result of these psychodynamics and clinical presentation, diagnosis of borderline syndrome was made. Because of his inability to talk in front of his parents, and his problem with peer relationships, it was recommended that he begin an adolescent group psychotherapy experience and that his parents engage in counseling.

In two parental sessions, mother was verbose and very emotional. Although verbally dominant, she was noted to avoid discussing important family issues. She described a distraught childhood, being abandoned by her family and raised in an orphanage. She and her husband met during World War II, when he was stationed in Europe. She described great difficulty in allowing her children to grow up, to the extent of not allowing G. to go alone on the school bus. Mother also shared fantasies of having her 27-year-old son marry and then have his wife move in with the family, so that she could raise her grandchildren. Father was quite peripheral during the sessions, allowing himself little expression of feelings, and indicating a lot of unmet dependency needs in his own childhood. Both parents were moderately obese and brother was said to be overweight also.

The therapist attempted to establish a contract in which the parents would allow G. to go to school on the bus and to practice music. In return G. would be responsible for doing his homework and bringing up his grades. However, in the next session mother said they did not present the agreement to G. as they felt that he would be unable to fulfill his part. During that session, the parents also showed much evidence of dependency on each other. The parents canceled two subsequent sessions and then were scheduled for a parallel parents' group, which was to begin in the future and which would meet at the same time as the adolescent group, with a different therapy team.

G. attended group psychotherapy for a period of three years and nine months, keeping 146 of 184 scheduled sessions. He generally called in advance to cancel the majority of sessions that he missed, usually because of extracurricular activities.

The group met once a week for 1 hour and 15 minutes. There were two coleaders [the same male therapist (LHR) throughout, and four different female cotherapists, each of whom worked with the group for a minimum of six months]. The male and female peer members, aged 15 to 18, presented with a variety of emotional difficulties, with diagnoses ranging from character disorder to psychosis.

During G.'s initial sessions, he remained generally anxious and passive and was spontaneous only to the extent of whispering asides to the male therapist, next to whom he tried to sit whenever possible. Occasionally he would joke as a form of distraction, particularly when the group was talking about meaningful feelings. By his third month in the group, although still anxious, he began to participate more appropriately when the group talked about earning poor grades in school, despite having the intellectual ability to perform better. By the fifth month of group, he spoke of his concerns of not being allowed to return to school the following year because of continuing poor attendance and talking back to teachers. He also spoke of concern in not being accepted for summer band, but minimized the emotional concomitants of this, although obviously it was quite important to him. During the month, he informed the group that he would be allowed to attend school in a different district, and his family had moved into a smaller apartment so that this would be possible. Despite this change, he was expelled from school just prior to the end of the school year, because of his continuing behavioral difficulty.

He gradually became more verbally active within the group, but still gave much evidence of diminished self-confidence and difficulty in relating meaningfully with peers. However, he related an incident of talking to some girls he had met at a dance, and this apparently was his first spontaneous heterosexual relationship.

During the end of the summer, B., a male homosexual, became a new member of the group and his presence initially increased G.'s anxiety concerning sexual identity. G. had been looking forward to returning to his new school, in hopes of making a successful adjustment this time. When he realized that B. attended the same school, G.'s initial response was embarrassment, and he dealt with this by ignoring B. Otherwise G.'s adaptation was positive, particularly since the school had a liberal dress code, which enabled G. to sport a full beard. (The male leader also had a beard.)

During the next month, G. became more verbal, particularly in response to peers having similar problems in talking about the bind in which they found themselves at home. He felt that if he left home, his father would do so shortly thereafter, thus implying that the parental relationship was held together primarily by G.'s presence.

G.'s parents were seen in a parallel parents' group from his eighth to his fourteenth month of therapy. His mother became a dominant member verbally, and rejected many of the suggestions made to her concerning tuning in to her own feelings and behavior within the family. When the parents and adolescents met for a combined session (multiple family therapy) during G.'s eleventh month of treatment, his parents did not attend. G. was present, but chose not to join in the group discussion of handling anger within the family.

G. became gradually more outgoing and started to share feelings, and in return the group gave him positive feedback for his improvement. They pointed out that instead of just speaking to the therapist, he was able to talk to the group as a whole and also was able to communicate with other members at certain times during the sessions. Shortly thereafter he began to sit in places other than next to the therapist. However, he would still engage the therapist after the sessions, with questions of a sexual nature, such as about masturbation and birth control. Brief answers were given, and it was suggested that he bring these topics up at the group session. However, he was unable to do so at that time.

During the fourteenth month of therapy, another combined session was held with parents and teenagers. G.'s mother was quite dominant and verbal and perseverated on the patient's past behavior, not acknowledging the changes that had occurred in the interim. She was resistant to accepting the group's confrontation of how she was dealing with this. During the session, G. indicated he wanted to become more responsible. As an example, he decided he would try to waken himself each morning to go to school. His parents felt that he would not do this, and the group tried to establish a one-week contract for this to occur. Mother became upset, interfered with establishing the agreement, and left before the session was over, while the group was still working on the contract.

However, by the next month, G. was indeed getting up each morning without help from his parents. At this time the parallel parents' group terminated, and the parents were seen thereafter only during multiple family sessions. Although mother had apparently been resistant to suggestions for change, she subsequently employed some of the advice she had previously turned down.

G. continued to do relatively well in school and decided that he would no longer snub B. on the school campus, despite fears he had of other people identifying him as a homosexual because of his association with B.

In the following month a minimarathon of four hours' duration was conducted, at the group's request. Because the group felt that many important feelings were beginning to be dealt with requiring a longer meeting, the therapy team incorporated the flexibility necessary for scheduling this extended session. During this time, G. was able to talk at length of concerns about his masculinity, observing that a masculine role model was limited at home because of father being emotionally distant and brother being obese and socially withdrawn.

During the seventeenth month of therapy, G. was hitchhiking in a prohibited area and observed a police car in the vicinity. He panicked, thinking that the police would come after him. Then he began to run, which of course made the police suspicious, and they indeed did come after him. He was arrested and detained briefly. During the following group session, he expressed significant anxiety about the incident as it was his first encounter with the police since he began group therapy. He was able to verbalize how his previous shoplifting episode was an attempt to get attention for his discomfort with himself. He also understood how he set himself up to be caught, particularly with this last encounter, and was pleased with his ability to see the relationship between his feelings and behavior.

A couple of sessions later, B. "sculpted" his family and demonstrated his interactions with various members. G. identified with B.'s ambivalent feelings toward his mother, and thereafter began to accept his feelings of wanting to distance himself from the overprotective aspects of the symbiotic part of his relationship with his mother. As he began to develop a more separate self, he would compete with the male therapist for group leadership. This was explored and related to G.'s wanting to see his father as a more dominant male, who could engage with him in a give-and-take manner.

During the next multiple family meeting, G. and his parents indicated a clearer communication within the family and shared pleasure at G.'s improvement in school, in his pursuing his interest in music, and in his obtaining a part time job. There was some anger expressed by G. because his parents did not allow him to use the car by himself, even though he had earned his driver's license.

During the next session, G. shared with the group his first sexual experience in a relevant and humorous way. He described having met a girl and subsequently they decided to try a sexual encounter, although neither of them had done so previously. After much research, they decided to take a bus to a three-dollar motel. There was much mutual anxiety during the bus trip and a marked increase in anxiety when they reached the registration desk of the motel. G. was unable to recall how he signed the register, other than as Mr. and Mrs. something or other. On going from the desk to their room, they kept looking around to see if anyone they knew was watching them. When they finally got into the room, they tried to consummate the sexual act, but were unsuccessful because of their shared anxiety. The group was very accepting and supporting of this incident, indicating that under those circumstances it was not unusual for failure to occur. G. was very appreciative of the feedback and felt good that he could be accepted even when describing failure. He also thereafter was more active in discussions with sexual themes.

By the nineteenth month of therapy, he began verbalizing ideas of completing the two years he had remaining in high school and then going to college. During a session when B. spoke of his low self-image, G. was quite supportive and gave good advice concerning B.'s positive relationships with others. G. began to utilize this approach as new members would arrive in the group, by being supportive in terms of their probability for change. He also continued to talk about how disappointed and angry he felt toward his parents for not allowing him the use of the car.

During the next multiple family session, G. spoke of the significant amount of anger that was present among family members. He described how he and his mother communicated by trying to outshout each other and eventually father would become quite angry and intervene. The group confronted the family with the need for each member to listen more attentively to the others and to consciously keep their voices down. The group also indicated that if father got involved in something that should be dealt with between G. and his mother, either G. or his mother should confront father concerning this. Father said the reason that he was uncomfortable with G. driving the car was that he had no car insurance. This seemed to relieve some of G.'s tension, as he had felt that the reason had been parental distrust of him. Thus, communication was becoming clearer within the family. Because of mother's protective anxiety, the group discussed the necessity of her learning that even though her intention was to protect her child from pain, it was important to the emotional growth of her child to experience frustration himself and to learn how to deal with this.

During a subsequent group session, a member spoke of her parents not acknowledging her having become a young lady and continuing to treat her as a child. A Gestalt technique was utilized to demonstrate this interaction in which the girl was able to relate to her mother in the here and now in a different manner than had previously been the case. She also spoke of her awareness of the uncertainty in both her own and her parents' expectations of how she should function. G. identified with this and became quite comfortable and supportive in relating with this member. G. then spoke of his own self-concept, particularly his weight problem and family acceptance of obesity. He talked of feelings of inadequacy, particularly in relating to females, because of his appearance. The group discussed being overweight as a possible way of appearing unattractive and thus a defense against involvement with the opposite sex.

G. spoke of his concerns about his mixed ethnic origin and began to bring a white pet rock to the group meetings. During the next few sessions, the group discussed positive qualities of each member and reinforced constructive changes that were noted. Following this, G. no longer brought his rock and stated that "she" had met a black rock and married. The group interpreted this as the resolution of G.'s ethnic concern related to his acceptance by his group peers.

At the next combined adolescent/parent meeting, G.'s mother voiced anger at the group, indicating she was always picked on and not listened to. This was in response to her feeling that G. interrupted her frequently when she would try to explain something to him. The group pointed out that her explanations were lengthy harangues or lectures which turned G. off. No additional combined sessions were held because of lack of interested parents.

G. began bringing candy to the group, providing a nurturing role, and being somewhat parental in trying to meet members' dependency needs. He also began dating more, but usually took a male friend along on his dates, and the friend usually would wind up with the girl by the end of the evening. The group confronted G. with this type of behavior, relating this to his fears of intimacy and his feelings of inadequacy. He responded by sharing his fear of being hurt or hurting the other person emotionally. This was also related to his concerns about the fragility of his parents' marriage, including his impression that his parents were involved too often in a mutually antagonistic relationship.

The group also began talking more about peer heterosexual relationships, and most members, including G., revealed their relative lack of skill in relating to the opposite sex. Role playing was employed in illustrating ways of using the telephone and in initiating conversations with the opposite sex. G. benefited from this in his subsequent improvement in communicating with females.

During this time, G. was earning good grades in school and was pleased with his musical accomplishments. The group reinforced his more positive self-concept.

By the twenty-sixth month of therapy, G. was able to talk about the positive aspects of crying and of becoming angry. He was able to understand the constructive aspects of emoting. Thereafter, he became less maternal and more appropriately peer oriented in sessions.

At this time, G. began mild experimentation in using marijuana and other drugs. The group members discussed their roles as future parents and how these would differ from those of their parents. G. indicated he would allow his children to separate and become autonomous at earlier ages and then also "separated" from his use of drugs.

By the twenty-ninth month of therapy, G. was working on his ambivalent feelings about forming close relationships and related this to past fears of abandonment. He realized that as he was approaching adulthood, he was becoming more independent and feeling comfortable about this. He then became more trusting of his peers in the group and brought a pet tarantula to one session to represent his ability to handle fearful objects.

During his thirty-third month in therapy, he began to take a more sustained leadership role in the group. A new female member spoke of having a negative self-image, and G. shared with her, in a supportive way, how similar he had been and the ways in which he was able to elicit change. He also began talking more about his sister. He indicated his brother had moved out of the house but soon returned. G. stated that his sister had obtained a divorce and that his parents might also divorce. However, he was able to realize appropriately that this would be their decision and not his, and so was beginning to delineate appropriate boundaries between himself and his parents.

At the end of his third year in group, G. began rehearsals in the school orchestra for a musical comedy production. When the male lead became ill, G. immediately auditioned for the role. Although he had no prior experience and there were only two weeks of rehearsal remaining, he won the role. He asked that LHR attend a performance, giving the wrong time so that he would arrive early and be introduced to the cast. Coincidentally, G.'s parents attended the same performance, and they asked LHR to sit with them. The three shared a thoroughly enjoyable evening and were delighted with G.'s versatility. From a previously shy and withdrawn teenager, he was now able to sing, dance, act, and display excellent comic timing, all in front of an audience.

He continued to manifest self-confidence by beginning to lose weight. When a pregnant member joined the group and spoke of setting herself up for rejection by boys, G. shared how he had behaved similarly with girls. He reinforced her decision to plan to give the baby for adoption, agreeing that it would be unfair to both mother and child for the girl to raise the child herself.

He also related how he was able to continue to avoid getting involved in parental conflicts unrelated to him. Although he thought his parents continued to try to implicate him in their difficulties, he was able to avoid the temptation.

In his thirty-eighth month of therapy, videotapes were made in preparation for a forthcoming national professional meeting. G. was one of the few members to appear for all videotaping sessions. G. enjoyed seeing the reruns and was able to give constructive criticism about himself and others. The group was also to be a part of a live presentation at the meeting, but only G. and a female peer attended, as most of the others were not allowed to participate by their parents. G. enjoyed interacting with the audience in an exhibitionistic controlling manner and discussed feelings and relationships openly.

During the next month, G. became more involved with female peers without overt fear of rejection. He also felt good that his father was accepting him as a man by sharing "dirty" jokes with him.

In the fortieth month of therapy, G. was pleased to receive his acceptance by a college and he began to talk, with ambivalence, about terminating from group therapy. Several sessions later, he graduated from high school and shared with the group that rather than being overjoyed, he experienced some sense of loss in leaving his classmates. This was discussed in the group as related to his working through feelings of separation from the group. He was also quite pleased that his parents were being more appropriate in allowing him to separate from them by giving him more independence, even allowing him to drive himself to the group, although there was still no car insurance. He also spoke of separation anxiety in a progressively decreasing manner and talked more of his eager anticipation to begin college.

During his last group session, G. terminated in a meaningful and emotional way. He verbalized his appreciation for the help and understanding he had received and felt he wouldn't have "made it" otherwise.

He visited the group during three school recesses, the last occurring one year after termination. During these sessions he described a successful completion of his first year of college and his progress toward a career as a professional musician. He also indicated that his mother had been hospitalized for a suicide gesture as an outgrowth of continuing marital conflict. G. indicated he felt sorry for her but realized it was her problem, and he was glad that she was in therapy.

DISCUSSION

G. presented a borderline personality syndrome, as described by Masterson (1972). G. had been involved in a symbiotic relationship with his mother as had his older brother. However, G., with therapeutic intervention over a long period of time, was able to progressively separate. Also instrumental was his parents' allowing this to occur eventually, despite their early and repeated attempts at obstruction.

G. initially was a shy, withdrawn, obese adolescent whose initial clinic appearance was precipitated by stealing towels. His previous acting out (poor school performance, poor social skills) had essentially been ignored, and this overt behavior was probably a desperate plea for help. His racially mixed background, overprotective parents, and difficulty with establishing individuation all helped create identity difficulties.

G. required much support from the therapist and identity with the therapist, during the early portion of therapy. This was related to Masterson's Phase I of testing and controlling acting out (school problems, episode of running from the police, etc.). His positive transference included growing a beard, using humor and sarcasm, and becoming progressively more comfortable. He then went into Phase II of working through depression and underlying low self-concept, and many of his peers were quite helpful to him in resolving some of his internal conflicts. B. helped G. overcome his fears of latent homosexuality, and female members of the group were instrumental in helping him overcome fears of relating with members of the opposite sex. His use of the tarantula and the rock enabled him to show peers and authority figures how he overcame feared objects and adjusted to his mixed ethnicity. When G. entered Phase III, that of separation, he became essentially a coleader of the group, reaching his zenith when he became the leader of the live group session during the professional meeting. The male–female coleader team concept also helped him work through conflicts with his parents in allowing separation. In these ways the group functioned as a significant transitional object in separation–individuation. All of these factors enabled him to function differently from his parents in an emotional sense. His progressive weight loss and acting role also helped him acquire a body image and self-concept decidedly different from that of other family members and from himself when first seen.

G. essentially went from his oral narcissistic initial appearance, with diminished self-worth, to progressive separation from mother, during which time he could relate more sensitively to peers in the group; and then when he was able to take risks, to extend this to peers outside the group.

In general, the parents were dealt with less frequently as G. got older, reinforcing the need for separation.

In therapy, particularly with adolescents, it is instrumental for the therapist to have a working relationship with the parents. In this particular case, when parents could realize that the therapists could respect their resistances and not try to take their child from them, they were able to function in a healthier direction by allowing their child to become gradually more autonomous. Residential treatment was not recommended for G. because it was felt that mother would have interpreted this as enforced separation and so would have probably terminated therapy.

Some speculations are offered concerning G.'s family. Mother entered individual psychotherapy following a self-harm gesture after G. started college. It would be interesting to speculate on the relationship of her psychopathology to her early deprivation, subsequent conflictual marital relationship, her overprotectiveness toward her sons, and her overt depression after allowing G.'s separation. Mother's predisposition to depression could certainly have included her having few friends or other outside interests, with her primary investment being her family. G.'s brother did not have treatment and continued in a symbiotic relationship with mother.

REFERENCES

Masterson, J.F. (1972), *Treatment of the Borderline Adolescent: A Developmental Approach.* New York: John Wiley.

Part III

Clinical Applications for Special Populations

Chapter 7
Application of Group Therapy in Secondary Schools

IRVING H. BERKOVITZ, M.D.

The group discussion format as a facilitating milieu for acquisition of new knowledge about self and others and for change of attitudes and behavior has been one of the beneficial pioneer developments in the mental health field of the last 50 years. Most applications have occurred in the clinical setting, but useful versions have burgeoned also in schools and colleges. This has occurred at the elementary school level as well as the secondary, but this chapter will confine itself to the adolescent school years, namely junior and senior high school, grades 7 through 12, ages 12 to 17.

Various books and articles have appeared pertaining to the uses of group counseling and guidance with adolescents in schools. Prominent among these have been those by Driver (1958), Warters (1960), MacLennan and Felsenfeld (1968), Mahler (1969), Glass (1969), Ohlsen (1970), Berkovitz (1975a), and Gazda (1976). Gazda and Larsen (1968) reported a comprehensive appraisal of group counseling research during the period of 1938 to 1968, while Berkovitz (1975b) reviewed 1967 to 1971.

Earlier authors and practitioners derived many of the procedures and concepts used in school group counseling from those worked out in clinical groups. In large measure, use of the clinical model was applicable and useful, but several important changes became necessary to allow more successful work in the school setting. At the same time it became evident there were certain important comparative advantages to using group methods in the schools.

Usually the term "therapy" is avoided in the school context as too clinical; the term "counseling" is preferred. There are many definitions of school group counseling, but I shall cite only one. Mahler defines group counseling as:

> [T]he process of using group interaction to facilitate deeper self-understanding and self-acceptance, so that individuals can loosen their defenses sufficiently to explore both the meaning of behavior and new ways of behaving. The concerns and problems encountered are centered in the developmental tasks of each member rather than on pathological blocks and distortions of reality [Mahler, 1969, p. 11].

In recent years, many disturbed young people are counseled in school groups, and the exclusion of "pathological blocks and distortions of reality" may not be realistic.

There are various kinds of groups in schools other than counseling. These may be task-oriented groups set up to focus on sex education, problems of transition to junior high school or transition to graduation, issues of entering college, or leadership. Some teachers may use group process in the classroom. In each of these contexts, there are differences in size of group, length of meeting, degree of permissiveness and spontaneity, severity of problems, responsibilities of leader, range of topics, and other features.

ADVANTAGES OF GROUPS IN THE SCHOOL SETTING

Groups in the school setting have several advantages.

1. Young persons (and families) who would not accept or follow through a referral to a community agency are often able and willing to accept an in-school counseling group. There is not usually the implication of illness with school groups, and there is no financial obstacle. As a result, severely disturbed adolescents often receive useful, and occasionally life-saving, assistance in school groups, which they might not otherwise receive.

2. Insights and confrontations not tolerated in group sessions occasionally result in a member's abrupt departure or nonattendance at future sessions. In a school group, unavoidable contact in the course of the school day and week with other group members and/or the leaders may inadvertently provide an opportunity for reassurance

and/or clarification so that the young person can return to the group, or not be as angry and fearful. School absence to avoid such contact has not been reported. Rather, school groups have usually improved school attendance (Awerbuch and Fraser, 1975).

3. Many facts about each group member, and their attitudes, are often known by the other adolescents or the school personnel in the group. These data may be useful in the sessions if it can be provided without creating undue hurt and antagonism. Often the additional information will shorten and deepen useful counseling.

4. In addition, other school personnel outside the group, who are available to the leader, also have information or observations about the group members that could be useful in that person's counseling. Perhaps there is more likely to be trust of a school colleague than an outside clinic person, who would have to send letters or obtain data by phone with all the attendant communication difficulties.

5. Teacher comments about positive change in the group members who are in their classes, when communicated to the members directly or to the group leaders, can be an important reinforcing influence to maintain group attendance as well as to bolster self-esteem in those young people, who are usually not aware of their positive assets.

DISADVANTAGES

Unfortunately, there are occasionally disadvantages of groups in schools.

1. A group session can lessen emotional control and increase motoric activities such that inappropriate behavior may disturb the concentration or calm of the other parts of the school environment.

2. Sensitive material is occasionally leaked to persons outside the group, breaking the rules of confidentiality and damaging individuals' reputations or sense of privacy, or depreciating the group in the school context. This will need attention in the group when discovered and occasionally requires the exclusion of a group member. If the damage created threatens the functioning of the group, there may be a need to intervene with the people damaged, such as a student falsely rumored to be pregnant or a teacher labeled as "homosexual."

3. Faculty members can be scapegoated if insufficient control is maintained in a session. Some group leaders insist that teachers be referred to only by the subject they teach rather than by name. This

is one way of reducing some of the damage, but trying to prevent students from talking about teachers is to ignore the important place of the teacher in the life of a young person. Feelings are often displaced from other adults, especially parents, to the teacher. Also some critical feelings may be appropriate to that teacher as a person. If some remarks about teachers do get repeated outside the group, this may create enemies for the group, as well as unfairly hurt teachers' feelings and reputations.

4. Some staff criticize the group either from feeling that disturbed children should not be rewarded with "playtime" or from resenting counseling in general. These staff can spread negative attitudes that may hurt the group members directly or indirectly.

5. If persons on the staff do not respect the group, or if the leader has insufficient status in the school, the group may seem undesirable and interruptions may occur during sessions, preventing an adequately private atmosphere in which to develop a useful introspective attitude for considering behavior.

6. Occasionally noisy interactions during some sessions can disturb nearby classrooms or offices and result in criticism or require undue moderation of enthusiasm in the group.

7. Parents who see counseling groups as "the work of the devil" or "communistic" may complain to the school board or other authorities, and cast the entire group program into disrepute or even have it canceled.

CASE EXAMPLES

At this point let me present some anecdotal descriptions of the kinds of useful interaction and change that can occur in school groups. An example of improved self-awareness occurred in a high school group conducted by the dean of girls:

> Cynthia would probably have been classified as a school phobic. One day she came in furious at a teacher. One of the group members noted a similarity between the way she described the teacher and the way she described her father. I suggested role playing. Cynthia was to play her father or the teacher, and Lucy played Cynthia. Lucy portrayed Cynthia accurately, and Cynthia got the message. She said, "Do I really push him like that?" [Evans, 1975, p. 100].

An example of likely characterological change emerging from confrontation occurred in a high school group conducted by a social worker on the school staff.

> Bernice's participation in the group for the first few months was minimal . . . she giggled, acted silly, whispered, or discourteously interrupted. . . . Her pattern was to arrive late— . . . claiming she had needed to attend the previous class. She said her grades were bad enough. . . .
>
> I learned from her teachers that Bernice's grades were, indeed, caused by her absences from classes. The teachers also reported the same provocative behavior and immaturity in the classroom, such as giggling when others made a serious effort.
>
> One day, when Bernice arrived a full hour late, an important encounter was occurring. Bernice loudly and intrusively asked what was going on. My answer was that if she'd come on time she'd know. A reaction followed. Bernice cried and had hysterics. She accused us of picking on her and singling her out for attack and said she could not understand the reason.
>
> I interpreted to her how she had invited the attack. Bernice wanted to leave the group but she requested two individual sessions. In these, I encouraged her to return and work out her negative feelings before discontinuing. When she came back to the group, the members supported her staying—and she stayed. She began to participate more realistically, and faced the part she had played in provoking others [Natterson, 1975, pp. 53–54].

There is a special value in a school counselor and an agency social worker providing coleadership, as demonstrated in the following experience.

> A very bright, capable, and attractive black girl had come from an almost wholly black elementary school to a junior high school comprising many ethnic groups. When she entered the group, she was underachieving and in difficulty because of open hostility to her teachers, who she felt were prejudiced. She expressed hatred for her new school and a desire to go to an all-black junior high school. The group, which was ethnically mixed and co-led by a black counselor and a white social worker, repeatedly discussed the whole problem, separating out its various aspects and focusing on what Althea herself could do about it.
>
> The school counselor was aware of prejudiced attitudes on the

> part of some teachers, yet she did not permit this to be used as an excuse for self-destructive defiance or withdrawal. She both supported and confronted Althea in group and out of it. Eventually, Althea became much more self-assured and comfortable dealing with students and teachers of other ethnic backgrounds (Anglo, Chicano, and Japanese). Her academic work improved, and she eventually emerged as one of the natural leaders of the school. In all of this, the ongoing counselor was of crucial importance. A group led wholly by nonschool personnel could not have played the same role [Kaplan, 1975a, p. 179].

Yet, some group members may need more than group alone can provide, as evidenced by a member of an inner city high school group.

> Nothing could be done about Cynthia's problems: an alcoholic mother, runaway father, brothers and sisters who were drug addicts, gang members, thieves, and constantly in and out of trouble with the police. All she could do was tell us about it. All we could do was listen and offer whatever we could. She must have gleaned something from the sessions, because she came every week for two years, except for illness. She often came to school just to attend group and left immediately afterward [Leong, 1975, p. 82].

GROUP MANAGEMENT

There are many details to be considered in discussing the beginning and maintaining of effective groups in schools. Many are similar to those needing attention in office or clinic groups (Berkovitz, 1972), while other details, especially administrative ones, may need special attention.

The issue of confidentiality and violations thereof are different in school groups. This may be because the members are in contact with each other in classes or other activities throughout the school day. This helps members provide support to each other between sessions, but may also aggravate any angry exchanges that occurred in the session. Usually when confidentiality is stressed at the start of the group it is observed, but angry or careless violations can occur. When violations do occur, corrective attention in the school milieu, may be needed for example, if a staff member has been maligned.

The school group, rather than being a separate unit, is located in the social network of the school and at times the peer network of the school enters and interacts with the group material. In some cases the insights of the group discussion can have immediate application in action in the school milieu, without regard to issues of confidentiality. The following is an example.

> In one group a young male student took the lead in discussing his feelings about being cut off from expressing his concern and affection for the girl he impregnated because she had excluded him from making any of the arrangements for the abortion. His girl friend had, however, involved another boy, who was known to the group member and also to a girl in the group, to convey the message, "When he got me pregnant he wasn't available to help me." In the discussion other girls helped the boy to understand the possibility that his girlfriend might have feared his rejection and therefore defensively ruled out asking for his assistance. He was encouraged to leave the group session early so that he could wait outside his girl friend's classroom to tell her how much he cared and offer his help [Sperber and Aguado, 1975, p. 197].

For a school group program to be most effective, it is desirable to have a school group counseling committee. Ideally, this committee should include administrator, teacher, and psychological personnel and should introduce and oversee the group counseling program. Such a committee is likely to gain faculty acceptance and manage a smoothly running program, because if any negative reaction does develop in staff this support group can deal with these complaints. This committee can also screen referrals or give follow-up reports to the faculty to maintain faculty support (Lewis and Thomson, 1975). In some schools one counselor may be given extra time in his or her schedule to manage the program, handle crises, take care of absences of group leaders, handle room scheduling, and so on (Leong, 1975). Occasionally an outside consultant is able to do this (Hill, 1975).

The use of a single counselor to supervise the program is not as good as having a committee with wider representation. Occasionally the head counselor or a vice principal can manage the program alongside other duties. It is unfortunate when the program proceeds only at the whim and the willingness of individual counselors or teachers. In one school (Evans, 1975) the dean of girls conducted five to six groups per day, and so at times was less available to other personnel or students. Useful though this was, counselors did not follow her example.

The length of the session needs to coincide with the length of a classroom period, 40 to 50 minutes. In the school context it is important that the group not meet at the same time each week, resulting in the same class being missed every week. Teachers can become antagonistic and the student can lose credits. The group usually is scheduled to meet at a different period each week so that a class is missed only every sixth week. Groups arranged to meet before or after school or at lunch have not been as successful.

The problems of missing a class may be complicated by the teacher's attitudes. If the teacher is antagonistic, he or she may not make arrangements for the student to keep up with the class work. This may require intercessions by the group leader and/or the liaison school person. A parallel issue is a system whereby the student has a reminder of which day and time the group meets that particular week (a card filled out every six weeks is one way).

Selection of members for the group may be controllable if the leaders can resist demands from teachers and administrators to place every needy student in the group. Six to eight active defiant boys (and/or girls) will tax the therapist and prevent optimum progress of the group. Six to eight apathetic teenagers will also be difficult. Ideally there should be a balance of personalities in a group. Among the six to eight members there should be a mixture of very active, less active, more verbal, and less verbal. In some localities, inadvertent inclusion of rival gang members can cause a crisis requiring changes of membership. The number in a group can vary from six to ten, depending on the problems of members. Occasionally, a lunchtime group of 20 to 30 has succeeded under special circumstances (Pannor and Nicosia, 1975).

Another rule that may require some attention is the desire of teenagers to smoke during sessions. This is not usually allowed on the secondary school campus except in special smoking rooms or areas. Occasionally refreshments can be provided by the group leader or the individual members may bring in their own refreshments. A session may also be held in a local snack shop or restaurant for a special celebration, such as the final session of the year or on birthdays. This kind of shared orality and nurturing can be useful to improve communication and cohesion.

Members may leave the group before the end of the session in response to strong emotions, friction between members, or inability to remain concentrated on a task. The leader may have to judge the severity of possible danger to the student and arrange for appropriate safeguards.

There are many other issues that can arise during the life of a group, for example, "silent periods, group drop-outs, the member who reveals too much, physical threat to one of the members of the group, questions asked after the group terminates, a tape recorder, etc." (Glass, 1969).

PROCESS IN THE GROUP

Very often groups, whether short or long lasting, go through somewhat definable stages. One study demonstrated three such stages in a group of 14- to 15-year-old undisturbed students in a large, mixed comprehensive school in southeast London, England (Clark, 1975). Sessions lasted 45 minutes with the teacher as the leader.

1. *Primitive stage.* Members remained highly dependent on teacher or fragmented into a collection of unrelated subgroups or conflicting individuals. Silences often occurred, or solidarity developed through an attack on the leader or a group member.

2. *Developing stage.* Pupils seek solidarity in subgroups but reach out to establish contact with the group as a whole. The search for significance and autonomy is now pursued with great confidence and more respect for what others have to contribute. Sex groupings occur with teasing, pranks, games, refreshments, joke telling.

3. *The mature stage.* Pupils discover a sense of solidarity that permeates the whole group while at the same time each member feels that his presence and his contribution are genuinely valued by the others. Groups attain this stage and step back. This stage was characterized by spontaneous enjoyment and fun and especially playing games, verbal and physical. The relationship between boys and girls was much freer and unselfconscious and participation on an equal footing and pairing was open and enjoyed by all. Conversation was not a "natural tool," and when the group process seemed blocked, the leader would perform an act such as placing an article (a bar of chocolate, dice, a pack of cards, a balloon, a small ball, etc.), and would give no instructions. When there was complaint of boredom, the leader pointed out forcibly that "the group is what we all make it."

At times it is helpful for leaders to have planned activities available, whether art materials, a game, or a structured exercise. Bates (1975) has described activities that she called mild and moderate. Among the mild techniques she described are discussion of birth order, or first memories. Moderate techniques include among others role playing, autobiographies, significant experiences, and psychodrama. Other authors have introduced discussion topics, such as boy/girl relationships, speaking to one's parents, making friends, spending time alone, and so on, but without making it closely structured, "keep to the subject" type discussion. There can be the dilemma of adding sufficient structure, but without sacrificing the values of an interactive, participatory experience.

Especially with very active younger adolescents, behaviorally reinforced kinds of groups have been reported. These usually require an observer to measure each member's amount of certain types of interaction in order to give rewards for certain kinds of behavior (Bardill, 1977). Some groups in clinical settings have used the lyrics of popular teenage music as a stimulus to discuss feelings such as sadness, jealousy, anger (Vanderkolk, 1976; Frances and Schiff, 1976).

Termination of a group can be an important phase in emotional learning. The young persons must learn to deal with experiencing loss and grief. These are crucial emotions, especially in the lives of disturbed children. Each group's type of termination will differ. The following presents the example of a junior high school group of six to twelve boys.

> During the tenth meeting, the psychiatrist announced that the group would terminate after a few more meetings. In the next-to-the-last meeting they decided to have a round robin of dirty jokes. . . . they once again wanted to reassure themselves that they could be with an adult and indulge in expressing sexual fantasies without being severely punished. . . . Elaborate plans were made for a party for the last meeting. Food was brought in by the mothers. The food and drink were gorged. . . . They decided to tell dirty jokes, and an exact repetition of all the jokes of the previous meeting ensued. Handling of loss and separation was done by different boys in their own different ways. One boy eulogized the psychiatrist as if he had died. Some of the more kinetic boys started acting up. One boy, who was going to move out of the community shortly, acted this out by isolating himself in a tent-like structure in the room [Vanderpol and Suescum, 1975, pp. 280–281].

Older teenagers are usually more verbal and less "kinetic" and occasionally discuss other loss experiences.

LEADERSHIP

Very often the group style evolves from the personalities of the members in the group, but the leader still sets the rules and the tone. Young people look to the leader for expected rules. This type of leadership is different from that needed in a classroom. Group counseling needs to allow for more spontaneous, less structured kinds of discussion than is usual in the classroom. This can be difficult for school personnel whose training has been only for the classroom. The following vignette is an example of the use of emotional insight rather than only behavioral control.

> Our first group meeting of seventh grade girls was in a laboratory; no other space was available. As we seated ourselves in a circle, some of the girls began fooling around with lab equipment, and Mrs. H. told them firmly that they could not handle it. Several of them then began to flick their fingers and hands on each other's arms and legs, while a general air of restlessness pervaded the circle. Mrs. H. looked at me, and I read her question clearly. Should she intervene again? I asked if the girls knew why they were here. Some said Mrs. H. had asked them. More flicking, changing into hitting. I asked what they were saying with their hands and feet. This appeared to startle them. One girl said, "Nothing. We do it all the time." I pressed further, and a discussion developed about how they express friendliness this way. They also agreed maybe it was a way of handling embarrassment at being here. This moved into a further discussion of how sometimes it ends in fights (which was one of the reasons some of the girls had been referred for group). Meanwhile, as the group talked about it, the actual behavior ceased. I breathed a sigh of relief that what I thought I knew about group process and feelings had worked at this crucial moment. Later, Mrs. H. and I talked about what happened in terms of when one had to use direct adult authority to control a group (safeguarding property and preventing personal injury, for instance) and when and how group process could be developed to deal with issues [Kaplan, 1975a, pp. 177–178].

Similarly, it is often necessary to help educational personnel to listen impartially to young people who air their negative feelings about trusting, either adults or peers. Coleaders whenever possible can assist and monitor each other, because a group of teenagers can be too much for one person to observe and interact with at many important moments.

There may be difficulties for some counselors to shift from a one-to-one traditional counselor-to-student relationship to the counselor-to-group relationship. The group leader must listen and pick out themes that can stimulate the flow of discussion.

The counselor must be willing to accept ideas that may be at odds with his own. If the group is functioning well, it may be that members are providing each other with some significant new awareness. Such awareness is better accepted from peers than from the counselor. However, if a very antisocial point of view seems to be embraced by a majority of the group members, it may behoove the counselor to present an alternative view, if possible, not in a strongly judgmental way. For example, one junior high school group was defending the values of stealing. It was as if these students had never before had presented to them the pros and cons of stealing as a way of acquiring material things. It was unlikely that criticism or contradiction by the middle-class counselor would have had a receptive hearing. Possibly a parable or some attempt to encourage an orientation toward the future might have been influential to some of them. In most school groups there are usually one or more members of the group who present an alternative, more constructive point of view.

Occasionally, personal examples from the leader's own life experience may be useful to show the group both the humanity of the leader and that he or she too was once a teenager. These self-revelations need to be given carefully, judiciously, and minimally; otherwise, they can sound "preachy." In most but not all cases the counselor ought not to form an alliance with a group member against the parent, even if at times the parent seems to be at fault. On the other hand, other members of the group may criticize that parent or empathize with the youngster in a way that may be of help. However, if instances of child abuse are disclosed by members, the leader will have a dilemma, since it is legally required that such instances be reported. (Each state has it own reporting regulations and procedures. These need to be known by the therapist or counselor.) The members of the group may appreciate the reporting, but the abused child may have greater difficulty at home.

It must be remembered that counselors can make mistakes. These mistakes must be honestly acknowledged if they are important, such as calling a member by the wrong name, getting inappropriately or excessively angry at a student, ignoring one student and favoring another during a particular session. Sometimes, reasons for the mistake may be demanded by the members, or the counselor may wish to give reasons if they are known. Showing this kind of honesty can often serve as modeling for the group: that one can make mistakes and still do an effective job and continue to deserve respect.

Leaders are often uncertain how to handle questions asked of them by members of the group, whether these be informational or personal. If one wishes not to answer, to avoid rejection of the child it may be best to answer in a minimal way, or to apologize. There may be times when giving information, but not a long lecture, can be useful for the group and add an important piece of learning. If one has been obviously disturbed by the question, frank discussion may be useful to avoid the therapist's undue anger.

At times the counselor may feel guilty that he is not able to spend more time with the youngster who wants and needs to have a closer relationship. It is important at such times to have referral resources or some agency where such needy young people can receive more time for discussion. Some youngsters may have to be given individual counseling (or therapy) instead of, or in addition to, the group.

TRAINING OF GROUP LEADERS

While we have talked thus far as if the counselor is the leader of most group counseling in schools, staff other than counselors are often group leaders. These may include the school psychologist, a head counselor, vice principals, or deans of students (Evans, 1975); the school nurse (Elkin, 1975); teachers (Sperber and Aguado, 1975); and teacher aides.

There are many examples of nonschool personnel being invited onto campus to conduct groups, usually in collaboration with school personnel (Berkovitz, 1975a). Most school personnel, including those in the psychological services, are usually more familiar with one-to-one counseling than with group counseling, and there needs to be in-service training to help school personnel reorient themselves to lead groups. In addition to the introductory in-service training, it is desirable to have ongoing supervision and support to discuss the various crises and vicissitudes that may arise during the life of the group. This can be provided by in-school personnel if such are available or by outside consultants (Vogel, 1975; Jacobs and Deigh, 1975). There may have to be some very basic discussion of psychological processes or of adolescent psychology for school personnel who have not had a wide clinical experience (Berkovitz, 1980a).

Among school psychologists, some have clinical expertise while others have mostly test administering skills. Of equal importance in group counseling programs is the ability to relate well to other school personnel, especially administrators and teachers. Without this skill, there may be hindrance to instituting an effective program, at least under the auspices of the psychologist. The school counselor is frequently the overworked frontline mental health person in schools. He or she is less fully trained than the psychologist and frequently has a load of 300 to 500 students. Therefore, it is often difficult for counselors to make time in their schedules to do group counseling. Incomplete training in this area results in unwillingness, as well. Schools in which a counselor has been given the time to be in full or part-time charge of group counseling have had greater success for their program (Leong, 1975). The school nurse is often very cognizant of mental health needs in a school, and when sufficiently motivated and given time in her schedule, she too can become a valuable leader of group counseling programs (Elkin, 1975).

Teachers are obviously busy with classroom tasks, but in some secondary schools they may have a free period. Some very motivated teachers have been available in these free periods to lead group counseling, with proper supervision. In one project teachers and psychologist-trainees from a nearby clinic were co-leaders of groups especially for students selected by the teacher from his classroom. There did not seem to be problems with confidentiality or role issues (Sperber and Aguado, 1975).

Administrators have served as group counselors less often because of the demands of their jobs and the inability to spend 50 minutes away from other duties. In addition, as administrators, they are more often accustomed to handling crisis in a direct managerial way. It is harder for some to listen without offering immediate assistance. Nonetheless, some deans of students (Evans, 1975; Evans, Johnson, and Thompson, 1975) and occasionally principals (Robinson, 1975) have conducted groups very effectively.

ROLE OF CONSULTANTS

When professionals from agencies outside the schools enter the school to conduct groups, there is a need for a close liaison with at least one school person to arrange for referrals, administrative sanction, room assignment, and other issues. These outside professionals may be members of any of the mental health disciplines: psychiatrists, psychologists, social workers, psychiatric nurses, rehabilitation counselors, and so on, as well as at times, probation workers, welfare department workers, police officers, or other volunteers.

School personnel may have mixed feelings toward "outsiders" on campus. The most careful consultative expertise and consideration of feelings have to be used. If properly handled, more often the school staff will welcome the assistance of community personnel. Some information has to be provided to nonschool personnel as to principles of consultation (Berkovitz, 1980b), details of school rules, and school customs. Some agencies have used role-playing to help their personnel when they are to enter the school sector (Gitterman, 1971).

The school administrator, as the protector of the campus, needs to have some knowledge of the training of these volunteers. The matter of financing of outside resources is frequently of concern also. Some school districts are prepared to pay a small part of the cost of the group leaders on campus (Kaplan, 1975a). At other times, funding agencies, public agencies (Berkovitz, 1975a), or even corporations have been willing to fund the services of some nonschool professionals in conducting groups on school campuses.

TYPES OF REFERRALS

The types of students referred to or seeking groups may vary from those who (1) have identified problems (i.e., emotionally disturbed, underachieving, behavior disorders); (2) have nonpathological problems of adolescence (i.e., shyness, mild parental conflict, desire for discussion of growth issues, obesity); or (3) have special education needs (i.e., mental retardation, deafness, blindness, cerebral palsy, other physical handicaps, and more severe emotional problems).

Each of these populations may require some adaption of previously stated practices of group process with appropriate monitoring of the level of anxiety and the level of controls necessary for the individuals in the group. Some groups may involve the leader's time outside the group in relating with parents, other agencies, and personnel within the school. Parent groups are useful, especially with certain groups of students such as the handicapped. These parent groups may be conducted by knowledgeable personnel within the school or in cooperation with community agencies.

TYPES OF GROUPS

The junior high school years (grades 7–9, ages 12–14) are the most difficult for most teenagers. Awkwardness, embarrassment, and confusion are problems for at least 50 percent of this age group (Offer and Offer, 1975). Teachers are not sure at times if they are babysitters or academicians. Group counseling at this age is most difficult, but very crucial and exciting when successful. Senior high school groups (grades 9–12, ages 14–17) may be more attentive and productive compared to junior high school groups, but there may be some immature students in these as well. High school groups may often be more task oriented and last for less than a semester. These may be leadership groups, groups for adolescent pregnant females, groups for weight reduction, career planning, and so on. After-school clubs, while directed toward specific interests, can certainly involve some elements of new emotional learning and interpersonal assistance, especially from knowledgeable faculty advisors or students.

Various styles and techniques may prevail with different group leaders, involving psychodrama or role-playing, behavioral contingencies, use of recordings, films, trips, and even speakers. Some groups may be a mixture of informational and psychological orientation. For example, some groups have been offered for teaching coping and study skills, assertiveness and social skills, reality therapy, and transactional analysis. Descriptions of these programs are often difficult to evaluate because important variables are not always taken into sufficient account. (1) Often a group needs to last more than 10–20 weekly sessions to allow for measurable change in members. (2) Individual changes during the life of a group may not be evident until one to two years later or residuals are difficult to measure. (3) Do the groups include young people with diagnosed psychological problems? (4) Are the personnel conducting the groups from outside agencies working with or without collaborative school personnel? (5) Questionnaires or instruments used to measure changes are often difficult to compare from one study to another.

TYPES OF SESSIONS

The first session is one of the most crucial. "It is during the first session that the counselor presents what his expectations are, what the goals of the group are, and what the rules of the meeting will be. He indicates to the students (both directly and implied) what he will tolerate and what he will not and how well he will be able to handle the group" (Glass, 1969). When the leader of the group is from an outside agency, it is desirable (and often legally required) that there be a school person as co-leader. It is best to keep rules to a minimum, but basically there be no hitting or destruction of property, some respect for each person's wish to talk, and a commitment to confidentiality.

With junior high school groups especially, the establishment of some control and attentiveness to each other and to the leader may take all semester, but may be the most important part of the group learning. There may be chaos, movement, fighting, distraction, and so on, for the bulk of the meetings. The leader may have to snatch useful pieces of self-disclosure or interaction and attempt to highlight them in the hope that somebody in the group catches something from it. The following vignette of Lewis, in a high school group was impressive in this regard.

> He was absolutely impossible. Playful, mischievous, constantly jiving around, talking loudly, and never serious about anything. Lewis controlled every group in which he participated. In a sense, he ruined every one of them. His presence in a group was the kiss of death for the counselor and set the tone for the entire group. No personality was strong enough to subordinate his. Nothing worked to stop his destructive antics—not threats or anger from the counselor, not appeals to his good nature, no amount of pleading or cajolery, no amount of feigned indifference.
>
> After almost two years of rampaging and running amok through the group, Lewis somehow graduated. At commencement his mother enthusiastically and sincerely thanked the counselor for the remarkable change she had seen in Lewis since he had been in the program [Leong, 1975, pp. 83–84].

GROUPS FOR SPECIAL PROBLEMS

Many groups have been designed to raise the grade point average (GPA) of underachieving students. Low GPA can often be an accompaniment of transient or chronic emotional disorder but can be related as well to poor study habits, poor home facilities for studying, test anxiety, or a problem between teacher and student. As a result, many types of groups do achieve a rise in GPA. However, there are many changes other than rise in GPA which may be a prime goal for the group interventions. For example, 69 gifted, underachieving high school sophomores were given four semesters of weekly group counseling. Compared with a control group of 85, no difference was found in the GPA, but the counseled students were rated by teachers as being less resistive and more cooperative in the classroom and less absent from class (Finney and Van Dalsem, 1969).

Test anxiety desensitization at junior high school level, using eight sessions of relaxation, visualization, and discussion, significantly improved GPA (Empey, 1977). One group reported that they were "more likely to have a specific time and place to study and that the program had increased their efficiency and time spent studying" (Harris and Trujillo, 1975).

Other student behavior and reactions have been the subject of group counseling procedures. Four seminars of group assertion training with 36 shy junior high students increased assertive skills in role-playing (test) situations. Junior high school students were trained in groups to learn "empathy, genuineness, and confrontation" as a preparation for group counseling. After two years this group "compared to other students . . . had a greater ability to solve problems, cooperate with others, listen more effectively to what others were communicating and exhibit more leadership behavior" (Gray and Tindall, 1974). Another study demonstrated that coping skills training as a cognitive–behavioral therapeutic intervention significantly reduced the manifestation of inappropriate classroom behavior and improved social skills of youngsters with serious learning problems (Hamelberg, 1981).

There have been several studies of groups to help ethnic minorities. A short-term school group for six Hispanic eighth grade girls reported "the increased ability to tolerate anxiety, to verbalize cross-cultural conflicts and to be able to turn to each other for support . . . " (Hardy-Fanta and Montana, 1982).

A group of 30 black students was compared to a control group in pre- and posttests. "After one year of group counseling, experimental groups showed significant gains in vocabulary, reading, English usage, occupational aspiration and vocational maturity . . ." (Gilliand, 1968).

A group of 20 ninth grade Mexican-American students of college potential in a minority high school in a low socioeconomic area met for a lunchtime conference daily during the freshman year, twice per week in the sophomore year, and occasionally during the junior and senior years. Topics of discussion ranged far and wide, although the primary focus was on why education was important, how to get into college, and special problems of the Mexican-American students. Of the 35 students, 30 entered college and did well; seven received scholarships (Klitgaard, 1969).

In a junior high school subject to student friction during desegregation:

> [A group was formed] of 12 of the 7th, 8th and 9th graders who were considered "natural leaders" by the counselors. These were the ones who had most often been referred to the counseling office for disciplinary problems on campus. The composition was ⅓ Black, ⅓ Hispanic and ⅓ Caucasian. For two months this group met weekly. These were the informal leaders among the students who had know of each other but had never sat down to talk to each other. The discussions were frequently heated. Especially notable was the learning of verbal expression and understanding, as an alternative to physical violence. Several of the students had been subjected to physical abuse in their families. This seemed to encourage their use of physical violence as a solution to tension and threat on campus. In the group discussions, however, they were able to explain to each other the risk of these physical responses. For example, one Black boy said "If that teacher bothers me one more time, I'm going to pop-off and hit him." A formerly overly aggressive Caucasian boy then said, "Don't do that man! You'll be the one who gets hurt." The members of the group began to be helpful to each other on campus. When they saw one of them about to get into trouble, they would help each other to avoid fighting. One even began to break up interracial fights on campus. They recommended that there be more groups next year: "If there's a chance to talk, then you don't have to fight" [Berkovitz, Carr, and Anderson, 1983].

Many types of groups have been established on campuses to deal with drug abuse (Flacy, Goda, and Schwartz, 1975). Some school systems have set up counseling groups for pregnant adolescents to try to improve understanding and decrease the number of repeat pregnancies. In peer counseling programs the training groups, in which older high school students are taught to counsel younger students, often provide a form of group counseling for these student counselors (Hamburg and Varenhorst, 1972; Varenhorst, 1974). Multiple family group therapy has been useful in some school settings (Durell, 1969), as well as simultaneous group counseling with adolescents and their parents (Shaw and Mahler, 1975).

Special education units for handicapped students use group counseling with varying effectiveness and special adaptations. Groups have been effective with adolescents who are (1) educable mentally retarded (i.e., IQ53–77) (Ringelheim and Polatsek, 1955; Stacey and De Martino, 1957; Lodato, Sokoloff, and Schwartz, 1964; Mann, Beaber, and Jacobson, 1969; Humes, Adamczyk, and Myco, 1969; Lee, 1977), (2) autistic/schizophrenic (Epstein, 1977), (3) with multiple handicaps (Empey, 1977), (4) epilepsy (Appolone and Gibson, 1980), (4) muscular dystrophy, (Bayrakal, 1975), (5) stammering (Laeder and Francis, 1968; Rustin, 1972), or (5) deafness (Sarlin and Altshuler, 1968; Bonham, Armstrong, and Bonham, 1981).

EVALUATION

As mentioned in previous studies, criteria used for evaluation vary widely and include change in GPA, school attendance, disruptiveness, empathy, and so on. Kaplan (1975b) evaluated 27 groups in junior and senior high school (310 students). Groups met weekly for 30 to 40 sessions per school year. The focus of the group discussions was fairly unstructured but included problems of achievement and difficulties with adult authority. Groups were co-led by an agency social worker and usually a school counselor. In the junior high school, students were referred for poor school performance (24%), poor school attendance (18%), problems with school authority (7%), difficulties in family relationships (10%), inadequate peer relations (6%), immature behavior in school (7%), and various other reasons (28%).

Change at the end of that school year was determined by ratings from group leaders, collateral school personnel, usually a grade counselor, vice principal, school nurse, or the teacher. It was of interest that compared to the elementary (20 groups) and the high schools (7 groups), the junior high school (20 groups) had the lowest percentage of students considered improved. There was a 57.6 percent improvement as seen by co-leaders and collateral personnel, and 60.6 percent as seen by co-leaders only. The percentage of group members showing improvement rose steadily in proportion to the member of group meetings attended, at all three school levels. The highest was 84 percent improvement for those attending over 20 meetings. A high percentage (71.8%) were judged improved in family and school centered problems.

SUMMARY

This chapter details some of the wide scope, variety, and usefulness of the application of group therapy/counseling in secondary schools. As with group methods in any organizational context, there has to be an adaptation of the particular group program to the organizational context, mores, and expectations. In the school context, administrative measures and relations have to be enlisted that facilitate the coexistence of the group counseling program, the prime educational task, and classroom structure. Once this has been negotiated, a group program can function in a very productive way. Some monitoring and maintaining of sanctions and quality still need attention. Mental health consultants from community agencies can often be useful in all aspects of a program. All categories of school personnel—administrative, teaching, nursing, or psychological—can conduct effective groups, especially with support consultation. The goals of groups have been for growth enhancement and amelioration of behavior, educational performance, or mild psychopathology. Some improvements in familial problems have been reported. Severe psychopathology usually needs referral to agencies outside the schools. Mental health consultation to school personnel deserves high priority, and the use of group counseling in the schools represents one of the important preventive mental health measures for children and adolescents.

REFERENCES

Appolone, C., & Gibson, P. (1980), Group work with young adult epilepsy patients. *Soc. Work Health Care*, 6(2):23–32.

Awerbuch, W., & Fraser, K. (1975), Chronic absenteeism decreased by group counseling. In: *When Schools Care, Creative Use of Groups in Secondary Schools*, ed. I.H. Berkovitz. New York: Brunner/Mazel.

Bardill, D.R. (1977), A behavior-contracting program of group treatment for early adolescents in a residential treatment setting. *Internat. J. Group Psychother.*, 27:389–400.

Bates, M. (1975), Themes in group counseling with adolescents. In: *When Schools Care, Creative Use of Groups in Secondary Schools*, ed. I.H. Berkovitz. New York: Brunner/Mazel.

Bayrakal, S. (1975), A group experience with chronically disabled adolescents. *Amer. J. Psychiat.*, 132(12):1291–1294.

Berkovitz, I.H. (1972), On growing a group: Some thoughts on structure, process, and setting. In: *Adolescents Grow in Groups: Experiences in Adolescent Group Psychotherapy.* ed. I.H. Berkovitz. New York: Brunner/Mazel.

——— ed. (1975a), *When Schools Care, Creative Use of Groups in Secondary Schools.* New York: Brunner/Mazel.

——— (1975b), Indications for use of groups in secondary schools and review of literature. In: *When Schools Care, Creative Use of Groups in Secondary Schools*, ed. I.H. Berkovitz. New York: Brunner/Mazel.

——— (1980a), Improving the relevance of secondary education for adolescent developmental tasks. In: *Responding to Adolescent Needs*, ed. M. Sugar. New York: Spectrum, pp. 51–72.

——— (1980b), School interventions: Case management and school mental health consultation. In: *Treatment of Emotional Disorders in Children and Adolescents,* eds. G.P. Sholevar, R.M. Benson, & B.J. Blinder. New York: SP Medical & Scientific Books, pp. 501–520.

——— Carr, E., & Anderson, G. (1983), Attending to the emotional needs of junior high school students and staff during school desegregation. Contributions of mental health consultants. In: *The Psychosocial Development of Minority Group Children*, ed. G.J. Powell. New York: Brunner/Mazel.

Berlin, I.N. (1974), Mental health programs in the schools. In: *American Handbook of Psychiatry*, 2nd ed., ed. S. Arieti. New York: Basic Books, pp. 735–744.

Bonham, H.E.E., Armstrong, T.D., & Bonham, G.M. (1981), Group psychotherapy with deaf adolescents. *Amer. Ann. Deaf*, 126:806–809.

Caplan, G. (1970), *The Theory and Practice of Mental Health Consultation.* New York: Basic Books.

Clark, D.B. (1975), Group work with early school leavers. *J. Curr. Stud.*, 7:42–54.

Driver, H.I. (1958), *Multiple Counseling: A Small Group Discussion Method for Personal Growth*: Madison, WI.: Morona Publications.

Durell, V.G. (1969), Adolescents in multiple family group therapy in a school setting. *Internat. J. Group Psychother.*, 19:44–52.

Elkin, M. (1975), The school nurse organizes a group counseling program in a high school. In: *When Schools Care, Creative Use of Groups in Secondary Schools,* ed. I.H. Berkovitz. New York: Brunner/Mazel.

Empey, L.J. (1977), Clinical work with multihandicapped adolescents, *Soc. Casework*, 58:593–599.

Epstein, N. (1977), Group therapy with autistic/schizophrenic adolescents. *Soc. Casework*, 58:350–358.

Evans, A. (1975), The administrator as group counselor. In: *When Schools Care, Creative Use of Groups in Secondary Schools*, ed. I.H. Berkovitz. New York: Brunner/Mazel.

——— Johnson, A.V., & Thompson, M. (1975), An administrator team as group counselors to an opportunity class. In: *When Schools Care, Creative Use of Groups in Secondary Schools*, ed. I.H. Berkovitz. New York: Brunner/Mazel.

Finney, B.C., & Van Dalsem, E. (1969), Group counseling for gifted underachieving high school students. *J. Coun. Psychol.*, 16:87–94.

Flacy, D., Goda, A., & Schwartz, R. (1975), Assisting teachers in group counseling with drug-abusing students. In: *When Schools Care, Creative Use of Groups in Secondary Schools*. ed. I.H. Berkovitz. New York: Brunner/Mazel.

Frances, A., & Schiff, M. (1976), Popular music as a catalyst in the induction of therapy groups for teenagers. *Internat. J. Group Psychother.*, 26:393–398.

Gazda, G.M., & Larson, M.J. (1968), A comprehensive appraisal of group and multiple counseling. *J. Res. & Develop. Ed.*, 1:57–132.

——— ed. (1976), *Theories and Methods of Group Counseling in the Schools*. Springfield, IL: Charles C Thomas.

Gilliand, B.E. (1968), Small group counseling with negro adolescents in a public high school, *J. Coun. Psychol.*, 15:147–152.

Gitterman, A. (1971), The school, group work in the public schools. In: *The Practice of Group Work*, eds. W. Schwartz & S.R. Zalba, New York: Columbia University Press.

Glass, S.D. (1969), *Practical Handbook of Group Counseling*. Baltimore: B.C.S. Publishing.

Gray, H.D., & Tindall, J. (1974), Communication training study: A model for training junior high school peer counselors. *School Coun.*, 22:107–112.

Gurman, A.S. (1967), Group counseling with underachievers: A review and evaluation of methodology. *Internat. J. Group Psychother.*, 14:463–473.

Hamburg, B.A., & Varenhorst, B.B. (1972), Peer counseling in the secondary schools: A community mental health project for youth. *Amer. J. Orthopsychiat.*, 42(4):566–581.

Hamelberg, L. (1981), The effect of coping skills training on the classroom behaviors of students with serious learning problems. *Diss. Abstr. Internat.*, 41:4979-A.

Hardy-Fanta, C., & Montana, P. (1982), The Hispanic female adolescent: A group therapy model. *Internat. J. Group Psychother.*, 32(3):351–366.

Harris, M.B., & Trujillo, A.E. (1975), Improving study habits of junior high school students through self-management versus group discussion. *J. Coun. Psychol.*, 22:513–517.

Hill, E. (1975), The school mental health consultant as a coordinator: A new role concept. In: *When Schools Care, Creative Use of Groups in Secondary Schools*, ed. I.H. Berkovitz. New York: Brunner/Mazel.

Humes, C.W., Jr. (1971), A novel group approach to school counseling of educable retardates. *Train. Sch. Bull.* 67:164–171.

——— Adamczyk, J.S., & Myco, R.W. (1969), A school study of group counseling with educable retarded adolescents. *Amer. J. Ment. Defic.*, 74:191–195.

Jacobs, S.M., and Deigh, M. (1975), The use of demonstration student groups in teaching group counseling. In: *When Schools Care: Creative Use of Groups in Secondary Schools*, ed. I.H. Berkovitz. New York: Brunner/Mazel.

Kaplan, C. (1975a), Advantages and problems of interdisciplinary collaboration in school group counseling. In: *When Schools Care, Creative Use of Groups in Secondary Schools*, ed. I.H. Berkovitz. New York: Brunner/Mazel.

——— (1975b), Evaluation: Twenty-seven agency-school counseling groups in junior and senior high schools. In: *When Schools Care, Creative Use of Groups in Secondary Schools*, ed. I.H. Berkovitz. New York: Brunner/Mazel.

Klitgaard, G.C. (1969), A gap is bridged. *J. Sec. Ed.*, 44:55–57.

Laeder, R., & Francis, W.C. (1968), Stuttering workshops: Group therapy in a rural high school setting. *J. Speech & Hear. Disord.*, 33(1):38–41.

Lee, J.A. (1977), Group work with mentally retarded foster adolescents. *Soc. Casework*, 58:164–173.

Leong, W. (1975), A total commitment group counseling program in an inner city high school. In: *When Schools Care, Creative Use of Groups in Secondary Schools*, ed. I.H. Berkovitz. New York: Brunner/Mazel.

Lewis, K. (1975), Activities of group leader and group member clarified by videotape evaluation. In: *When Schools Care, Creative Use of Groups in Secondary Schools*, ed. I.H. Berkovitz. New York: Brunner/Mazel.

Lewis, P., & Thomson, M. (1975), Small group counseling in secondary schools. In: *When Schools Care, Creative Use of Groups in Secondary Schools*, ed. I.H. Berkovitz. New York: Brunner/Mazel.

Lodato, F.J., Sokoloff, M.A., & Schwartz, L.J. (1964), Group counseling as a method of modifying attitudes in slow learners. *School Coun.*, 12:27– 29.

MacLennan, B.W., & Felsenfeld, N. (1968), *Group Counseling and Psychotherapy with Adolescents*. New York: Columbia University Press.

Mahler, C.A., (1969), *Group Counseling in the Schools*. Boston: Houghton Mifflin Co.

——— (1975), Group counseling. In: *When Schools Care, Creative Use of Groups in Secondary Schools*, ed. I.H. Berkovitz. New York: Brunner/Mazel.

Mann, R.H., Beaber, J.D., & Jacobson, M.D. (1969), The effect of group counseling on educable mentally retarded boys' self-concepts. *Except. Child.*, 35:359–366.

Natterson, I. (1975), Special advantages of group counseling in the school setting. In: *When Schools Care, Creative Use of Groups in Secondary Schools*, ed. I.H. Berkovitz. New York: Brunner/Mazel.

Ohlsen, M.M. (1970), *Group Counseling*. New York: Holt, Rinehart & Winston.

Offer, D., & Offer, J.B. (1975), *From Teenage to Young Manhood*. New York: Basic Books.

Pannor, H., & Nicosia, N. (1975), Structured problem solving to improve participation in a large high school group. In: *When Schools Care, Creative Use of Groups in Secondary Schools*, ed. I.H. Berkovitz. New York: Brunner/Mazel.

Ringelheim, D., & Polatsek, I. (1955), Group therapy with a male defective group. *Amer. J. Ment. Defic.*, 60:157–162.

Robinson, F.W. (1975), A principal benefits from weekly meetings with a selected group of students. In: *When Schools Care, Creative Use of Groups in Secondary Schools*, ed. I.H. Berkovitz. New York: Brunner/Mazel.

Roth, R.M., Mauksch, H.O., & Peiser, K. (1967), The non-achievement syndrome, group therapy, and achievement change. *Pers. & Guid. J.*, 46:393–398.

Rustin, L. (1972), An intensive group programme for adolescent stammerers. *Brit. J. Disord. Commun.*, 13(3):85–92.

Sarlin, M.B., & Altshuler, K.Z. (1968), Group psychotherapy with deaf adolescents in a school setting. *Internat. J. Group Psychother.*, 18:337–344.

Shaw, M.C., & Mahler, C.A. (1975), Simultaneous group counseling with underachieving adolescents and their parents. In: *When Schools Care, Creative Use of Groups in Secondary Schools*, ed. I.H. Berkovitz. New York: Brunner/Mazel.

Sperber, Z., & Aguado, D.K. (1975), Teachers and mental health professionals as co-leaders in high school groups. In: *When Schools Care, Creative Use of Groups in Secondary Schools*, ed. I.H. Berkovitz. New York: Brunner/Mazel.

Stacey, C., & De Martino, M. (1957), *Counseling and Psychotherapy with the Mentally Retarded.* Glenco, IL: Free Press.

Vanderpol, M., & Suescum, A.T. (1975), Discussion groups: Research into normal adolescent behavior in a junior high school. In: *When Schools Care, Creative Use of Groups in Secondary Schools*, ed. I.H. Berkovitz. New York: Brunner/Mazel.

Vanderkolk, C. (1976), Popular music in group counseling. *School Couns.*, 23:206–210.

Varenhorst, B.B. (1974), Training adolescents as peer counselors. *Pers. & Guid. J.*, 53:271–275.

Vogel, L.B. (1975), Support of group counselors' feelings. In: *When Schools Care: Creative Use of Groups in Secondary Schools,* ed. I.H. Berkovitz. New York: Brunner/Mazel.

Warters, J. (1960), *Group Guidance: Principles and Practices.* New York: McGraw-Hill.

Chapter 8
Group Psychotherapy with Learning Disabled Adolescents

JUDITH MILNER COCHÉ, PH.D.
JAMES H. FISHER, M.DIV.

Since the mid-1970s developmental psychologists, clinicians, and educators have pioneered issues in diagnosis, academic intervention, and emotional restructuring for the youngster whose capacity to learn is either neurologically or functionally impaired, or both (Abrams, 1980). This chapter considers the value of peer group psychotherapy in treating both the academic and the emotional handicaps of the learning disabled adolescent between the ages of 12 and 21. The following is the most acceptable definition of the disorder:

> Learning disabilities is a generic term that refers to a heterogeneous group of disorders manifested by significant difficulties in the acquisition and use of listening, speaking, reading, writing, reasoning, or mathematical abilities. These disorders are intrinsic to the individual and presumed to be due to central nervous system dysfunction. Even though a learning disability may occur concomitantly with other handicapping conditions (e.g., sensory impairment, mental retardation, social and emotional disturbance) or environmental influences (e.g., cultural differences, insufficient/inappropriate instruction, psychogenic factors), it is not the direct result of those conditions or influences [National Joint Committee on Learning Disabilities, 1981].

LITERATURE REVIEW

Although there is no other program known to the authors that is significantly similar to their own approach, a research review did produce contributions dealing with two central issues: what is the value of a school-based psychotherapy program? and what is the value of grouping adolescents with each other in maximizing therapeutic effectiveness?

Glasser (1969), whose reality therapy approach was instrumental in conceptualizing the authors' program, states that the major problem of the schools is that of student failure. Unless professionals can provide schools where children can succeed through reasonable use of their capacities he believes that little can be done to solve the major problems of our country. He advocates teaming between classroom teachers, psychologists, and remedial instructors to aid the student in experiencing academic as well as affective success within his school year. Fisher (1983) describes the necessity to structure a school program that meets the needs of adolescents who typically present six difficulties.

1. Emotional problems revolve around feelings of frustration, impotence, fear, anger, depression, alienation, boredom, emptiness, unrelatedness, and being handicapped.
2. Lack of understanding about the nature of the handicap (which can be receptive, integrative, expressive, or diffuse) manifests itself in many types of baffling disabilities ("Can't read, can't write, can't talk too good either").
3. Compensatory defense mechanisms, many of which are self-defeating, make psychic change more difficult.
4. Inability to test reality well limits his skill in making good judgments and results in being emotionally bruised by interactions with others in home, social, and educational environments.
5. Poor self-concept is universal.
6. Lack of trust in authority figures is typical.

Likewise, Gordon (1970) discusses the necessity to reverse a negative self-image in helping the neurologically disabled adolescent: "it is not the handicap itself that will limit our NH (neurologically handicapped) adolescents, but it is their attitude about themselves that will determine whether they will go ahead successfully or not" (p. 51). In sum, it is evident that any academic program that hopes to reverse a lifelong pattern of academic failure for a youngster must structure the inevitability of psychic change *into* its academic day.

Affective Education Within a School Setting

The authors' school is not the first to adopt the model of combining affective and cognitive parts to the learning process. West, Carlin, Baserman, and Milstein (1978) describe a Montreal-based program for eight adolescents combining tutoring and group discussions. Brochu (1977) sent a clinical team to France to a school of 2,000 late adolescents with school problems and incorporated weekly group psychotherapy sessions. Garfield and McHugh (1978) describe the learning counseling model, a small group-based technique used with adolescent underachievers in the Pittsburgh area. Finally, Lamia (1977) reports a study in which 70 Catholic high school seniors were given "psychological education" as part of their curriculum. Of the models described here, all but Lamia report extremely successful intervention. Lamia reports that students in the treatment group became less withdrawn and had more positive self-perceptions than control students, but found no significant differences on dimensions including authority conflict and integrative capacity.

Group Psychoherapy for the Problem Learner

Theory on cognitive development (Elkind, 1970), as well as emotional development (Blos, 1962; Erikson, 1968), describes the process by which the youngster differentiates himself from his parents and turns to same-aged youngsters as a new reference group. Kronick (1975) cites special difficulties encountered by the learning disabled youngster at this developmental phase. Although it is imperative that adolescents be able to discuss their feelings, they may feel unable to do so within the family, not only because of their age but also because many families with a learning disabled child have particular difficulty communicating with affection, respect, and authority to the disabled adolescent (Miller, 1982). Therefore, structuring a peer group to discuss emotional issues becomes a logically sound treatment option, and one that is employed in a variety of settings besides dealing with the learning disabled.

There are a number of research-oriented studies based on

various sorts of school counseling for groups of varying ages and symptoms. For example, Arnold and Simpson (1975) report mixed effectiveness ratings for a transactional analysis therapy group for school-age emotionally disturbed boys. Horstmann (1977) researched the efficacy of employing high school group counseling sessions to improve group interactions and the ability to deal with feelings, and related these variables to improved individual psychosocial competence scores in a normal senior high school population. Behavioral group counseling with youngsters of various ages in various settings is also a popular them (Mistur, 1978), as is group counseling based on self-concept improvement (Armstrong, 1978), and group counseling based on a child development model (Bleck, 1977).

Jacks and Keller (1978) report a humanistic approach at a private educational facility for adolescents with learning disabilities that combines academic and affective educational dimensions. Although group counseling is part of the program, groups are described as theme centered and time-limited. There is also a "guide group," but this is described as an informal rap session and is conducted by a teacher. Kilman, Henry, Scarbro, and Laughlin, (1979) describe group counseling for elementary age underachievers, with a large increase in reading skills and in emotional vitality compared to the control groups. Likewise, Gisondo (1978) employed school-based counseling groups with 96 learning disabled elementary school age children but found individual counseling to be as effective in post counseling testing on the WRAT. In his chapter on child and adolescent group psychotherapy Kraft (1983) includes adolescents and underachievers, but neither he nor Sugar (1975) mention the learning disabled population. This literature review explains what may have looked like an oversight, but is more likely a statement of the scarcity of an effective model, and moreover requires therapists highly skilled in group dynamics, human development, individual psychodynamic theory, and work with the learning disabled adolescent.

THE STRUCTURE AND CONCEPTUAL FRAMEWORK OF THE AUTHORS' GROUP PSYCHOTHERAPY MODEL

The function of the school, where the authors have developed their model, is to provide a systems-oriented environment in which all aspects of the learning disabled adolescent can be treated. About 100 students, ages 12 to 21, are enrolled yearly. They graduate with a high school diploma, and most go on to employment, college, or a combination of the two. Students generally live at home with family. The school also offers a transitional college year between high school and college, in which the learning disabled young adult receives academic and emotional remediation to accommodate his disability to a college setting.

The group therapy program is integrated into the academic day and every student attends. A maxium of eight students of similar age meet twice weekly for the academic year. Three adults colead: a master's or Ph.D. level psychologist or social worker and a teacher trained in therapeutic interventions are present at all meetings. Once a week they are joined by one of three clinical consultants who are Ph.D.s or M.D.s. Student membership is very heterogeneous with regard to length of attendance, gender, type of learning disability, and verbal articulateness. Confidentiality is maintained, as is usual in clinical practice, but faculty are informed of group issues that are cogent to their work with a particular student. "Taking information out of group" is met with severe criticism by other group members.

Group topics can be formulated in a number of ways. Either the student, or any of his teachers may request that a topic be discussed. For example, a new student was overheard calling other students "weird," and this was raised as a group topic. Or, a student "kept forgetting" to bring in homework, and this was raised as a discussion topic in the group. Finally, one student can bring something about another student to the leader's attention. For example, a 15-year-old male hyperactive student was observed climbing into the luggage rack of the local train. Other students were embarrassed by his lack of control and hyperactivity, and confronted him with his behavior during a group therapy session.

Four goals underlie the group therapy structure:

1. Development of communication skills in both cognitive and affective areas
2. Learning how to deal with authority figures in effective ways
3. Development of a variety of problem-solving skills
4. Assuming increased responsibility for one's learning and behavior, including an understanding and acceptance of one's learning disability

In order to achieve these goals, an amalgamation of theoretical preferences are blended to produce an action-oriented, systems-based intervention approach. Theoretical foundations emphasize four complementary themes in education and clinical intervention.

Reality Therapy (Glasser, 1965)

The therapy increases the capacity for the student to take responsibility for his own thoughts and behaviors. The therapist acts as an involved, interested "other" who is not afraid to be involved in the youngster's development. Stress is placed on behavioral change and on present behavior.

Group Dynamics and Family Systems Theory (Cartwright and Zander, 1968; Coché, 1978; 1980)

A clear commitment is maintained to working with the three contextual systems for each individual student. The peer group, the school as an educational system, and the family are assumed to interact continually with and impinge upon one another. Students learn to assume the necessity of taking responsibility for themselves within the contextual realities of their lives. For example, the "luggage rack nester" mentioned previously was confronted not only because of his behavior as a source of embarrassment to students, he was also not completing homework and getting traffic tickets for which his parents were paying. The three areas of concern were presented to him in his group by members and leaders, and he was encouraged to discover what might have been churning inside him to produce this breakdown in his behavior.

Educational Therapy (Bauer, 1972)

Because the groups function to confront academic difficulties for each student at all times, classroom teachers are enabled to maximize the relearning process. Teachers function as educational therapists, working simultaneously in six aspects of the teaching process; securing and sustaining student attention; modifying teaching stimuli into patterns comprehensible by the student's more primitive perceptual apparatus, motor channeling, self-differentiation and reality testing, improving storage and retrieval techniques, and cognitive structuring. The interested reader is referred to Fisher (1983). The authors wish to emphasize that stress is placed on restructuring the cognitive system of the learner, rather than merely on increasing expertise in "school subjects."

Child Development Theory

Given the age span for students from puberty through young adulthood, it is essential that all teaching efforts be rooted in theory and research in normal adolescent development (Group for the Advancement of Psychiatry, 1969; Offer, 1969). Piagetian thought is highly regarded in the school where the authors work, and it is adaptable to the learning disabled youngster (Elkind, 1970). Erikson's thinking on emotional and interpersonal developmental tasks during adolescence is also directly applicable to these adolescents (Erikson, 1968). Finally, advances from neuropsychology prove valuable with neurologically impaired youngsters.

GROUP PSYCHOTHERAPY PRINCIPLES

Principles of group dynamics (Cartwright and Zander, 1968; Yalom, 1970) and group psychotherapy are applicable to a learning disabled population, but require adaptation in some instances. When applied successfully, students can participate at various levels of their learning in ways more helpful to them than in their prior life experience. Adaptations include a shortened group session and increased frequency to accommodate to shorter attention spans (45 minutes twice weekly). A second adaptation to the age level and to the disabilities is expressed in a higher level of structuring of group content matter by the group leaders than in a traditional psychotherapy group. Until the group becomes cohesive enough that mutual trust enables leaders to work with the student's defensive structure, group leaders focus members on content themes they have in common with each other. "Cohesion builders" include the student's past schooling failures and what they know about their own learning disability.

It is imperative to increase or, in many cases, to begin effectiveness in communication skills between members, and between members and leaders. Although this group therapy principle may sound simplistic, it is important to keep in mind that *every* entering student has a receptive, integrative, or expressive language disability of one form or another. And, it goes without saying that language is a central tool in psychotherapy. Furthermore, many learning disabled students are too embarrassed to admit that they do not understand when complex thoughts are being presented to them, and, like the turtle, retreat into their shells by remaining quiet about their confusion. Well-intentioned therapists uninitiated in the intricacies of the learning disabled student's defensive structure, often wrongly assume that students can comprehend complex thoughts and that they have the capacity to work with indirect communication, figurative language, and insight-oriented therapy. The present model assumes the need for extremely concrete interactions, short sentences, and unambiguous communication *until* the student indicates the capacity to share sarcasm, symbolic language, or self-reflective experiences. For example, one class was describing that Columbus managed to "keep his three ships together" in the islands, and a student wanted to know if he kept them together with nails. This author taught a young man (now in college) to interrupt adults politely whenever he didn't understand what they were saying to or about him, because his auditory perception disability prevented him from receiving communications his brain could process once received. A final example in the innocent misuse of humorous symbolism by a well-reputed therapist: the school received an irate call from a mother quite upset that Dr. X had accused her daughter of trying to molest him. Further investigation of the two-generational family learning disability revealed that Dr. X had jokingly told the girl that he thought she was "pulling his leg."

Moderate levels of therapist self-disclosure provide modeling functions for students in the group and in their lives outside of school. Dies (1977) discusses the factors involved in appropriate therapist disclosure and concludes that contextual clues are central in determining optimal use of the tool. Coché and Dies (1981) discuss the integration of research and theory into the practice of group psychotherapy, using therapist self-disclosure as an example of the ways in which research findings can aid in clinical practice. Research in other group settings indicates that leaders reveal themselves as people with real families, real emotions, and real handicaps, but do not share their own interpersonal conflicts within the therapy group (Coché, 1983). For example, one faculty member has been able to share her own auditory perception problem without insulting herself. She knows that when there are too many auditory distractions, she feels confused, looks stern, and students assume she is angry with them because she looks stern. A frank discussion with the students acted both to model her need to accommodate to her disability, and to achieve the accommodation.

A SYSTEMS APPROACH TO PSYCHOTHERAPY

In successful cases, a student who graduates or who completes the transitional college program has been a participant for at least two years in the intensive psychotherapy process, which leads to personal change both at the behavioral and experiential levels. Students call this process "being shrunk." In the groups, one often hears, "Uh-oh, here comes Fish (James Fisher) to shrink John," and usually other students join in the group therapy experience, helping by confronting a student, giving classroom examples, or supporting a tearful youngster. Although the group experience is the cornerstone for change, the group is augmented by individual school counseling and regular parent conferences in the school year. Additionally, when necessary, private psychotherapy referrals are either suggested by the school, or, on occasion, required for a child to continue attendance. When private therapy is requested, the preference is for a systems-based therapist who can team with the school and work with the family roles as well as with the youngster (Coché, 1978). For example, a suspected "fire setter" was recently admitted with no prior knowledge of the boy's history. When burned matches were found in the toilets, the private psychotherapy requirement was made because of the potential danger involved in the symptom. The parents were so relieved to have the boy remain at school that they were highly motivated to help in any way. The referral was made to a senior level family therapist with a working knowledge of the school.

For purposes of clarity, the authors have isolated eight stages that students typically go through in their therapy process in the groups and outside. The stages can only be considered a conceptual model—moreover, some students do not progress emotionally and are asked to leave. Therapeutic progress is only possible when trust between group members is high and when confidentiality is maintained. Thus, building cohesiveness becomes central at the beginning of the groups. Often a resistant family can successfully block the therapeutic progress of their youngster, even though family members are rarely in school. As Whitaker (1975) states:

> Current psychotherapy of adolescents is frequently based on the concept that the family should be a resource for the

> adolescent. The therapist's problem then would be to increase the lovingness, increase the availability, increase the denial of self within the family group so that the adolescent can fill his emotional needs before he leaves. I contend that this effort is a mistake. The family members also have a right to their living process; they have a right to group loyalty, as well as individual initiative and liberation. There is no reason why they should be subjugated to the rebellious defiance of the teenager. The family needs the therapist's support to be hostile and to be loving. They must demand the right to be a group and the right to be individuals. This should be the byproduct of a good experience in family therapy. It helps the scapegoat reenter his family of origin, complete his individuation in coordination with other family members, and graduate with honors [pp. 214–215].

EIGHT STAGES IN THE THERAPY PROCESS

The two-to-three-year therapeutic process as enacted by many students runs a typical course.

1. *Facade or honeymoon period.* Upon admission students often say: "The other kids are weird but I'm okay." Any disability is denied or intellectualized. The work seems easy compared to past failures.

2. *Initial labeling of learning disability by group therapist.* As the student begins to demonstrate the disabilities in class, group leaders confront the student with the disability, and discuss this in the group with other students.

3. *Reenactment of denial to avoid pain.* Many students get angry at the therapists, maintaining stalwartly that they are okay. The old intellectualization, denial, and withdrawal begins to falter as students cling to old ways of seeing themselves.

4. *Acting in, acting up, acting out.* Despair over the inevitability of the necessity for an internal shift in self-perception and self-esteem as well as interpersonal and academic change often produces some extreme behaviors for the adolescent. This stage is achieved either by allowing a personal, existential crisis to develop organically, or by "precipitating a crisis" through group confrontation.

5. *Fear of the unknown.* The group leaders begin to "join with" the student in the existential sense (Bugental, 1981). Encouragement is offered for the youngster to use previously untapped emotional

resources in confronting his fear of change. Students are prompted to talk with students who have gone through the pain, and to talk with family and faculty for support.

6. *Grieving over loss of old coping mechanisms.* As the internal shift occurs, students realize that they "will never be the same," and that growth implies leaving behind more childish coping skills and the increased responsibility of self-awareness. Most students see this as a "mixed blessing," and therapists allow the ambivalence honest expression in the group.

7. *Emotional readiness to shift self-perception.* Since there is considerable support and encouragement as a student begins to "clean up his act," the adolescent moves from his grieving to a position of tentative enthusiasm about using himself more effectively.

8. *Increased efficiency in channeling energies.* The changes in self and in outward behaviors begin to reinforce each other in a "growth spurt" that may encompass growth in the emotional, academic, athletic, interpersonal, or family relations areas. The changes are happening, they are evident to faculty, group members, and to family, and the student is encouraged to "keep up the good work" and to give himself credit for a job well done.

To bring the process to life, the authors have chosen a case with which they were both involved as group leader, clinical consultant, and family therapist. The case is accurate though names are changed, and is representative of the authors' approach when it is successful.

Case Example 1

Bill, aged 14, was referred from a prestigous East Coast preparatory school where members of his family were enrolled. His father, graduate of a fine New England college and graduate school, is a successful professional. His mother, also a college graduate, free-lances for local papers and appears attractive, articulate, and successful. Bill's younger brother was an honors student at the prep school where Bill had failed. Both boys were slated to carry on the upper-middle-class life-style and achievement orientation that was natural for the parents. In his first year, Bill quickly demonstrated his inability to comprehend written material past the fifth grade level. Psychological testing indicated superior intelligence, but this did not help Bill in his fruitless attempt to "mask" his disability through charm, wit, good looks, and diligence (stage 1).

Academically in this first year, Bill began a honeymoon period where he believed the school was too easy for him. He resented carrying "little kids' books," and going to a school where all of the *other* kids had learning problems. He planned to transfer back to his old prep school or to another. This massive denial consumed his energies and was evident to the staff, who knew that no traditional academic prep school would accept him with his record of past failure. In his first year, Bill had never discussed his disability with either parent or with his brother. This "family secret" was mutually maintained by the entire family system, which formed a protective shield around Bill's capacity to grow emotionally and develop academically. When asked, family members agreed to tell others that Bill was going to a "prep school with small classes." Bill was instructed not to discuss his special learning needs with friends or girl friends.

Bill's learning disability, a severe integrative thinking disorder, was mentioned in his therapy group within the early months of Bill's attendance. Bill chose to become more and more taciturn and withdrawn, holding his head down and folding his arms, covering himself with a jacket even on the warmest days. The group leaders acknowledged the difficulty Bill was having, and they suggested how he must be feeling (stages 2 and 3).The more overt the attempt by the group leaders to involve Bill, the more withdrawn and resistant he became within the group. This posture was evident throughout the first academic year, although Bill enjoyed immense popularity and social skillfulness outside of the group setting. In sum, Bill was stuck at stages 2 and 3 by the end of his first academic year.

In the next fall, Bill began to "act in" (stage 4). He became physically ill, had repeated attacks of the flu with 102-degree fevers and physical weakness. This tall, handsome, athletic youngster looked gaunt and mildly green, lost his powers of concentration and kept falling asleep. Because of the academic disaster his physical state created, a parent conference was called, and was attended by the authors, Bill and his parents, and Bill's teacher. Because the parents continued to attribute Bill's academic difficulties to his physical illness and seemed unable to conceptualize their son as disabled in any way, the therapeutic team gently explored with them what they believed to be the nature of Bill's learning problem and how they felt about it. Bill's father held steadfastly to the view that Bill would succeed if only he would "apply himself" and "take his work seriously," as the father had done in his school years. The therapists thus concluded that the father maintained massive denial of Bill's emotional pain in being unable to achieve to his father's standards. Moreover, the therapists were struck by the systemic shame in the family around having a disabled child, as evidenced by a total inability to discuss the issue after Bill had spent one and a half years at a school for learning disabled adolescents.

The therapists reflected to the family that their attitudes toward Bill's disability were dysfunctional, and that the family's cognitive set would have to change if any academic progress were to happen for Bill. When the team asked how the parents felt about the years of Bill's academic failures, the father remained stalwart, while Bill's mother became tearful. She shared her sadness and helplessness during these years, and intimated feeling responsible for her son's disability. She connected Bill's learning blocks to her own feelings of ineptness, and discussed that she expected herself to be able to produce freelance articles with ease. However, she admitted that she found the writing process frustrating and difficult. This was the first indication in over a year that the family was ready to take responsibility in dealing with Bill's learning problem.

The therapeutic team "joined" the family, encouraging them to discuss their feelings about the disability with Bill, and requesting that the issue be discussed honestly with Bill's younger brother. Therapeutically, the meeting functioned to allow the pain and fear to surface for Bill and his parents. Bill realized that, for the first time in his life, emotional honesty about the disability was possible in his family. Second, the team assured the parents that, given Bill's intellectual endowment, he could go on to a successful career, albeit at a college different from his father's.

In Bill's second academic year, he shifted to a desire to maximize personal growth by using the group therapy experience to advantage. At first, Bill's attempts were bizarre—he would attempt to participate in discussions about feelings that he did not understand. It was evident to all group members that Bill was a "greenhorn" in self-reflection and was sadly unable to connect thoughts to feelings, despite his efforts. Because of the high degree of trust between members in the group, Bill allowed others to help him. Members and leaders "provided the glue" by helping Bill make those early connections between his feelings and thoughts, until he became increasingly congruent in his presentation of self, and became less dependent on group members to do the thinking for him. During stage 6, this formerly reticent group participant openly showed his dismay at his plight in life and his fear of being unable to make it in his family and in the world. He was most upset about being compared to his younger brother, and was fearful that his girl friend would drop him if she knew he had a learning disability. The group encouraged him to tell his girl friend, which he did. This was the start of the new pattern of coping—speaking honestly about feelings and dealing with the fear by discussing it with others.

By the middle of his second year, Bill was squarely in stage 7. Academically, he surpassed earlier performances and began to compensate for the remaining integrative thinking disorder. He instructed his parents on which colleges were appropriate for him, and began the application process independent of their efforts to lead him to less appropriate institutions. In his therapy group, because of his intellect, good looks, and humor, he became a model for others. He would reminisce about his early days when he stayed in his shell like a turtle, and would confront other younger group members whom he saw doing the same thing. His athletic prowess had always been admirable, but was no longer at the expense of his inability to concentrate in class. He was voted valedictorian of his class, and went on to higher education (stage 8). He is now living independently of his parents, but often revisits the staff at the school. Younger students consider him a role model and are not sure how he achieved so much success. Neither is Bill, but he is delighted that he did.

The above account sounds almost pollyannaish in its happy end, but it is accurately described. Now in his early twenties, Bill still has an integrative thinking disorder. He did not and will not follow in his father's footsteps to Dad's alma mater. He is learning, instead, to own and to accommodate for a learning difficulty that he will always wish he did not have. Allowed to pursue its course unaborted, the eight-step process described here, within the context of the group principles and academic program related earlier, forces the student through the emotional "eye of the tornado."

SUGGESTIONS FOR THE CLINICIAN

Three suggestions can be offered that are applicable to clinicians intervening in the emotional world of learning disabled youngsters (ages 12–21) in all settings—private practice, schools, groups, or family therapy.

1. *Speak simply.* Assume first that the youngster only understands part of your verbal delivery, and check out with that youngster what he is getting from the statements made. Moreover, since many learning disabilities run in families, and since the topic is an emotionally charged one for the most auditorially sophisticated parent, speak clearly and succinctly in parental discussions as well. The clinician needs to assume responsibility for clear communication in all types of psychotherapeutic interventions. With the learning disabled, this factor in therapy is critical.

For example, one of the authors spoke to a youngster about her "blossoming maturity" and, in asking the girl what she remembered from the discussion, the girl repeated that she had been told that her mahogany was blooming. Needless to say, she had not understood the word "maturity."

2. *Allow time.* Cognitive changes depend on internal attitude shifts that involve substantive movement in self-perception and self-esteem on the part of the youngster and his parents. Allowing the family to take their time indicates the clinician's healthy respect for the natural human resistance in changing familiar cognitive, attitudinal, and behavioral patterns. For example, one bright youngster was in the program six years, and was still stuck at phases 1, 2, and 3. In the student's final semester, the team related to the parents that it might be necessary for the boy to flunk out of college before he could experience emotionally the need to accept his disability. Although the conference provided the crisis needed to move the student into phase 4, the team was prepared to let the family take their time in accepting the disability.

3. *Respect contextual change.* Internal changes within a youngster can only take hold within the context of that youngster's life. As a child struggles to shift his self-esteem, the support and readiness for change has a ripple effect within his nuclear family, friendship circles, and classrooms. The clinician who conceptualizes change as systemic and contextual can enable the student to predict and therefore to handle the changes in the systems of his life. Moreover, the clinician can push for internal changes for a youngster by enabling contextual systems to change before the child's does.

For example, in order for the young fire setter (mentioned earlier) to change manipulative and indirectly hostile ways of relating to others, the clinician worked with the parents on the ways they allowed the boy to have too much power within the family. Moreover, other students were invited to report any burned match smell to the faculty, and to confront the boy on their feelings of fear and anger in having a fellow student deface school property in a potentially dangerous manner.

CONCLUSION

This chapter has dealt briefly with attempts by other authors to combine affective education and group dynamics techniques in working with the learning disabled adolescent population. It has dealt in depth with a model, first by describing theoretical foundations, next by describing three group psychotherapy principles, and then by describing through a case history, eight stages in the therapy process. Finally, as Erikson (1968) has stated: "We deal with a process (identity) located in the core of the individual and yet also in the core of his communal culture, a process which establishes, in fact, the identity of these two identities" (pp. 22–23).

One must agree with Erikson when one stops to consider the potential impact for the clinician in structuring growth experiences for youngsters who must integrate a lifelong disability into an adult identity that is both vibrant and realistic if that youngster is to impact meaningfully in his world (which is by definition, the future for everyone). That psychosocial strength depends on a total process that regulates individual life cycles, the sequence of generations, and the structure of society simultaneously, for all three have evolved together. Certainly clinicians, in structuring the interface between a developing youngster and his reference groups, have the potential to act as catalysts in the most profound sense.

REFERENCES

Abrams, J. (1980), Learning disabilities. In: *Emotional Disorders in Children and Adolescents.* eds. P. Sholevar, R. Benson, & B. Blinder. New York: SP Medical & Scientific Books.

Armstrong, J. (1978), The Effect of Group Counseling on the Self-Concept, Academic Performance, and Reading Level of a Selected Group of High School Students. Unpublished doctoral dissertation. Wayne State University, Detroit, MI.

Arnold, T., & Simpson, R. (1975), The effects of a TA group on emotionally disturbed school-age boys. *Transact. Anal. J.*, 5(3):238–241.

Bauer, J. (1972), The therapy in education therapy. *Acad. Ther.*, 8(2):1972–1973.

Bleck, R. (1977), Developmental Group Counseling Using Structured Play with Elementary School Disruptive Children. Unpublished doctoral dissertation. The University of Florida, Gainesville.

Blos, P. (1962), *On Adolescence, a Psychoanalytic Interpretation.* New York: Free Press of Glencoe.

Brochu, L. (1977), Psychiatric intervention in an academic environment. *Rev. Neuropsychiat. Infant. Hyg. Ment. Enfance,* 25(5–6):335–338.

Bugental, J. (1981), *The Search for Authenticity.* New York: Irvington Publishers.

Cartwright, D., & Zander, A., eds. (1968), *Group Dynamics: Research and Theory,* 3rd ed. New York: Harper & Row.

Coché, J. (1978), The appliction of family role research to family therapy practice. Paper presented at the XIX International Congress of Applied Psychology, Munich, West Germany.

——— (1980), Social roles and family interaction. In: *Children in Cooperation and Competition,* ed. E. Pepitone. Lexington, MA.: Lexington Books.

——— (1983), Psychotherapy with women therapists. In: *Psychotherapy with Psychotherapists,* ed. F. Kaslow. New York: Haworth Press.

——— Dies, R. (1981), Integrating research findings into the practice of group psychotherapy. *Psychother.: Theor., Res. & Pract.,* 18 410–415.

Dies, R. (1977), Group therapist transparency: A critique of theory and research. *Internat. J. Group Psychother.,* 27:177–200.

Dwyer, W. (1979), The case for group counseling as the means for eliminating erroneous zones. *Element. School Guid. & Coun.,* December:145–148.

Elkind, D. (1970), *Children and Adolescents. Interpretive Essays on Jean Piaget.* New York: Oxford University Press.

Erikson, E.H. (1968), *Identity, Youth and Crisis.* New York: W.W. Norton.

Fisher, E. (in press), Teaching figurative language. *Acad. Ther.*

——— (1983), Therapeutic interventions and educational strategies for learning disabled students. *Hill Top Spect.,* 1(1):1 & 4.

Garfield, L., & McHugh, E. (1978), Learning counseling. *J. Higher Ed.,* 49(4): 381–392.

Gisondo, J. (1978), Learning Disabilities Remediation Using Individual or Group Techniques in Clinic and School Settings. Unpublished doctoral dissertation. Hofstra University, Hempstead, New York.

Glasser, W. (1965), *Reality Therapy.* New York: Harper & Row.

——— (1969), *Schools Without Failure.* New York: Harper & Row.

Gordon, S. (1970), Reversing a negative self-image. In: *Helping the Adolescent with the Hidden Handicap,* ed. L. Anderson. Los Angeles: Academic Therapy Publications.

Group for the Advancement of Psychiatry (1969), *Normal Adolescence.* New York: Charles Scribner's Sons.

Horstmann, N. (1977), The Role of Group Interactions and an Integrated Problem-Solving/Feelings Approach in the Development of Competence. Unpublished doctoral dissertation. University of Maryland, College Park.

Jacks, K., & Keller, M. (1978), A humanistic approach to the adolescent with learning disabilities: An educational, psychological and vocational model. *Adol.,* 13(49):61–69.

Kilman, P., Henry, S., Scarbro, H., & Laughlin, J. (1979), The impact of affective education on elementary school underachievers. *Psychol. in the Schools,* 16(12):217–223.

Kraft, I. (1983). Child and adolescent group psychotherapy. In: *Comprehensive Group Psychotherapy,* 2nd ed., eds. H. Kaplan & B. Sadock. Baltimore: Williams & Wilkins.

Kronick, D. (1975), *What About Me? The LD Adolescent.* Novato, CA.: Academic Therapy Publications.

Lamia, M. (1977), A Preventive and Treatment Program for Adolescents: Psychological Education. Unpublished doctoral dissertation. California School of Professional Psychology, San Diego, California.

Miller, B. (1982), *A Comparative Study of Role Behaviors Within Families Containing a Learning Disabled Adolescent.* Unpublished doctoral dissertation. Temple University, Philadelphia.

Mistur, R. (1978). *Behavioral Group Counseling with Elementary School Children: A Model.* Unpublished doctoral dissertation. Case Western Reserve University, Cleveland, Ohio.

National Joint Committee on Learning Disabilities (1980), Position paper, unpublished.

Neill, J., & Kniskern, D., eds. (1982). *From Psyche to System. The Evolving Therapy of Carl Whitaker.* New York: Guilford Press.

Offer, D. (1969), *The Psychological World of the Teenager.* New York: Basic Books.

Sugar, M. (1975), *The Adolescent in Group and Family Therapy.* N.Y.: Brunner/Mazel.

West, M., Carlin, M., Baserman, B., & Milstein, M. (1978), An intensive therapeutic program for learning disabled prepubertal children. *J. Learn. Disab.,* 2(8)511–514.

Yalom, I. (1970), *The Theory and Practice of Group Psychotherapy.* New York: Basic Books.

Whitaker, C. (1975), The symptomatic adolescent—An AWOL family member. In: *The Adolescent in Group and Family Therapy,* ed. M. Sugar. New York: Brunner/Mazel.

Chapter 9

The Clinical Practice of Group Psychotherapy with Delinquents

RICHARD R. RAUBOLT, PH.D.

INTRODUCTION

Delinquents have played a major role in the development of adolescent group therapy. Certainly they have been the target of many therapeutic interventions on both an individual and group level. Up to the 1970s the delinquent continued to be the major focus in the development of theory and technique in the adolescent group theory field. We may, perhaps, begin to understand how this has occurred by referring to MacLennan and Felsenfeld (1968) who describe how adolescents, in general, come to treatment: "Teenagers attend treatment groups for one of three major reasons: (1) they recognize the need for help and are willing to seek it out, (2) they obtain other kinds of gratification in treatment, or (3) they are forced to attend. Very few attend for the first reason" (p. 54).

The delinquent, in particular, fits the last category. They came to treatment not out of any felt need to change, but rather under parental or, more likely, court mandate. This large, captive, resistive population has led to the development of new strategies for management and treatment.

Individual therapy, often so difficult to conduct for the troubled but nondelinquent adolescent (Josselyn, 1951; A. Freud, 1958; Blos, 1962), has proven even more problematic for the delinquent (Eissler, 1949; Hoffer, 1949; Johnson, 1949). This difficulty in treating the delinquent is directly related to the establishment of a therapeutic contract. To enter treatment is to admit the weaknesses and problems that are so actively avoided via provocative behavior. Admitting such feelings to oneself is difficult, but to admit them to an adult is to capitulate to a resented authority.

Those two forces—large numbers of patients with similar problems and the limited effectiveness of individual treatment—led to the development and utilization of group psychotherapy.

Gersten (1952), describing the advantages of group therapy with this population, suggests that it makes therapy available to greater numbers while also more closely resembling actual life situations and social living than does individual therapy. This latter point is important when working with delinquents as "they need persons with socially acceptable standards and conduct with whom they can identify. Group therapy can be an effective means of providing that need" (p. 315). Gadpaille (1959) also believes that in addition to the practical considerations of attempting to treat large numbers of patients, group psychotherapy has unique advantages for delinquents. Perhaps of greatest significance for the conduct of treatment is that group therapy takes into account the fact that these youngsters are frequently at war with adults. The group situation recognizes that many of these youngsters feel that such a war is an uneven battle and that peer support is often required. Such support allows for the delinquent adolescent to have a new opportunity of interacting with an adult authority figure from a position of relative strength. Group therapy also offers special emphasis on group interaction where delinquents commonly manifest significant problems.

The special approach that group therapy provides in the treatment of adolescent delinquents can also be seen in the goals of such an intervention as seen by Averill, Cadman, Craig, and Liner (1973), in which they help group members:

> 1) Become more comfortable in their relationships with adults and peers; 2) recognize and identify the feelings and impulses aroused in their relationships with others; 3) learn that many of their fears, wishes, impulses and thoughts which they considered unique are common to many people; 4) become aware of the feelings, impulses, tensions and anxieties which cause them to act up or act out; 5) develop the ability to tolerate their feelings, without acting until they can appropriately assess present reality; 6) learn to express their feelings, wishes, fears and hopes openly and directly in

> words to discover that more rewarding and gratifying relationships can take place [p. 17].

DELINQUENCY: DEFINITIONS AND DESCRIPTION

Before exploring the various models of group therapy used with adolescent delinquents, let us define the types of delinquents being treated and conceptualize the psychodynamic and developmental issues involved in delinquency.

Schulman (1957) has developed categories of "dissocial behavior" in delinquency that are relevant to our study: "1) delinquency associated with intellectual retardation or organic brain pathology, 2) delinquency associated with incipient or early psychosis, 3) delinquency primarily related to neurotic conflicts (internalized conflict), and 4) character-disordered delinquency (externalized conflict)" (p. 197).

The last types, the neurotic delinquent and especially the "genuine" or character-disordered delinquent, have received the most attention. Group treatment models designed for these two groups have also influenced the wider practice of adolescent group therapy. According to Spiegel (1958):

> The neurotic delinquent suffers from insecurity, deep anxiety and feelings of guilt. Engaging in antisocial behavior allows the youth to express unresolved conflicts and provides relief from anxiety. . . . The child in this group has developed the capacity to internalize conflict, and his antisocial behavior is reactive to his conflicts. He is able to experience anxiety and guilt, and his interpersonal relationships, although ambivalent, are warmer and more meaningful than those of the psychopath [p. 267].

It is this latter characteristic that Slavson (1947) considers a necessity for group treatment. He has coined the term "social hunger" to describe the yearning for emotional communion with others, a desire to belong with people, and a capacity for being affected by interpersonal experiences.

Although no explicit and clear rationale has been put forth, the character-disordered delinquent has received the most attention in both the theory and practice of adolescent group psychotherapy.

While a full-scale analysis of the antisocial delinquent is beyond the scope of this work, it is helpful to examine some of the characteristic behaviors and attitudes of this type of youngster. (The interested reader is referred to Aichhorn (1925, 1935), Szurek (1942), Eissler (1949), and Friedlander (1949) for a more complete description of the dynamics involved in the antisocial personality.)

The antisocial, delinquent adolescent by definition may be characterized as acting without foresight, without thought. The immediacy of the moment is paramount. Since the impulsive adolescent fails to plan ahead and is guided by the supremacy of feelings, his or her behavior is often reckless, inconsistent, and frequently dramatic. Action is considered magical and therefore a solution to any discomfort. There is, in fact, a psychopathology of thought. Dulit (1975), for example, has commented on the limited capacity for abstraction found in impulsive, delinquent adolescents. As a result, there is overutilization of direct concrete action; abstract assumptions, propositions, and hypotheses are notably absent.

To compound the problem, there are few superego controls and the adolescent appears oblivious to societal proprieties. Conscience pales before the apparent immediacy of current needs and satisfaction. These defeats in conscience, however, appear to be selective rather than pervasive. Such a process can also point up significant ego deficits where the capacity for object relations, judgment, and intactness of stimulus barriers are impaired.

Quite frequently both superego and ego weaknesses stem in part from parental fostering of impulsive behavior. Parents may reveal overt or direct modeling of delinquent behavior. They may also offer covert stimulation to impulsive acting out. Johnson (1949) was the first to identify this concept, which she described as "superego lucanae." In essence, many of these parents secretly hold antisocial attitudes and impulses, which they do not act out themselves. Instead, they indirectly encourage their children to act out these impulses for them. This covert stimulation may be reflected in inconsistent and ambivalent discipline, which implicitly suggests approval of the behavior. Conversely, these parents may also communicate an expectation that their son or daughter may commit delinquent actions.

Keeping these differences between the neurotic delinquent and the antisocial delinquent in mind, let us now turn to the various group therapy models used in the treatment of these populations.

The Permissive Approach

August Aichhorn, S. R. Slavson, and Betty Gabriel worked with delinquents in a manner that may be described as democratic and permissive. The restraints on behavior were to come from the group members themselves and not from adult leaders.

Of these writers, Slavson's model of activity group therapy has most heavily influenced the field. Let us again examine this model for treatment of adolescent delinquents. According to MacLennan (1951):

> Activity group therapy is a method of treatment which aims at strengthening the ego, changing the identifications and improving the self-image, thus enabling the patient to function more adequately. This improvement is achieved through the relationship with the therapist and group members and through reality testing in a permissive and accepting group climate [p. 160].

The patient is given the freedom to act within the limits of his or her own superego demands and ego resources. The judgment for conduct resides with the patient. Through such a process it is believed that the patient develops responsibility for his or her own behavior through self-confrontation.

In utilizing this neutral, accepting approach with delinquents, Slavson (1947a) has been careful to specify which patients will respond to this approach and which should be excluded:

> We found that "delinquents" with psychopathic personality structure do not respond to group treatment. Group therapy, whether activity or interview, is based upon the patient's needs to be accepted, his desire to belong to a group and his striving to be well thought of by others. This we describe as social hunger. In extreme behavior disorders, and psychopathic states this social hunger is either very weak or non-existent. There is, therefore, no foundation on which to base group treatment [p. 423].

This permissive approach would appear to be most successful and appropriate for the type of delinquent we have designated as neurotic, where there is some anxiety and guilt present as well as some relationship capacity. Slavson has not, however, been the only clinician to use a permissive approach, although the literature reveals he is one of the few (Schulman, 1957; Shellow, Ward, and Rubenfeld, 1958) to specify which populations he feels it should or could be used with.

Gersten (1951, 1952) completed a formalized evaluation of a modified form of activity group therapy. This approach included activities and an invitation for free discussion. However, according to Gersten: "Although the leader provided an atmosphere of permissive acceptance and devoted himself to recognizing and reflecting the feelings of the subjects, he did not restrict himself to applying only the strictly non-directive methods of counseling" (p. 39). Instead, the leader sought and selected films and readings that might aid with discussions. He did, however, try to "follow the principles and techniques of Slavson, in as far as the methods were applicable to the subjects of this study" (p. 39). The types of delinquents involved in this study were not clearly described.

Thorpe and Smith (1952) also used a nondirective, permissive model with delinquents in which they suggested that the leader's role should reveal warmth, understanding, and "dissident features" from the institutional authorities. The group they described moved from testing the leader on the limits of his permissiveness to acceptance of the therapist and an expressed desire for "group therapy."

Peck and Bellsmith (1954) describe a permissive approach in their work with delinquents that included a "permissive encouraging environment for hostility and guilt-tinged material" (p. 64). They note, like Slavson, that other group members provided a limit-setting tone, which was thought to be more acceptable than if it came from adults. Unlike Slavson, however, they included a wide variety of disturbances such as early or latent schizophrenia, psychopathy, and acute neurosis. They limited such severely disturbed delinquents to no more than two to a group. They found their approach successful in treating those adolescents not amenable to individual treatment.

A similar permissive approach in using the strengths of the group can be seen in the guided group interaction method (McCorkle, 1954; Empey and Rabow, 1961; Elias, 1968). Applying group therapy principles to a correctional setting McCorkle (1954) found:

> If participants are not degraded or excluded from the group because of their impulsive, aggressive behavior, the "group

> climate" must be lenient, accepting and structured to give support to all. Freedom must exist for each participant to evolve his own role in the group, to learn to understand his present role, and opportunities must exist to develop new roles. . . . It is inevitable, if these goals are reasonably achieved, for free emotional expressions to follow with the characteristic modes of adjustment of all participants exposed to one another and the therapists [pp. 200–201].

Using a permissive, interview approach, Epstein and Slavson (1962) incorporated a modified form of analytic group psychotherapy with delinquents. A major reason for this change, while not stated, may have been the inclusion of seven character disorders and one neurotic in the group of eight boys. Again, freedom was a key element and resistant group behavior disappeared as the boys tired of it. Initially there were no attempts at interpretation; the leader's only role was to introduce a topic for discussion that did not directly involve the boys. This was continued until a "breakthrough" occurred when one such topic of discussion (the sound of a plane) led to a discussion of planes, then bombs, and finally death dreams. At this point the therapist (Epstein) began educating the boys on the difference between the conscious and unconscious mind. Such a process led to "inversion" (i.e., the reversal of the blame from projection onto the environment to self-understanding and self-confrontation).

This approach led to the development of para-analytic group psychotherapy (Slavson, 1965) and leads us to consider another model of adolescent group therapy, the psychoanalytic.

The Psychoanalytic Approach

For two or three decades analytic group psychotherapy has been the primary force in the field of group psychotherapy. Briefly, the major technique of this form of treatment is to analyze transference and resistance as it occurs in the individual member, group as a whole, or to the therapist. Such a group model stresses the belief that the members of all therapy groups regularly and unconsciously reenact significant yet inappropriate patterns of behavior and feelings in group interaction. The therapeutic focus of change is believed to rest in analysis of these neurotic patterns of behavior and feelings, which leads to their modification or replacement by more realistic and spontaneous behavior. In dealing with delinquent adolescents this classical model was questioned and often modified to meet the treatment requirements of this population. Such modifications were not uniformly accepted as necessary and have served as a major point of controversy for group therapy with delinquents.

Let us begin with the para-analytic technique first developed for delinquents and then recommended for all adolescents (Slavson, 1965; Brandt, 1973). According to Slavson, it is essential for the therapist of adolescents in general and delinquents in particular to provide tools for living, techniques for dealing with life situations. This is accomplished by fusing analytic group psychotherapy with guidance, counseling, advice, and "teaching as indicated."

Slavson presents nine points that clearly delineate this para-analytic approach: (1) the interviews have to be an admixture of uncovering, exploration, evaluation, discussion, and medium of didacticism; (2) the pressing actualities (top realities) as well as unconscious and preconscious ones from the content of group interviews; (3) the therapist must not press for uncovering the unconscious and should use every opportunity to impart information that adds to the patient's "psychological literacy"; (4) the evocation of only minimal anxiety is essential for involvement in treatment, if treatment is permitted, beyond which point it has to be avoided, allayed, or diverted; (5) a degree of introspection and uncovering therapy has to precede or run parallel with the acquisition of psychologic literacy; (6) regressive "free association" alone is not suitable in work with adolescents, for it may overload their, as yet, not fully integrated ego; it must be diluted by associative ideas stemming from realities and current lives and needs; (7) the therapist's role is an incredibly more active one than in strictly analytic psychotherapy; (8) para-analytic group psychotherapy addresses itself to the integration and support of the ego; (9) para-analytic psychotherapy is a combination of psychoanalytic psychotherapy, counseling, guidance, and orthopedagogy (p. 329).

Hersko (1962), while not calling his approach para-analytic, developed a similar modification of traditional analytic group psychotherapy, this time with delinquent girls:

> The usual group therapeutic approach must be modified because of the incomplete ego development of adolescent patients . . . the greatest handicap to successful psychotherapy lies in the deliquent's low tolerance which maintains

> anxiety at a relatively low level. This automatically limits the depth and goals of the therapeutic process. Ego defences should be supported and integrated rather than weakened by the therapist [p. 170].

In both these approaches there is an emphasis on freedom of expression and the development of a supportive, accepting environment that recognizes the limitations of delinquent adolescents' coping ability. Limit-setting is minimal and there appears to be a respect for the group as a self-maintaining unit, which limits its own behaviors. The therapist's role, however, is more actively supportive and involved.

Not all analytic group therapists, however, have shared the belief that classical psychoanalytic procedures are ineffective with delinquent adolescents. Schwartz (1960) set up a project to evaluate the effectiveness of the more traditional approach with delinquent boys. Such analytic processes as transference, emergence of insight, acceptance of reality, and revelation of the unconscious were seen to be operating. In such a classical model permissiveness was expressed in a nonjudgmental and accepting, although clarifying manner: "At every opportunity, the therapist expressed the thought that if they talked and understood what they felt inside, they would not need to act out and could thereby control their lives" (p. 211).

This model was described as successful, for the boys were less tense and anxious; they were able to understand the differences between thinking and doing, and they began to help each other in a noncritical manner.

Franklin and Nottage (1969) also used a classical psychoanalytic approach with delinquent boys that met five times weekly (due to low frustration and poor impulse control) with the goal of reconstruction of character structures. Gratifying relationships were seen as the key to successful treatment as they were in marked contrast to the life experiences of group members.

This form of group therapy was felt to be successful in exposing the boys' deep-seated distrust and fearfulness and stimulating interest in observing and understanding themselves.

Evans (1965, 1966), while utilizing a psychoanalytic approach, used a model developed at the Tavistock Clinic. This approach, although nondirective in style, focused on the unconscious motives for group behavior by describing current active defenses and feared catastrophes and by interpreting current here-and-now behavior. The goals of these groups were to enable the delinquents to tolerate frustration, to deal with anxiety and conflicts, and to seek solutions that did not affect society adversely.

Modifications in this technique became necessary due to their intense and rapid swings of feelings toward the therapist. The ambivalence that adolescents display toward adults is very much in evidence in delinquent groups. Given these mixed feelings about therapy they need external controls to provide them with some stable framework and security while they sort out their thoughts and feelings.

Since this issue of controls is a crucial one that serves as a major point in the distinction between the permissive and the direct approach, Evans's suggestions for limit-setting are worth study. According to Evans (1965):

> With adolescent groups the therapist does need to set limits of behavior to facilitate the effective therapy. At times adolescents, especially delinquents, behave in such a way that the therapist must choose between limiting their behavior or abandoning a work group or regarding them as unsuitable for treatment. . . . Equally important it should be remembered that controls or setting the limits are also construed as concern, so that the adolescent is not allowed to go to a point of no return and be rejected [pp. 269–270].

A Directive Approach

While a permissive approach in the various forms we have surveyed has been a major force in the field of group therapy with delinquents, many clinicians have not found this style effective in their work. Schulman (1957) perhaps sums up this position best when he writes:

> The therapist who undertakes to treat the emotional distortions in the severely antisocial adolescent becomes aware quickly of the inappropriateness of usual psychotherapeutic methods. This is particularly noticeable in group psychotherapy since personal interaction, cooperation, and tolerance—all very much a part of group experience—are in direct conflict with the dissocial, antagonistic, exploitive orientation of these adolescents [p. 30].

The key change suggested by Schulman is regarding the issue of control. The therapist in such a model must be in control of the group and actively use that power to encourage ego synthesis and self-control.

Shellow, Ward, and Rubenfeld (1958) adopt a similar position when they state "group therapy must be 'tailor made' to the problems of these patients because of their desperate struggle against authority and the intensification of that struggle in an institutional society" (p. 271). As a result, like Schulman, they suggest the establishment of sensible limits where the therapist overtly represents institutional authority. They go on to write, in greater detail, on the use of such authority and also clarify their position in regard to a permissive approach:

> Our accepting the role of authority and helping the boys learn to live with authority deviates from other approaches used in dealing with delinquent adolescents, such as Thorpe and Smith (1952). They describe the operational sequence occurring in groups of delinquents when the therapists' role is characterized by warmth, understanding and permissive disidentification from institutional authority. While our view acknowledges the essential importance of support and permissiveness, we feel that Thorpe's and Smith's approach is better suited for the more mature neurotic described with relatively good controls rather than the impulsive and relatively infantile character disorders with which we work [p. 265].

The last point is significant for it recognized the necessity of fitting the therapy to the patient and not vice versa. It also serves to clarify the differences, as we have noted between the neurotic delinquent and the character disorder of a "genuine" delinquent.

Limit-setting is an important function in these groups of character-disordered delinquents and represents a directive, active position for the group therapist. Straight and Weekman (1958) in this regard spell out three "pillars" for hospitalized delinquents that speak to this issue: (1) individuation of limits, (2) active intervention in fights and withdrawals from groups as necessary for control, (3) use of tangible incentives for remaining in the group (i.e., extra activities such as parties with girls).

Rules must be established and strictly enforced as permissiveness with delinquents tends to perpetuate the acting out of omnipotent fantasies in the group situation. Appropriate limit-setting, on the other hand, enhances reality testing and impulse control.

This issue of the use of control and authority is noted by other clinicians as well (Stranahan, Schwartzman, and Atkins, 1957; Healock, 1965) which led to modifications in the standard approaches. Perhaps the best explanation and summary of this position is rendered by Jacobs and Christ (1967): "Qualities of defiance and resentment of authority, characteristic of teen-agers in general are particularly exaggerated in this population and make traditional techniques inappropriate" (p. 237).

Jacobs and Christ go on to suggest three modifications of standard practice: (1) provision must be made for outlets for tension, such as arranging for food, and so on; (2) a formal structure for planning arrangements must be instituted; and (3) setting limits for actions permitted and prohibited with the leader in a role of authority.

The permissive and directive models of therapy with delinquents do overlap. For example, the differences in leadership style are largely a matter of degree. These two styles have, however, been a continuing issue in the field. I believe one of the reasons for this may well be that the standard approach in group therapy from the beginning has been a permissive, nondirective, democratic one. Changes from such a position had to be justified, explained, and defended. It is interesting to further note that these same issues occupied therapists dealing with another type of delinquent: the "defective delinquent."

There have been few reports regarding this population (Cotzin, 1948; Yonge and O'Connor, 1954; Snyder and Sechrest, 1959), and they are almost evenly divided over the need for the provision of structure for group discussion and establishing limits for behavior. Both groups, the permissive and directive, report favorable results, but again the directive approach appears more effective with the severely antisocial, characterological problems. Here we are dealing with severe behavioral problems complicated by the fact that the delinquents described are functioning far below the dull normal range of intelligence (e.g., below 70). In addition to problems of impulse control, there are severe limitations in abstract reasoning, language usage, and learning potential. A directive approach relies less on these abilities than does a permissive approach. When form and structure are provided to such groups, behavioral change can become more specific and concrete, which facilitates the learning of new, more socially appropriate behaviors. Such a structure serves also to reduce unnecessary and unproductive anxiety.

Recent Advances

The literature on theories of group therapy with delinquents since the late 1960s has been sparse. In this literature the issue of a permissive, traditional versus directive approach is again evenly argued.

Didato (1974) sets four therapeutic goals, which, I believe, most group therapists of the various schools of treatment would accept:

> 1) To increase capacity to experience powerful affects (positive and negative, without acting them out) 2) to increase capacity for empathy 3) to strengthen identification with the therapist 4) to encourage new behavioral patterns in helping the group resolve intergroup conflict through nonphysical verbal means [p. 747].

The question again becomes how this might be best accomplished. To Didato this is accomplished in a traditional permissive format with a major focus on developing and encouraging empathy. Rachman (1974) also suggests that delinquents can be treated by traditional approaches: "however, since such a group includes the most resistant, poorly motivated, and difficult patients, the therapist must be willing to make a substantial emotional investment of considerable duration" (p. 21). Rachman justifies such a position by noting the need to reverse "negative fathering." Recognizing that many male delinquents have negative and conflictual relationships with their fathers, and with most authority persons in general, he set about to reverse this position by providing "positive fathering" (i.e., warmth, strength, and firmness). While using a traditional insight-oriented approach Rachman, also engaged in judicious self-disclosure, provided refreshments during group sessions, and utilized action techniques such as role playing and confrontation.

Bratter (1974, 1976) has taken a more active, problem-oriented approach that is a modified version of reality therapy. His focus has been on altering problem behavior through the use of confrontation and individual behavioral contracts. Limit-setting is considered a must and is also the focus in the development of "responsible behavior." The traditional model is rejected as ineffectual with impulse disorders. The primary goal of their program is to create constructive change in the individual's condition as quickly as possible. The program stresses the growth and development of the individual, who with the assistance of his peers, determines those goals to which he wishes to strive.

In discussing limit-setting and confrontation, Rachman and Raubolt (1983) have identified several types of confrontation useful in group therapy with delinquents: (1) Gradual confrontation—the ongoing challenge of individual by group or leader, geared to the individual's capacity to integrate interventions. There is no emergency situation or immediate need to change. (2) Intensive confrontation—persistent "therapeutic pressure" is applied to an individual or group to face the impulsive delinquent behavior. The situation is considered very serious (approaching an emergency). Change is considered necessary. (3) "The showdown session"—delinquent behavior is an emergency situation. Immediate, dramatic action is necessary. The entire session is devoted to intense confrontation with the goal of a breakthrough in behavior. Usually a time-extended session is necessary for this procedure.

While limit-setting and confrontation are considered important parameters in group therapy, judicious use is suggested. Utilization of such approaches is best based on the personality structure of the individual and where other responses (empathy, interpretation, information giving) do not deal effectively with the problem.

A clear diagnostic formulation for treatment is highlighted by Scott (1979) in his work with delinquent behaviors of narcissistic adolescents. Scott believes group treatment is important in providing the adolescent with a setting where he can learn to share the parental figure with others. Support and recognition of the "reality ego" are considered important elements and are utilized as part of a narcissistic transference.

The above noted articles address treatment issues with character-disordered delinquents but there has been little work cited on the neurotic delinquent. Recently, in a brief report, however, Eaker and Allen (1982) describe an "ingratiating" delinquent whom they believe responds well to therapy. This type of youngster is described as bright, adjusting to school, motivated, in control of reality, and physically and emotionally mature.

While not identified as such, Raubolt (1983) describes a similar youngster who responds to brief, problem-focused therapy. The use of active techniques when coupled with a clear therapy contract with the delinquent member was found to be particularly effective. The contract for therapy minimized somewhat the manipulation involved and gave the group members greater feelings of self-control and support for independent action.

Corder (1983) also suggests use of written contracts in group therapy with antisocial adolescents. These require the adolescent to list at least two goals for himself and also involve the parents/guardians in the therapy process by requiring their signatures (as well as those of the adolescent and therapist) on the contract.

In addition to these individual contracts Corder (1983) also clearly delineates group participation guidelines. In a most interesting and helpful two-way feedback, she identifies ways "to tell other people what you think about what you say and do" (p. 90).

OVERVIEW

In reviewing the literature on group psychotherapy with delinquents, certain points became evident and are worthy of special recognition. (1) Delinquency became a major social problem, as manifested by the dramatic increase in court cases and arrests, from 1948 through 1959 (Neumeyer, 1961). Despite this increase and a heightened sensitivity to the problem (West, 1967), there is only passing reference to the social forces at work in the 1940s, 1950s, and early 1960s.

The major emphasis in theory was the practice of group therapy with delinquents, *not* on understanding the dynamics of delinquents (Schulman and to a lesser extent Slavson would be exceptions here); nor was there any attempt to explain the reasons or causes of delinquency in the group therapy literature. A third major reason was the dominance of psychoanalytic practice and theory that spoke only to intrapsychic causes.

(2) In the practice of group psychotherapy with delinquents two different treatment approaches emerged, the permissive and the directive approach. It is interesting to note that both these forms of group treatment describe similar sequences and patterns. A major impetus for adolescent group therapy, then, has been the unique

character of delinquent reactions, particularly resistance to treatment. While I have noted how these resistances gave support for the development of various group approaches for this population, there is the need to clearly define the pattern of the resistance involved.

Redl, based on his work in the Detroit Group Project and Pioneer House in the mid 1940s describes five forms of resistance. (1) Escape into love where a personal relationship with the leader is used to placate the leader but to avoid real personal change. (2) Protective provocation is used to incite the leader, get him angry so that he repeats actions or words other adults have used against delinquent group members. They ask for punishment. (3) Escape from guilt through displaced conflict where the group members show improvement and a willingness to talk over problems only to act out and cause trouble outside the group situation. (4) Role confusion is created when the adult leader is attacked for minor incidents, and accused of disloyalty to avoid their own acceptance of the group leader. (5) Escape into health represents a smokescreen where laudable, sudden improvements are established in a very short time to defend against any real impact of the therapeutic efforts.

Gadpaille (1959) also offers a sequence of resistance in delinquent therapy groups. His stages include (1) open defiance, in which there are open expressions of distrust of the therapist's motives and interests; (2) testing, which is close to consciousness and includes acting out as well as expressions of hatred and resentment against adults often in vulgar language, most commonly the telling of "dirty" stories, and (3) silence. In summarizing the nature of resistances with delinquents in group therapy, Gadpaille (1959) provides the following cogent observation:

> It appears characteristic of delinquent groups that they are capable of employing with great versatility a host of highly organized resistances against external dangers. . . . The more or less unstructured and disorganized response to these unaccustomed anxieties is clear evidence that the primary direction of the defensive organization in delinquents is against projected sources of danger [p. 284].

These resistances are common to delinquent groups in general regardless of the particular leadership style adopted. While most of the articles describing adolescent therapy groups are focused on delinquents there has been a significant change in the field since the late 1960s. As noted earlier, articles describing delinquent therapy groups have been sparse since this time. Certainly, one explanation has been the increase in concern with the special legal and developmental problems of drug abuse. Many adolescents who have come to the attention of the legal system have done so for drug-related crimes.

Significantly, the national attention until very recently has not been directed to delinquency but rather to drug abuse. With such national attention has come an increase in programs and numbers of adolescents being seen. In other words, social forces again appear to have influenced the direction of adolescent group psychotherapy.

REFERENCES

Aichhorn, A. (1925), *Wayward Youth.* New York: Viking Press, 1935.

——— (1935), *Delinquency and Child Guidance: Selected Papers,* eds. O. Fleishmann, P. Kramer, & H. Ross. New York: International Universities Press, 1964.

Averill, S.C., Cadman, W.H., Craig, L.P., & Liner, R.E. (1973), Group psychotherapy with young delinquents. *Bull. Menn. Clin.,* 37:10–70.

Blos, P. (1962), *On Adolescence: A Psychoanalytic Interpretation,* New York: Free Press.

——— (1975), The second individuation process of adolescence. In: *The Psychology of Adolescence,* ed. A. Esman. New York: International Universities Press.

Brandt, D.E. (1973), A descriptive analysis of selected aspects of group therapy with severely delinquent boys. *J. Amer. Acad. Child Psychiat.,* 12:473–481.

Bratter, T.E. (1974), Confrontation: A Group Psychotherapeutic Treatment Model for Alienated, Acting Out, Unmotivated, Adolescent Drug Abusers and Addicts. Unpublished doctoral dissertation, Columbia University, New York.

——— (1976), Group psychotherapy: A restructuring of the probation process. *Correct. & Soc. Psychiat. & J. Behav. Technol. Meth. & Ther.,* 22:(1):1–5.

Corder, B.F. (1983), A structured group for undersocialized, acting-out adolescents. In: *Handbook of Short-Term Therapy Groups,* ed. M. Rosenbaum. New York; McGraw-Hill.

Cotzin, M. (1948), Group psychotherapy with mentally defective problem boys. *Amer. J. Men. Defic.,* 53:268–283.

Didato, S.V. (1974), Delinquents in group therapy. In: *Progress in Group and Family Therapy,* eds. C. Sangu & H.S. Kaplan. New York: Brunner/Mazel.

Dulit, E.P. (1975), Adolescence. In: *Personality Deviation and Development,* ed. G.H. Wiedeman. New York: International Universities Press.

Eaker, H.A., & Allen, S.S. (1982), A factor-analytic study of a group therapy screening scale for children and adolescents. *J. Clin. Psychol.,* 38:742–743.

Eissler, K.R. (1949), *Searchlights on Delinquency.* New York: International Universities Press.

———(1958), Notes on problems of technique in the psychoanalytic treatment of adolescents. *The Psychoanalytic Study of the Child,* 13:223–254. New York: International Universities Press.

Elias, A. (1968), Group treatment program for juvenile delinquents. *Child Welf.,* 47:281–286.

Empey, L.T., & Rabow, J. (1961), The Provo experiment in delinquency. *Amer. Sociol. Rev.,* 26:679–695.

Epstein, N., & Slavson, S.R. (1962), Future observations on group psychotherapy with adolescent delinquent boys in a residential treatment. *Internat. J. Group Psychother.* 12:199–210.

Evans, J. (1965), Inpatient analytic group therapy of neurotic and delinquent adolescents:; Some specific problems associated with these groups. *Psychother. Psychosomat.,* 13:265–270.

——— (1966), Analytic group therapy with delinquents. *Adolescence,* 1:180–196.

Franklin, G., & Nottage, W. (1969), Psychoanalytic treatment of severely disturbed juvenile delinquents in a therapy group. *Internat. J. Group Psychother.,* 19:165–175.

Freud, A. (1958), Adolescence. *The Psychoanalytic Study of the Child.* 13:255–278. New York: International Universities Press.

Friedlander, K. (1949), Latent delinquency and ego development. In: *Searchlights on Delinquency,* ed. K.R. Eissler. New York: International Universities Press.

Gabriel, B. (1939), An experiment in group therapy. *Amer. J. Orthopsychiat.,* 9:593–602.

——— (1943), Group treatment of six adolescent girls. *Newsletter, Amer. Assn. Psychiat. Soc. Workers,* 13:65–72.

——— (1944), Group treatment for adolescent girls. *Amer. J. Orthopsychiat.,* 14:593–602.

Gadpaille, W.J. (1959), Observations on the sequence of resistances in groups of adolescent delinquents. *Internat. J. Group Psychother.,* 9:275–286.

Gersten, C. (1951), An experimental evaluation of group therapy with juvenile delinquents. *Internat. J. Group Psychother.,* 1:311–318.

——— (1952), Group therapy with institutionalized juvenile delinquents. *J. Genet. Psychol.,* 80:35–64.

Healock, D.R. (1965), Modifications of standard techniques for outpatient group psychotherapy with delinquent boys. *Amer. J. Orthopsychiat.,* 3: 371.

Hersko, M. (1962), Group psychotherapy with delinquent adolescent girls. *Amer. J. Orthopsychiat.,* 32:169–175.

Hoffer, W. (1949), Deceiving the deceiver. In: *Searchlights on Delinquency,* ed. K.R. Eissler. New York: International Universities Press.

Jacobs, M., & Christ, J. (1967), Structuring and limit setting as techniques in the group treatment of adolescent delinquents. *Commun. Men. Health J.,* 3:237–244.

Johnson, A. (1949), Sanctions for superego lacunae of adolescents. In: *Searchlights on Delinquency,* ed. K.R. Eissler. New York: International Universities Press.

Josselyn, I.M. (1951), *The Adolescent and His World.* New York: Family Services Association of America.

MacLennan, B. (1951), The Analysis of Group Psychotherapy Techniques with Negro Adolescent Girls. Unpublished doctoral dissertation, London University, U.K.

——— & Felsenfeld, N. (1968), *Group Counseling and Psychotherapy with Adolescents.* New York: Columbia University Press.

McCorkle, L.W. (1954), Guided group interaction in a correctional setting. *Internat. J. Group Psychother.,* 4:199–203.

Neumeyer, M. (1961), *Juvenile Delinquency in Modern Society.* Princeton, NJ: Van Nostrand.

Patterson, R.M. (1950), Psychiatric treatment of institutionalized delinquent girls. *Diseases Nerv. Syst.,* 11:272–282.

Peck, H., & Bellsmith, V. (1954), *Treatment of the Delinquent Adolescent.* New York: Family Service Association.

Perl, W.R. (1963), Use of fantasy for a breakthrough in psychotherapy groups of hard-to-reach delinquent boys. *Internat. J. Group Psychother.,* 13:27–33.

Rachman, A.W. (1969), Talking it out rather than fighting it out. *Internat. J. Group Psychother.,* 19:518–521.

——— (1974), The role of fathering in group psychotherapy with adolescent delinquent males. *Correct. & Soc. Psychiat. & J. Behav. Technol. Meth. & Ther.,* 20(4):11–22.

——— Raubolt, R. (1983), The clinical practice of group therapy with adolescent substance abuses. *Current Treatment of Substance Abuse and Alcoholism,* ed. T.E. Bratter. New York: Free Press.

Raubolt, R. (1983), Brief, problem-focused group psychotherapy with adolescents. *Amer. J. Orthopsychiat.,* 53:157–165.

Redl, F. (1948), The phenomenon of resistance in therapy groups. *Hum. Rel.,* 1:307–313.

Schulman, I. (1952), The dynamics of certain reactions of delinquents to group psychotherapy. *Internat. J. Group Psychother.,* 2:334–343.

——— (1957), Modifications in group psychotherapy with antisocial adolescents. *Internat. J. Group Psychother.,* 7:310–317.

Schwartz, M. (1960), Analytic group psychotherapy. *Internat. J. Group Psychother.,* 10:195–212.

Scott, E.M. (1979), The female delinquent narcissistic personality disorder; A case illustration. *Internat. J. Group Psychother.,* 4:503–508.

Shellow, R., Ward, J., and Rubenfeld, S. (1958), Group therapy and the institutionalized delinquent. *Internat. J. Group Psychother.,* 8:265–275.

Slavson, S.R. (1947a), An elementaristic approach to the understanding and treatment of delinquency. *Nerv. Child,* 6:413–424.

——— (1947b), Activity group therapy with character deviations in children. In: *The Practice of Group Therapy,* ed. S.R. Slavson. New York: International Universities Press.

——— (1947c), Differential dynamics of activity and interview group therapy. *Amer. J. Orthopsychiat. Group Ther. Brochure,* 16:293–302.

——— (1965), Para-analytic group psychotherapy: A treatment of choice for adolescents. *Psychother. & Psychosom.,* 13:321–331.

Snyder, R., & Sechrest, L. (1959), An experimental study of directive group prescription with defective delinquents. *Amer. J. Men. Defic.,* 64:117–123.

Spiegel, L. (1958), Comments on the psychoanalytic psychology of adolescents. *The Psychoanalytic Study of the Child,* 13:296–308. New York: International Universities Press.

Stranahan, M., Schwartzman, C., & Atkins, E. (1957), Group treatment for emotionally disturbed and potentially delinquent boys and girls. *Amer. J. Orthopsychiat.,* 27:518–527.

Straight, B., & Weekman, T. (1958), Central problems in group therapy with aggressive boys in a mental hospital. *Amer. J. Psychiat.,* 114:998–1001.

Szurek, S. (1942), Notes on the genesis of psychopathic personality trends. *Psychiatry,* 5:1–6.

Thorpe, J.J., & Smith, B. (1952), Operational sequence in group therapy with young offenders. *Internat. J. Group Psychother.,* 2:24–33.

West, D.H. (1967), *The Young Offender.* New York: International Universities Press.

Yonge, K.A., & O'Connor, N. (1954), Measurable effects of group psychotherapy with defective delinquents. *Brit. J. Psychol.,* 100:944–952.

Chapter 10

Group Psychotherapy with Alcohol and Drug Addicted Adolescents: Special Clinical Concerns and Challenges

THOMAS EDWARD BRATTER, ED.D.

GROUP PSYCHOTHERAPY WITH ADDICTED ADOLESCENTS: CONTROVERSY, CONFUSION, AND CONFLICT

When reviewing 1,100 group psychotherapy publications for 1980 and 1981, Silver, Lubin, Miller, and Dobson (1981) and Silver, Miller, Lubin, and Dobson (1982) located fewer than 10 publications that discussed group psychotherapy concerns for addicted adolescents. Credentialled mental health practitioners are hesitant to provide intensive long-term group psychotherapy for adolescent substance abusers and addicts. While responding to a volume devoted to adolescent addiction, Tyson (1982) cogently provided some reasons why few psychoanalysts elect to work with this subpopulation. "Drug-dependent adolescents typically have been viewed as double pariahs, thought to be neither suitable in terms of the requirements to come, to pay, and to associate freely, nor analyzable in terms of suffering from an inner conflict for which help is sought" (pp. 667–678).

Most psychotherapists who work with addicted adolescents can recognize that avoidance, denial, mistrust, and resulting paranoia are basic adjustment reactions but do not know how to challenge deliberate deceit and distortion. Since the theory and practice of group psychotherapy with alcohol and drug addicted adolescents currently has not been quantified, there has been no systematic effort to devise innovative and effective therapeutic tools to neutralize these resistances to treatment. In addition, addicted adolescents in their desperate effort to maintain the status quo have antagonized and alienated the group psychotherapist whom they disrespect and insult personally. Imhof, Hirsch, and Terenzi (1983) explain the psychodynamics when the substance abuser who feels worthless works with the therapist who represents the paragon of virtue:

> The resultant good–bad dichotomy is a serious threat to the ego identity of the patient, and the first order of psychic business for the patient is to reverse the imbalance. More specifically, the patient (unconsciously) begins to employ any strategy available to provoke, cajole, humiliate, and deceive the therapist—in essence to make the therapist more like himself, or worse than himself. Without the concurrent presence of the therapist's skill and understanding of the dynamics at work, including his own countertransferential and attitudinal postures, the proposed treatment may be short-lived, and the probable negative results all too frequently ascribed to the patient alone [pp. 501–502].

Undeniably, working with addicted adolescents can be a draining, depressing, and discouraging experience for the group psychotherapist. Stolorow (1975) discusses the vengeful way that addicted adolescents abuse themselves: "By actively producing his own failure and defeat and actively provoking humiliation, abuse and punishment, the masochistic character experiences the illusion of magical control and triumphant power over his object work. . . . Such illusion of magical control enable the masochist to deny his narcissistic vulnerability by retaining the fantasies of infantile omnipotence" (p. 445).

Professionals are aware of the numerous occupational hazards that can occur when working with angry adolescent addicts. Bratter (1973) suggests the clinical challenges and inconveniences with this specific subpopulation exceed those of other treatment groups. Often there are impromptu problems that must be resolved during the group session. Sometimes it is impossible to formulate any intermediate to longer term treatment goals because these adolescents can be relentless in their testing of therapeutic limits. Frequently crises demanding the group leader's immediate attention occur at times other than scheduled sessions. The group psychotherapist may need to inconvenience himself by disrupting his professional and personal life to respond to life-threatening acting out. Substance abusers can overwhelm the group therapist by their acts of desperation, feelings of depression, and their dependency needs. Addicted adolescents can be creative in devising ways to hurt and destroy both themselves and those who care about them because they perpetually engage in devour-or-be-devoured, drug-related behavior. Parents may attempt to sabotage the group, and can become threatened when adolescents begin to assert themselves to achieve independence, at which point parents may refuse to pay the bill.

Before electing to work with this most demanding, often depressed, drug-dependent subpopulation, which engages in death defying behavior, the group psychotherapist needs to examine his beliefs: To what extent am I prepared to become involved; what constitutes appropriate therapeutic limits; do I possess the creativity, commitment, resilience, and concern to attempt to help these immature, impulsive individuals who refuse to play by anyone's rules but their own?

THE "PERSONA": THE CURATIVE CONTRIBUTION OF THE GROUP PSYCHOTHERAPIST WHO WORKS WITH ADDICTED ADOLESCENTS

Jung (1928) defines the persona as the mask or image the individual consciously or unconsciously projects to others. It is precisely the persona of the group psychotherapist that becomes the compelling curative factor for desperate, drug-dependent adolescents. This finding has been contraindicated by psychoanalytic literature, which has been confined to treatment populations other than acting out, addicted adolescents. Freud (1921), Slavson (1943), and Bion (1961), for example, have stressed the neutrality of the group psychotherapist. While exploring the implications of Freudian analytic abstinence, Newton (1971) concludes that "the role requirement of abstinence is . . . designed to mean that the therapist is called upon to deny himself and his patient any gratification which does not further the work of psychotherapy. Conversely, this requirement means that the therapist abstains from any frustration of his patient which does not advance the psychotherapeutic task" (pp. 399–400). Yalom and Lieberman's (1971) conclusion regarding the noxious impact of group leaders who were "intrusive, confrontive, challenging, while at the same time [were] demonstrating high positive caring" (p. 21) needs to be reevaluated in terms of its applicability for adolescents whose impulsive behavior can create a life-or-death situation. Liff (1975) raises a valid clinical concern when he discusses charismatic group leaders who "in their eagerness to heal and cure, tend to violate the dignity as well as the privacy of the person—his right not to participate, to be quiet, to withdraw without ridicule, humiliation, reprisal, or rejection of the leader himself or of any other group members" (p. 119). This brief, though representative, review of the psychoanalytic literature urges the group psychotherapist to retain the treatment status quo and not to tamper with the traditional analytic mantle of objectivity and detachment. The anonymity of the group mental health specialist encourages the formation of the transference reaction that is the analytic tool not only to the understanding but also the resolution of unconscious intrapsychic conflicts. With this type of prohibition from the most respected psychoanalytic practitioners such as Wolfe and Schwartz (1959, 1962) it is understandable why any countertransferential behavior has been discouraged. The group leader generally is trained not to become involved, not to offer opinions, and not to display any emotion.

Initially, it is precisely that "charisma," the persona of the group psychotherapist that creates the conditions necessary for positive and profound personality change. One of the first to appreciate this fact was Thomas Wolfe (1936), the novelist, who agonizingly examined his lost youth. "The deepest search in life, it seemed to me, the thing that in one way or another was central to all living was man's search to find a father, not merely the lost father of his youth, but the image of a strength and a wisdom external to his need and superior to his hunger, to which the belief and power of his own life could be united" (p. 39). Confirming Wolfe's contention, Liff (1975) has written, "The search for the strong supportive, and protective figure who conveys absolute sureness fits into the magical thinking and messianic wishes of hundreds of thousands of people. The high charismatic leader promises miracles, if his followers will only submit to his dominance" (p. 116). Lonely, lost, drug-dependent adolescents desperately need to believe in the power of someone else initially to help them extricate themselves from chemical bondage.

It is my contention that unless the group psychotherapist is willing to assume a most uncomfortable and awesome role of becoming the parent surrogate, powerful provider, addicted adolescents simply will not consider the possibility of becoming abstinent because the thought is too frightening. Rachman (1974) is correct in his assessment: "In attempting to produce magical results, the therapist may be joining the group's magical wishes for an omnipotent parent" (p. 152). It needs to be stressed that while initially charisma is the crucial catalytic ingredient to help addicted adolescents not only begin to dream but also to help themselves, this precise quality can impede group progress once abstinence has been achieved. Phelan (1974) believes that the adolescent group psychotherapist "needs to be more open with his own emotional responses, both to the group as a whole and to individuals within it, as circumstances dictate. He deliberately provides an example of the capability to feel and to express a range of emotions at appropriate times, spontaneously yet without loss of self-control" (p. 240). The leader, thus, becomes a responsible role model or ego ideal for adolescents to emulate. As the group matures, stabilizes, and becomes self-actualizing, the leader subtly decreases his charisma, activity, and domination by assuming the more traditional therapeutic posture.

There is reason to believe those psychotherapists who can work with addicted adolescents effectively in a group setting possess a quintessential quality that the theologian Paul Tillich has defined as "caritas," which connotes a noncompromising and nonpossessive form of caring. Explicit is a "toughness"; the group therapist needs to force addicted adolescents to become abstinent, to become more realistic, to accept the responsibility for their behavior, and to want to improve themselves. Adolescents who are self-destructive and behave irresponsibly, according to Glasser (1969), need mental health professionals "who will not excuse them when they fail their commitments, but who will work with them again and again as they commit and recommit until . . . they finally learn to fulfill a commitment. When they learn to do so, they gain respect, love and a successful identity" (p. 24). Should an adolescent tearfully report to the group, for example, that he was unable to complete an important assignment because his house was destroyed, the group leader might consider replying: "Had you thought the project was sufficiently important, you could have succeeded by studying by the light of the flames and the heat of the fire." While many might consider this to be a sarcastic and noncaring statement, the adolescent will hear the expectation of success and the refusal to accept any excuse, no matter how realistically legitimate, for continued mediocrity or failure. Implicit in a nonseductive way is a tenderness and concern that stresses improvement, accountability, and productivity. These suspicious and hostile adolescents appear to respond positively to an aura of antagonism and toughness. The often expressed missionary attitude, which states, "I love you despite of what you do and say, you poor, noble savage," can damage the treatment alliance beyond repair. The psychotherapist will be seen as a bleeding heart who deserves no respect. These adolescents are most sophisticated intuitively, and they know praise, warmth, and support are inappropriate therapeutic responses when they themselves are being deliberately hostile, dishonest, insulting, cruel, and provocative. When the group psychotherapist reciprocates the underlying feeling of contempt, he demonstrates convincingly that he simply will not tolerate any demeaning and outrageous behavior because he respects himself. Angry, addicted youth not only are confused but also become suspicious of the motives of those who are affectionate and sensitive. Bateson, Jackson, Haley, and Weakland (1956) in a seminal paper have referred to the sense of feeling pressured to adapt to the stronger person's sense of reality as the "double bind" where the child is forced to accept the mother's infantilizing and crippling perception of reality or be threatened by a loss of love (i.e., protection). In contrast, the psychotherapist who works with adolescents communicates a "never give up attitude" coupled with high expectations for improved performance (i.e., "You can do much better because after all why would I be working with you if I thought you were a loser–failure which is what you successfully have convinced the world and yourself you are!").

An essential ingredient to the treatment alliance is a nonpossessive form of crisis intervention in the extreme situations which Bratter (1975a) previously has labeled "the therapeutic eros." Brandes and Gardner (1973) add some pertinent comments regarding adolescent group psychotherapy: "Although many older adolescent and young adult patients say they *do*, most of them really *do not* want (and most of them cannot handle) erotic, physical expressions of caring from the therapist . . . they usually crave a relationship that is trusting, close, warm, sincere, and reliable, and accepting, on which they can build emotional strength to change and to grow psychologically" (p. 161). It can be salutary when the psychotherapist demonstrates a specific capacity and commitment to act assertively to ensure the ultimate survival and welfare of the adolescent by intrusively intervening at a time of impending crisis that involves either life-threatening behavior or an act of unmitigated illicit cruelty. A clinical vignette forcefully makes this point:

> During a probation group session for adolescents who have been convicted of serious crimes, a South Bronx eighteen-year-old confided his fear about an inevitable gang war which was scheduled for later that night. José resisted the group's attempt to persuade him not to return to the neighborhood because he reasoned his honor would be compromised. As the group ended due to a time commitment to vacate the building, José cheerfully said with a smile: "Tom, I know you are a powerful and intelligent person who cares so I know you will find a solution." I knew my options were limited. I was not prepared to go to the neighborhood and attempt to convince the warring gangs not to fight because I realistically feared for my safety. I elected to contact the local precinct to inform the police about the impending gang war. In doing so, I knew I would be violating confidentiality. I recognized the group might condemn me "after the fact" for interfering with their lives. I failed to discuss my plan with them because I had not thought of it during the group. Knowing all calls are recorded, I first inquired what the exact time was and then the badge number of the officer. I then identified myself by name and mentioned that I was a group psychotherapy consultant for the New York City Department of Probation. I told him I would hold him personally accountable if the area were not saturated with police cars and officers to prevent the gang war. José arrived late for the next group and immediately positioned himself in front of me with a grin. I feigned ignorance and concern. "Well?" José looked around the room before he responded slowly with much emphasis. "Tom's a sonofabitch! I never seen so many big mother-f—— cops! . . . What did you do, call the police?" "No," I replied casually. "I contacted my friends at the FBI and the CIA. I didn't want anyone to trace the source. Besides, I didn't want to go to any funerals!" The group seemed relieved that I had acted decisively to prevent the gang war. There was no criticism.

Adolescents, who mistrust authority, are too guarded to disclose any intended future illicit act or self-destructive behavior unless they want the group psychotherapist to intervene. When this occurs, the psychotherapist needs to interpret it as tangible proof that the adolescent wants limits set and also is beginning to trust the group. The concept of cathartic confession to purge feelings of guilt and anxiety rarely is valid with addicted adolescents. To demonstrate an active concern for survival is crucial for the group psychotherapist who works with individuals whose extreme impulsive and potentially self-annihilative behavior often can produce irrevocable damage. Bratter (1981) has written, "by virtue of a proscribed 'caretaker' or 'healer' role during the initial phases of group psychotherapy where malignant acting out is most prominent and self-destructive, invariably the therapist is thrust into an authoritarian posture" (p. 510). Rachman (1974), based on his earlier work with delinquent adolescents, suggests that the leader needs to establish a milieu where the positive attitudes of the father predominate. Rachman (1972) lists five considerations regarding the role for those who wish to work with adolescents in groups. The therapist (1) needs to present "himself as a potential model for ego identity . . ."; (2) needs to be "positive, caring, warm, understanding, and passionate—yet firm, assertive, definite and direct . . ."; (3) needs to develop "a humanistic person-to-person relationship . . ."; (4) needs to "take definite stands in the relationship, expressing and sharing his values, ideas, and beliefs . . ."; and (5) needs to encourage "the adolescent to have a meaningful dialogue with him and other members of the group" (pp. 117–118).

The psychotherapist, thus, becomes a parental surrogate and needs to understand the dynamics and responsibilities of this crucial role. Samorajczyk (1971) recognizes this need based on his work with alienated adolescents who "want to know where the limits are—and that someone 'gives a damn' enough to guide [them] in [their] search of what's expected of [them]" (p. 115). The psychotherapist is thrust into a charismatic role whereby he must define and enforce behavioral limits. Azima (1973) suggests that not all group psychotherapists have the capacity to work with adolescents and lists the following important personal qualities for the group psychotherapist who works with adolescents: "Adequate skills and experience, flexibility, spontaneity, enthusiasm, trust, honesty, optimism, a good sense of humor, an adequate frustration tolerance, and a dedicated responsibility to the care of the young" (p. 126).

PRETREATMENT CONCERNS: PSYCHOSOCIAL CHARACTERISTICS OF DRUG-DEPENDENT ADOLESCENTS

When working with drug-dependent adolescents, in particular, it is useful for group psychotherapists to understand individual dynamics that create existing pretreatment problems that must be resolved before any meaningful relationship can be established. Adolescents elect to medicate themselves because they have learned that any psychoactive substance can be the magical elixir to ameliorate painful feelings of frustration, fear, and failure. Drugs can provide an immediate, though ephemeral, escape from a reality felt to be too painful and pessimistic to endure. Beneath the facade of arrogance and grandiosity that adolescent addicts often project to protect themselves from a perceived cruel environment is an insecure, terrified child who feels too battered, bruised, and damaged to survive without being fortified by drugs. For many adolescents, drug taking tragically may be the only activity that guarantees a respite from suffering while producing a concurrent euphoria. If viewed from the substance abusers' perspective, drugs are a potent pharmacological solution to everyday problems and boredom that can both produce and prolong a pleasurable state.

Ingesting drugs produces an encapsulating cocoon that immunizes individuals from their feelings. As long as adolescents seek pharmacological solutions from their problems, they will form few, if any, meaningful interpersonal relationships. Adolescent alcoholics and addicts have segregated themselves from their more achievement-oriented families and friends. Substance abusers have done so because they recognize their illicit drug-related activities (i.e., securing money to purchase intoxicants or possessing psychoactive substances) are dishonest. In order to procure mind-altering chemicals, many have resorted to manipulation, deceit, and theft that have polarized them from those who are abstinent. Those who do not use drugs are viewed as the "enemy" by adolescent substance abusers because the former possess the power either to prohibit the use of chemicals or to notify the authorities. Persons who do not use drugs are reduced to the status of objects whose mission it is to gratify the sexual, monetary, survival, and comfort needs of the adolescent. Drug and alcohol addicted adolescents develop a self-protective aura of antagonism and arrogance that those who do not abuse psychoactive substances neither understand nor tolerate.

The group psychotherapist must assume no treatment alliance exists until one is established. Alienated adolescents agree to participate in treatment only after much external pressure from the environment has been applied. The therapist is viewed as the formidable enemy who will force them to stop their pleasurable drug-related activities, which Raubolt and Bratter (1974) describe.

CREATING A CLIMATE FOR GROUP PSYCHOTHERAPY: THE ROLE OF THE LEADER

The burden for creating an atmosphere conducive for group psychotherapy remains the total responsibility of the leader. Intuitively, there exists a countertherapeutic we–they dichotomy whereby the group intuitively bands together and refuses to say anything that could be incriminating about themselves or anyone else. Redl (1945) has recognized the tendency of the group to mistrust and be hostile to persons, especially authority figures, who are not members of the delinquent gang. Sager (1968) has written that for some "the injuries suffered have been of such a pernicious nature that some barriers to trust will inevitably remain. . . . This is especially relevant in work with young people where the generation gap, real or inferred, acts as an impediment to understanding. . . . The imaginative and productive utilization of peer relationships within a group gives promise of being a key factor in work with . . . adolescents (p. 429). Without exception, the first few sessions will be characterized by massive mistrust and alienation. A countertherapeutic climate will prevail until the group leader decides to confront deliberate deceit and demand honesty. Addicted and alienated adolescents are both dishonest and manipulative. These adolescents trust no one because they fear being hurt. Without direct and dramatic therapeutic intervention to shatter these prominent defenses, adolescent substance abusers will continue to replicate their lying, cheating, and stealing patterns of behavior. During the orientation sessions, the group psychotherapist has only one realistic and modest treatment goal, that is, to convince individuals to return for additional sessions. It is premature for the mental health specialist to issue any appeal, no matter how sincere, rational, persuasive, and idealistic for these drug-dependent persons to return so they can provide support and assistance to each other since realistically no group exists. It is appropriate, however, to reiterate the explicit agreement that had been discussed with the adolescent prior to admitting the individual to the group. Vannicelli, Canning, and Griefen (1984) have listed five points that pertain to adolescent alcoholics and addicts: (1) attendance, (2) notice before terminating, (3) commitment to remain abstinent, (4) promise to discuss relevant extramural issues as they relate to interpersonal relationships with the group, (5) agreement to limit outside contact with group members (p. 146). The group leader needs to insist that there will be no violence or threats of assault and that it will lead to automatic expulsion. There needs to be some consensus regarding the confidential nature of the group. Finally, the group needs to recognize that it is mandatory to respect the rights of others and one cannot interrupt another speaker. Otherwise, there will be an atmosphere of anarchy that will preclude group psychotherapy. While all these points are logical, it is important to recognize that addicted adolescents have been playing only by their rules and no one else's. The group therapist should assume that aside from their decision to use and abuse psychoactive substances, the only other characteristics these adolescents share is responding to the threat exerted by a significant other in their environment to attend the current session. It is likely, furthermore, that some have had either indirect or direct social contact with each other. When individual introductions are made, the psychotherpist can watch for any nonverbal signs of recognition such as eye contact, an abrupt change in posture, and/or change of expression, but should remain silent for the present. As long as the psychotherapist does not acknowledge any awareness of individual and group dynamics, these adolescents will underestimate the leader's sophistication and knowledge of them, which has been reinforced by the stereotypic thinking that "no straight adult can understand me." The leader's silences will be perceived by the members to connote either acceptance of the act or stupidity and naiveté. By virtue of their miscalculation, the group deliberately is lulled into a sense of security, which permits them to disclose more about themselves than originally intended. Once the more traditional treatment process begins, the group psychotherapist can use these data to penetrate the protective barriers of self-righteousness and deception erected by these desperate adolescents who previously have been immune from any therapeutic intervention or confrontation.

During this chaotic phase before the group congeals, it will not be unusual for an adolescent to arrive inebriated—a possible flaunting of authority by testing limits. Unless this act is viewed by the leader as potentially dangerous, disruptive, or defiant, it should be ignored because it still may be premature to begin treatment. If, however, the psychotherapist overreacts and issues an ultimatum that anyone who attends and is chemically intoxicated will be excluded from the next session, there will be inevitable acting out. No addict wants to attend any group where there will be pressure to cease all drug-related pleasurable activity. These adolescents, who are concurrently frightened by intimacy and threatened by the realization they will be forced to reduce their drug consumption, desperately wish to discover any legitimate excuse to leave the group. The psychotherapist needs to exercise both discretion and restraint; otherwise these adolescents will refuse to return. The referral source may be too ambivalent or unable to mobilize resources to ensure continuation of attendance.

Any topic, regardless of how frivolous (with the exception of drug-related issues such as who sells the "best dope" or any attempt to glamorize the act of self-medication), can be discussed. It is a legitimate group concern to inquire about the psychotherapist's personal experience regarding drugs. Once the adolescents have agreed to band together against the adult, the psychotherapist can acknowledge an awareness of the many manipulations. A spirit of mutiny has formed that needs to be quelled before it is possible to conduct group psychotherapy.

The crucial therapeutic test for the group psychotherapist occurs when someone, who is intoxicated, becomes provocative and belligerent, which will create a treatment crisis. The leader, however, has several treatment options that will affect the group. The psychotherapist needs to acknowledge the incident or else implicit approval of such behavior will be communicated. The therapist can ask innocently: "What is wrong with . . . ?" The group might attempt to protect the member, who is intoxicated, against the group leader by denying any impairment. Recognizing the conspiratorial implications, the group psychotherapist can verbalize disappointment that no one is honest or cares sufficiently to confront the individual about potentially self-destructive and disruptive behavior.

There are five effective clinical treatment strategies that depend on the composition of the group, its duration, and, of course, group dynamics: (1) to note the occurrence and issue a warning that any future acts of inebriation will be dealt with in unpleasant ways; (2) to request that the individual remain silent and not disturb the discussion; (3) to ascertain the group's reaction and elicit their recommendations; (4) to insist that the member tell significant other(s) about what transpired and have them contact the leader. Awad (1983) provides the rationale for permitting responsible adults to contact the therapist. Significant others are frustrated and angered by blatant acting out behavior and would like to share their perceptions with the therapist. While Awad is mindful of the confidential relationship that exists, he reports third-party information can permit the psychotherapist to gain a more accurate account of what is happening. These kinds of contacts rarely affect the relationship and, in fact, communicate to adolescents that all their behavior is a legitimate concern of the group. (5) To request that the inebriated person leave can create additional problems of management in the future. The adolescent could report this incident to the family, creating the false illusion of expulsion. Other members may appear intoxicated to force the leader to modify this stance or to discharge them for a session or two. The issue of sobriety and abstinence becomes an important treatment priority because it affects interaction as well as the achievement of individual goals. The psychotherapist needs to remember that should any feelings of personal insult or anger be communicated to the group at this juncture, it can retard or jeopardize the establishment of a meaningful treatment alliance and a sense of positive group solidarity. The intent of the resistance and the subsequent acting out probably was not to discredit or humiliate the psychotherapist but designed to permit the adolescent to prolong pleasurable pharmacological activities. When handling this crisis appropriately, the psychotherapist can gain respect by matter-of-factly mentioning why the individual elected to get "high" just before the group was to meet. If done skillfully, the group will be impressed by the cleverness of the mental health practitioner that may stimulate additional serendipitous confessions, which become the cement necessary to solidify treatment. This is a deliberate therapeutic act calculated to produce group honesty and cohesion. It is premature for the leader either to rejoice or to relax because the group now has progressed to the starting point of most other treatment populations. The leader cannot assume deliberate distortion and deceit have been discarded because all that has happened momentarily is these suspicious adolescents have reduced their mistrust and hostility of the group. These lonely and lost persons still depend primarily on drugs to offer immediate relief from the aches and agonies of adolescence but may begin to realize that people can fill the void of aloneness by offering companionship. It can be expected that after a particularly poignant and intimate disclosure the adolescent will decide to miss the next session. The absence is a legitimate topic for discussion and has one of three resolutions: (1) the group member can elect to do nothing and adopt a wait and see attitude; (2) a member or several members of the group can "reach out" to the absent adolescent to extend an invitation to return; and/or (3) the group leader can assume the initative either by calling or writing to express appreciation about the individual's courage for being honest or mention how much the group missed not seeing him.

The profound psychotherapeutic challenge for the group leader will be not only to convince adolescent substance abusers to discontinue their drug dependence but also to help them discover other options that will enable them to justify their existence to themselves while concurrently achieving self-respect. Until the group psychotherapist can convince adolescent addicts there can be a more rewarding existence than using drugs, it is unlikely they will modify their attitudes. Alcohol and drug addicted adolescents notoriously remain unmotivated and unconvinced about the desirability of constructive and creative change. If there is no intervention, interference, and/or involvement, these adolescents will continue to use and abuse drugs, a life-style from which escape is exceedingly difficult. What has been neglected is that these adolescents systematically have alienated themselves from positive persons and have elected not to prepare themselves for or participate in "straight society." They have developed few, if any, marketable skills and lack a consistent employment record.

RATIONAL AUTHORITY: A MOST UNCOMFORTABLE, BUT NECESSARY, ROLE FOR THE GROUP PSYCHOTHERAPIST

The group psychotherapist who works with adolescent alcoholics and addicts unavoidably is perceived to be a representative of the feared and powerful law enforcement/correctional establishment. No matter what the setting, whether it is an agency or an office, adolescents initially view the leader to be an extension of the "straight society." Berman (1982) succinctly states: "Any form of psychotherapy involves the use of authority" (p. 189).

The therapist possesses the power to *force* adolescents to terminate their pleasurable drug-related activities. Rather than waste time by denying the validity of adolescent perceptions, the leader needs to discuss this realistic concern. Jacobs and Christ (1967), who work with adolescent delinquents, ascribe limit-setting functions to the responsibilities of group psychotherapists. "The role of the leader as an authority had to be established and worked into the therapeutic contract" (pp. 237–238). Chwast (1965) notes that, "In treating offenders, the overall aim could be seen as one of shifting from recourse to open outer controls to the development of controls from within. One important way that this can be achieved is by helping some offender patients to develop appropriate guilt feelings. In this, fear and anxiety could sometimes serve as starting points" (p. 125). Should the group psychotherapist elect to remain passive, reflective, rather than becoming active and assertive, in all probability drug-dependent adolescents will not become abstinent. Rachman and Raubolt (1985) discuss the need for the leader to assume an active and directive role.

In order to persuade alienated adolescents to change, the group psychotherapist, according to Bratter (1975b), will need to become a rational authority so that they will remain against their wishes until they can tolerate tension, become less self-destructive, deescalate their drug dependence, understand the realistic demands of society, and accept the responsibility for their drug-related behavior. The application of rational authority by the group psychotherapist can help these adolescents begin to resolve their resistances to treatment, to build a therapeutic alliance, and to control their impulsive self-annihilative actions. By encouraging adolescent addicts to continue to attend groups, simultaneously they learn how to reorient their attitudes and restructure their relationships so they can exist within the social system. Soden (1961) has termed this process, which utilizes compulsion and rational authority, "constructive coercion."

Fromm (1947) offered a pragmatic operational description of rational authority, which forms the foundation for this discussion: The rational authority "need not intimidate . . . or arouse . . . admiration by magic qualities; as long as and to the extent to which he is competently helping, instead of exploiting, his authority is based on rational grounds and does not call for irrational awe. Rational authority not only permits but requires constant scrutiny . . . it is always temporary" (p. 7). While Fromm was discussing governmental leadership, the concept is most applicable to psychotherapy with adolescent substance abusers. Chwast (1957) adds another dimension to Fromm's rational authority: "In the curbing of antisocial behavior, only that much and no more outside control—authoritative intervention—is called for in a given situation as will meet the needs of the situation, if the rights of the individual to growth and fulfillment are to be respected" (p. 451). Rational authority utilizes confrontation to attempt to correct distorted thinking and to develop a more realistic assessment of self-destructive, drug-related behavior. To this end, Khantzian (1981) writes:

> Priority must be given to addressing drinking behavior, understanding quickly and empathetically its present determinants, and engaging the patient's cooperation to the greatest extent possible to establish control over the drinking. . . . Keeping the focus on control allows a strategy to develop that avoids premature insistence on permanent abstinence, or an equally untenable permissive acceptance of uncontrolled drinking. . . . The emphasis in this approach is on establishing control and giving the patient a chance to make a choice [p. 173].

The psychotherapist attempts to mobilize the group to serve as a rational restraining force by imposing a series of coercions and controls. Brill and Lieberman (1969) discuss the treatment rationale when they write "in the sense of providing a firm structure of the treatment relationship, setting limits, and providing controls that rational authority might minimize the addict's acting-out behavior, help him grow within the structure and internalize the controls he lacks, and, hopefully, help give up his destructive way of life" (p. 75). Redl and Wineman (1957) described therapeutic limit-setting as the "technique of authoritative Verbot. . . . We simply say 'No' and we say it in such a way that it is clear we mean it and don't soften it up by arguing, explaining" (p. 463). While working with addicted adolescents, the therapist often can share the life-saving function with the group. By delegating this responsibility to the membership, the psychotherapist extends the power and influence of the group. Stein and Friedman (1971) report that: "In group psychotherapy . . . the other members help the patient control his drinking. . . . The group members point out restrictions in the patient's ego functioning—his limitation in perception and awareness of things outside of himself, his difficulty in reality testing. With the support and help that the group offers, the patient can start to deal with these things" (p. 658).

While recognizing the potential treatment leverage afforded by extending the parameters of group psychotherapy to include extramural contact among the members in a quasi-supervised manner, the dynamics of corrective groups for alcoholics have been described by Trice (1956) and Hoff (1968); for heroin addicts by Volkman and Cressey (1963) and Yablonsky (1965).

FREEDOM OF CHOICE: THE PRIMARY PSYCHOTHERAPEUTIC PROPOSITION

Freedom of choice with the risks of failure and the rewards of success comprise the existential reality that especially pertains to adolescent addicts and alcoholics. Paradoxically, however, to act free by making decisions does not necessarily guarantee the goal of freedom. To choose to abuse mood-altering drugs inevitably will limit future freedom regarding choice of options. By consciously choosing a chemical life-style, individuals elect to become imprisoned by the act of addiction, which decreases their self-determinism and ability to choose. Alcohol and drug addiction provide a temporary feeling of euphoria without any behavior demands and investment other than to secure the intoxicants.

Constructive and creative change originates when individuals elect to actualize their potential. When persons exercise their will unencumbered by any compulsive behavior or similar restraint, they are free in the literal existential sense. Persons can assume and accept responsibility for their behavior. Individuals need to accept the proposition that freedom of choice entails a perpetual struggle to generate the energy required to resolve any crisis within oneself or from the environment. All intact human beings are capable of choice and decision. The ultimate goal of treatment defined rightly by Sutherland (1962) is to replace "compulsion with choice" (p. 371). By definition, addiction becomes a compulsive act that robs people of their free will. Addiction inevitably will trap its victims in a self-imposed no-exit quagmire. There are those adolescents who learn too late that any retreat from rational action (i.e., compulsive or obsessive behavior) promulgates a loss of freedom, hence, a loss of humanity.

The therapeutic implications would help adolescents explore their three behavioral options (i.e., inaction, action, and reaction), to the plethora of interpersonal and environmental stimuli. Drug-dependent adolescents in psychotherapy, furthermore, can confront the restricting feelings of helplessness, powerlessness, and resignation. In this respect, the group functions as a catalyst that helps adolescents to concretize their creative impulses and choices.

The act of self-medication can be viewed as a desperate attempt to perpetuate a constricting homeostatic constancy where change is absent. Addiction is accompanied by an arresting of developmental psychosocial maturation. The central clinical concern is how these adolescents will cope with freedom of choice. Those who elect to become dependent on drugs surrender much of their freedom. Carkhuff and Berenson (1967) write, "The essential task of all therapy is to enable man to act and to accept the awesome freedom and responsibility of his actions" (p. 77). Freud (1923) defined psychoanalysis as an attempt "to give the patient's ego freedom to choose one way or the other" (p. 104). Maslow (1962) labeled this dynamic the "third force in psychology," which places individual freedom and personal responsibility as its nuclei. Horney (1945) has defined the goal of psychotherapy to help the individual: "To assume responsibility for himself, in the sense of feeling himself the active, responsible force in his life, capable of making decisions and of taking the consequences" (p. 241). Schnee (1972) recognizes a psychoanalytic dilemma when he poses, but does not answer, the crucial question "Whether or not a human being is capable of freedom of choice" (p. 206). Krystal (1982) acknowledges, "Psychoanalysis has been relatively ineffective in dealing with problems of addiction because it tries to fit addicts into the procrustean bed built for neurotics" (p. 581). There appears to be a confusion about the "loss of control" proposition as defined by Jellinick (1960) and personal responsibility and choice (p. 41). It is necessary to understand the concepts of addiction and responsibility because they appear antithetical. The term "addiction" originates from the Latin *ad dicere,* which suggests surrender. Van Kaam (1968) concludes that, "This emphasis on surrender, or giving up, contains a first clue to the understanding of addiction, it seems to be related more to the passive than to the active dimension of man's life" (p. 59). The disease concept of alcoholism may appear contradictory to the notions of personal responsibility but is not. Fundamentally, the disease concept states that after the first drink has been imbibed, the alcoholic is unable to regulate consumption, which suggests a two-phase process.

In the first phase individuals retain the ability to refrain from taking the initial drink and, therefore, can remain abstinent. If it were possible, hypothetically, to follow an individual with a gun pointed to the back of his head with the threat as soon as he reached for the symbolic first drink, he would be shot, the person would not drink.

In the second phase, once alcoholics begin to drink they lose the ability to regulate the degree of consumption of alcohol. Bean (1981) has described this loss of control that characterizes alcoholics:

> The alcoholic begins to react, by fighting to regain control, and to explain to himself and others why he is behaving so badly. Repeated attempts to recover control predictably fail. This gradually destroys hope. Alcoholism destroys the person's belief that he is a normal, worthwhile person, for he finds himself repeatedly behaving destructively. Self-esteem deteriorates. The experience forbids the normal social wish to be able to drink socially. The alcoholic becomes guilt-ridden. . . . The alcoholic no longer believes in the possibility of a solution, and he retreats to the undifferentiated responses of regression, avoidance, magical thinking, and denial [pp. 75–76].

Clinically, Jellinick (1960) has identified certain individuals who encounter difficulty regulating and limiting their drug consumption *after* the first drink, pill, or injection to warrant the formulation of a rigid therapeutic mandate of absolute abstinence with no exceptions. Davies (1962), Bigelow and Cohen (1972), and Armor, Polich, and Stambul (1973) adversely affected the field of treatment when they contended that some alcoholics would be able to resume their "social drinking." Caddy, Addinton, and Perkins (1978) believed that moderate or controlled drinking could be a desired treatment goal. Pendery, Maltzman, and West (1982) challenged not only the Sobells' (1978) methodology but also the scientific conclusions. The Pendery team confirm the earlier Ewing and Rouse (1976) study that concludes controlled drinking is not a viable goal and abstinence must be stressed. Those studies that permit moderate use ignore the reality that a significant number of individuals lose the capacity to monitor their drug consumption after they make the choice to start. Rather than risk unwittingly placing those individuals in a no-win position, unquestionably it is more prudent for the group psychotherapist to insist that abstinence is achievable. Unless the leader believes that addicted adolescents, indeed, can control their behavior, the chances of helping them extricate themselves from a drug-dependent life are significantly reduced.

THE GROUP AS A SOCIAL SUPPORT SYSTEM: IMPLICATIONS FOR TREATMENT AND A PLEA FOR INNOVATIVE CONCEPTUALIZATION

Undeniably, the leader is the catalyst to create a climate conducive to group psychotherapy for alcohol and drug addicted adolescents. The group becomes the most potent therapeutic tool which enables the credentialled professional to extend his influence to help addicted and alienated adolescents adopt more responsible, reasonable, and realistic behavior while they simultaneously learn how to use their assets, rather than continue to abuse them, which Bratter (1972) has discussed. The group serves four curative and crucial functions which provide the necessary conditions to help adolescents escape from pharmacological bondage.

1. The group can serve as a rational restraining force for those adolescents who have elected to engage in potentially dangerous and self-destructive drug-related behavior (Bratter, 1971). Some members either will begin to imitate or want to please the group therapist. Strategically, the leader needs to reinforce any positive and productive growth by providing these adolescents with status within the group. These "converts" can be praised for their constructive change in such a way that they are encouraged to become responsible role models. These recovering adolescent addicts begin to function as ego supports for the group, which concurrently strengthens their resolve to continue to grow and develop. Increasingly, the leader begins to depend on their constructive and candid reaction to the attitudes and behavior of those who remain intransigent. It is salutary for the leader to praise and congratulate any successful behavior by joking: "Gee, it seems as if Lisa wants my job!" The members who have become abstinent form a nucleus, and with the approval of the group therapist can exert positive peer pressure for the resistant members to change so more meaningful and intimate material can be discussed. A serendipitous payoff may be that the "strong" members voluntarily provide some sort of surveillance for those who continue to engage in self-destructive, deviant, and dishonest drug-related behavior by virtue of their contacts in the adolescent society. These members can function as quasi-counselors and quasi-consultants to help the more pathological members control their impulsive behavior. The group psychotherapist must decide how to use this vital information most effectively. I have found it most beneficial to protect the anonymity of

the source, to distort the data somewhat, and then to confront the individual directly in the group. If, for example, I learn that an adolescent has been selling LSD, I would make a most ambiguous statement that: "I am distressed to hear you have become a salesman." If pressed for more details, I might deliberately mention a transaction involving marijuana to protect the confidence. Generally, the offender is astonished that I know what is happening and may exhibit some paranoid behavior that I will exaggerate. I can say sarcastically: "Hell, if I know about you, maybe your parents and the police also are aware because many people apparently are talking about you." Playing detective and then deliberately distorting information can be justified because the therapeutic transaction literally is reduced to a life-or-death proposition. As an incentive, the group leader can offer the adolescents who have become relatively positive the opportunity to have their own corrective emotional experience discussed either before or after the larger group convenes—if this is practical and desired.

2. The group collectively learns how to help everyone begin to identify negative attitudes in social contacts, how to avoid placing oneself in a no-win situation, and how to unlearn being dependent on mind-altering psychoactive substances. By confronting another member, adolescents become more aware of their behavior, feelings, and attitudes, which help them to anticipate the payoffs and consequences of their current decision. A confrontational approach is indicated that initially dramatizes the self-destructive behavior and then focuses on ways to assist the adolescent to recognize his potential. Bratter (1976) has identified seven sequential guiding principles of confrontation which (1) "attack the malignant dysfunctional aspects of behavior; (2) penetrate the facade of justification of behavior; (3) force the individual to accept responsibility for behavior; (4) help the individual evaluate behavior; (5) assist the individual to be aware and to anticipate the payoffs and consequences of behavior; (6) challenge the person to mobilize personal resources; and (7) define a direction so that the individual can continue to grow and develop" (pp. 168–169). While this type of confrontation can be painful, it also is tangible proof that others care, which contributes to a nurturing and corrective experience. This kind of confrontation provides the original impetus for adolescents to improve, grow, and develop.

3. The group becomes a corrective emotional experience. Adolescent members learn how to care responsibly for each other as

persons rather than as objects who can be manipulated to gratify narcissistic needs. Adolescents become involved with each other by investing in another member's recovery simultaneously with their own. The group begins to depend upon and trust each other, which results in a new orientation. Rather than seeking a pharmacological solution to their problems, they begin to rely on peers. The group now provides its own momentum and incentive to change so that the leader can adopt more traditional ways of responding rather than feeling burdened by the awesome responsibility of caring for and controlling the members.

4. The group becomes a caring community. Raubolt and Bratter (1976) have defined the caring community as follows:

> In adolescent groups . . . members are encouraged to become directly and intimately involved with each other beyond the structured group. Instead of restricting "help" to the adult leader, the group becomes responsible for themselves. Adolescent members exchange phone numbers and are encouraged to call each other in times of crisis, loneliness, or desire to use drugs, etc. Additional plans are often drawn up in the group which require specific contacts between sessions. These may range from a wake up to a phone call to a member not attending school . . . or if necessary, peer supervision of free social time for the extremely self-destructive member. In either instance, members freely agree to the commitment required and welcome the opportunity to establish significant honest relationships that transcend the more formalized group sessions. The assumption is made that these contacts will be positive and responsible. Adolescent members recognize that they will be expected to discuss this with the overall group [p. 12].

Speck (1965) writes about a tribal community for healing purposes. Relatives, neighbors, and friends are brought together to form a social network of sharing and caring. Speck and Attneave (1971) suggest that "By strengthening bonds, loosening bonds, opening new channels, facilitating new perceptions, activating latent strengths and helping stamp out, ventilate, and excise pathology, the social network is able to become the life sustaining community within the social matrix of each individual" (p. 332). Problems of living are viewed from the macrocosmic perspective requiring the creating and involvement of a social system that seeks to create a support system predicated on interdependence, honesty, commitment, and flexibility.

It is inevitable that extramural relationships will be formed, which may be the sustaining ingredient when the group members recognize that they no longer can associate with their former friends who still are drug dependent. There is a painful transition when the adolescent must reject negative people (sometimes family members), who will provide temptation to regress, while looking for more positive persons. It is important to recognize that relationships formed in group psychotherapy differ dramatically from those made in an institution because the community-based friendships begin with a commitment to improve and change rather than to perpetuate pathology. These adolescents have learned how to relate to and respect each other as individuals who have assets and liabilities so the formulation of friendships can be viewed as an affirmation of the positive values of group psychotherapy. Greenblat, Becerra, and Serafetinides (1982) and Leavy (1983) recognize that social networks can act as support systems that enhance mental health. Group psychotherapists who elect to work with addicted adolescents, in particular, need to acquaint themselves with the newly recognized phenomenon because it will permit them to be more creative and effective. Elsewhere, I have discussed special clinical psychotherapeutic concerns for alcohol and drug addicted individuals (Bratter, 1985). This chapter is an attempt to help group psychotherapists who work with addicted adolescents to recognize that there are creative solutions to situations previously thought to be untenable when using a psychoanalytic framework.

REFERENCES

Armor, D.J., Polich, M.J., & Stambul, H.B. (1973), *Alcoholism and Treatment.* Washington, DC: Rand Corporation.

Awad, G.A. (1983), The middle phase of psychotherapy with antisocial adolescents. *Amer. J. Psychother.*, 37:190–201.

Azima, F.J. (1973), Transference–countertransference. In: *Group Therapy for the Adolescent*, eds. N.S. Brandes & M.L. Gardner. New York: Jason Aronson, pp. 101–126.

Bateson, G., Jackson, D.D., Haley, J., & Weakland, L. (1956), Toward a theory of schizophrenia. *Behav. Sci.*, 1:251–264.

Bean, M.H. (1981), Denial and the psychological complications of alcoholism. In: *Dynamic Approaches to the Understanding and Treatment of Alcoholism*, eds. M.H. Bean & N.E. Zinberg. New York: Free Press, pp. 55–96.

Berman, E. (1982), Authority and authoritarianism in group psychotherapy. *Internat. J. Group Psychother.*, 32:189–200.
Bigelow, G., & Cohen, M., (1972), Abstinence or moderation? Choice by alcoholics. *J. Behav. Res.*, 10:286–289.
Bion, W.R. (1961), *Experiences in Groups*. London: Tavistock.
Brandes, N.S., & Gardner, M.L. (1973), Therapeutic approaches. In: *Group Therapy for the Adolescent*, eds. N.S. Brandes & M.L. Gardner. New York: Jason Aronson, pp. 155–162.
Bratter, T.E. (1971), Treating adolescent drug abusers in a community-based interaction group program: Some philosophical considerations. *J. Drug Issues*, 1:237–252.
——— (1972), Group therapy with affluent, alienated, adolescent drug abusers. *Psychother.: Theoret., Res. & Pract.*, 9:308–313.
——— (1973), Treating alienated, unmotivated, drug abusing adolescents. *Amer. J. Psychother.*, 27:585–598.
——— (1975a), Responsible therapeutic eros: The psychotherapist who cares enough to define and enforce behavior limits with potentially suicidal adolescents. *Coun. Psychol.*, 5:97–104.
——— (1975b), Dynamics of group psychotherapy for heroin addicts: A confrontation orientation. In: *Proceedings of the Fifth International Congress for Group Psychotherapy*, ed. A. Uchtengagen. Berne, Switzerland: Hans Huber, pp. 360–367.
——— (1976), Confrontation groups: The therapeutic community's gift to psychotherapy. In: *Proceedings of the First World Congress on Therapeutic Communities*, eds. P. Vamos & J.J. Devlin. Montreal: Portage, pp. 164–174.
——— (1981), Some pre-treatment group psychotherapy considerations with alcoholic and drug-addicted individuals. *Psychother.: Theor., Res. & Pract.*, 18:508–517.
——— (1985), Special clinical concerns for alcoholically and drug addicted individuals. In: *Alcoholism and Substance Abuse: Strategies for Clinical Intervention*, eds., T.E. Bratter & G. Forrest. New York: Free Press, pp. 561–624.
Brill, L., & Lieberman, L. (1969), *Authority and Addiction*. Boston: Little, Brown.
Caddy, G.R., Addinton, H.J., & Perkins, D. (1978), Individualized behavior therapy for alcoholics: A third year independent double-blind follow up. *Behav. Res. & Therap.*, 16:345–362.
Carkhuff, R.B., & Berenson, B.G. (1967), *Beyond Counseling and Therapy*. New York: Holt, Rinehart & Winston.
Chwast, J. (1957), The significance of control in the treatment of antisocial persons. *Arch. Crimi. Psychodyn.*, 2:448–459.
——— (1965), Control: The key to offender treatment. *Amer. J. Psychother.*, 19:116–125.
Davies, D.L. (1962), Normal drinking in recovered alcohol addicts. *Quart. J. Stud. Alcohol.*, 23:90–99.
Ewing, J.A., & Rouse, B.A. (1976), Failure of an experimental treatment program to inculcate controlled drinking in alcoholics. *Brit. J. Addict.*, 71:123–134.
Freud, S. (1921), Group Psychology and the Analysis of the Ego. *Standard Edition*, 18:67–143. London: Hogarth Press, 1955.

——— (1923), The Ego and the Id. *Standard Edition*, 19:3–66. London: Hogarth Press, 1961.

Freudenberger, H.J. (1973), The therapist faces the new life styles of his patients. *J. Clin. Issues Psychol.*, 5:2–5.

Fromm, E. (1947), *Man for Himself: An Inquiry into the Psychology of Ethics*. New York: Holt, Rinehart & Winston.

Glasser, W. (1969), *Schools Without Failure*. New York: Harper & Row.

Greenblat, M., Becerra, R.M., & Serafetinides, E.A. (1982), Social networks and mental health: An overview. *Amer. J. Psychiat.*, 139:977–984.

Hoff, E.C. (1968), Group therapy with alcoholics. *Psychiat. Res. Report*, 24:61–70.

Horney, K. (1945), *Our Inner Conflicts: A Constructive Theory of Neurosis*. New York: W.W. Norton.

Imhof, J., Hirsch, R., & Terenzi, R.E. (1983), Countertransferential and attitudinal considerations in the treatment of drug abuse and addiction. *Internat. J. Addict.*, 18:491–510.

Jacobs, M.A., & Christ, J. (1967), Structuring and limit setting as techniques in the group treatment of adolescent delinquents. *Commun. Ment. Health*, 3:237–244.

Jellinick, E.M. (1960), *The Disease Concept of Alcoholism*. New Haven, CT: College & University Press.

Jung, C.G. (1928), *Two Essays on Analytical Psychology*. London: Ballière, Tindall & Cox.

Khantzian, E.J. (1980), The alcoholic patient: An overview and perspective. *Amer. J. Psychother.*, 34:4–19.

——— (1981), Some treatment implications of the ego and self disturbances in alcoholism. In: *Dynamic Approaches to the Understanding of Alcoholism*, eds. M.H. Bean & N.E. Zinberg. New York: Free Press, pp. 163–188.

Krystal, H. (1982), Adolescence and the tendencies to develop substance dependence. *Psychoanal. Inq.*, 2:581–618.

Leavy, R.L. (1983), Social support and psychological disorder: A review. *J. Community Psychol.*, 11:3–21.

Liff, Z.A. (1975), The charismatic leader. In: *The Leader in the Group*, ed. Z.A. Liff. New York: Jason Aronson, pp. 114–122.

Maslow, A.H. (1962), *Toward a Psychology of Being*. Princeton, NJ: Van Nostrand.

Meeks, J.E. (1974), Adolescent development and group cohesion. In: *Adolescent Psychiatry: Developmental and Clinical Studies*, Vol. 3, eds. S.C. Feinstein & P. Giovacchini. New York: Basic Books, pp. 289–297.

Newton, P.M. (1971), Abstinence as a role requirement in psychotherapy. *Psychiat.*, 34:394–402.

Pendery, M.L., Maltzman, I.M., & West, L.J. (1982), Controlled drinking by alcoholics? New findings and a reevaluation of a major affirmative study. *Science*, 217:169–175.

Phelan, J.R.M. (1974), Parent, teacher, or analyst: The adolescent-group therapist's trilemma. *Internat. J. Group Psychother.*, 24:238–244.

Rachman, A.W. (1972), Group psychotherapy in treating the adolescent identity crisis. *Internat. J. Child Psychother.*, 1:97–119.

——— (1974), The role of "fathering" in group psychotherapy with adolescent delinquent males. *Correc. Soc. Psychiat.*, 20:11–20.

——— (1975), *Identity Group Psychotherapy with Adolescents*. Springfield, IL: Charles C Thomas.

——— Raubolt, R.R. (1985), The clinical practice of group psychotherapy with adolescent substance abusers: Strategies for clinical intervention. In: *Alcoholism and Substance Abuse: Strategies for Clinical Intervention*, eds. T.E. Bratter & G. Forrest. New York: Free Press, pp. 338–364.

Raubolt, R.R., & Bratter, T.E. (1974), Games addicts play: Implications for group psychotherapy. *Correc. Soc. Psychiat.*, 20:1–10.

——— ——— (1976), Beyond adolescent group psychotherapy: The caring community. *Addict. Therap.*, 1:10–16.

Redl, F. (1945), The psychology of gang formation and the treatment of juvenile delinquents. *The Psychoanalytic Study of the Child*, 1:367–377. New York: International Universities Press.

——— Wineman, D. (1957), *The Aggressive Child*. Chicago: Free Press.

Sager, C.J. (1968), The group psychotherapist: Bulwark against alienation. *Internat. J. Group Psychother.*, 18:419–431.

Samorajczyk, J. (1971), The psychotherapist as a meaningful parental figure with alienated adolescents. *Amer. J. Psychother.*, 25:110–116.

Schaffer, H.H. (1968), Twelve month follow-up of behaviorally trained ex-alcoholic social drinkers. *Quart. J. Study Alcohol.*, 28A:610–622.

Schnee, J. (1972), Freedom of choice. *Amer. J. Psychoanal.*, 30:206–209.

Silver, R.J., Lubin, B., Miller, D.R., & Dobson, N.H. (1981), The group psychotherapy literature 1980. *Internat. J. Group Psychother.*, 31:469–526.

——— ——— ——— ——— (1982), The group psychotherapy literature 1981. *Internat. J. Group Psychother*, 32:481–554.

Slavson, S.R. (1943), *An Introduction to Group Therapy*. New York: Commonwealth Fund.

Sobell, M.B., & Sobell, L.C. (1978), *Behavioral Treatment of Alcoholism*. New York: Plenum Press.

Soden, E.W. (1961), Construction coersion and group counseling in the rehabilitation of alcoholics. *Fed. Probation*, 30:56–60.

Solomon, R.L. (1980), The operant-process theory of acquired motivation: The costs of pleasure and the benefits of pain. *Amer. Psychol.*, 35:691–712.

Speck, R.V. (1965), Psychotherapy of the social network of a schizophrenic family. *Family Proc.*, 6:208–214.

——— Attneave, C. (1971), Social network intervention. In: *Changing Families*, ed. J. Haley. New York: Grune & Stratton.

——— ——— (1973), *Family Networks: Retribalization and Healing*. New York: Pantheon Books.

Stein, A., & Friedman, E. (1971), Group therapy with alcoholics. In: *Comprehensive Group Psychotherapy*, eds. H.I. Kaplan & B.J. Sadock. Baltimore: Williams & Wilkins, pp. 652–690.

Stolorow, R. (1975), The narcissistic function of masochism (and sadism). *Internat. J. Psychoanal.*, 56:441–452.

Sutherland, R.L. (1962), Choosing as a therapeutic aim, method and philosophy. *J. Exist. Psychiat.*, 2:368–374.

Trice, H.M. (1956), Alcoholism: Group factors in etiology and therapy. *Hum. Organ.*, 15:33–40.

Tyson, R.L. (1982), Discussion adolescent addiction: Varieties and vicissitudes. *Psychoanal. Inq.*, 2:677–688.

Van Kaam, A. (1968), Addiction and existence. *Rev. Existential Psychol. Psychiat.*, 8:54–64.

Vannicelli, M., Canning, D., & Griefen, M. (1984), Group therapy with alcoholics: A group case study. *Internat. J. Group Psychother.*, 34:127–147.

Volkman, R., & Cressey, D.R. (1963), Differential association and rehabilitation of drug addicts. *Amer. J. Sociol.*, 69:129–142.

Werkman, S.L. (1974), Value confrontations between psychotherapists and adolescent patients. *Amer. J. Orthopsychiat.*, 44:337–344.

Wolfe, A., & Schwartz, E.K. (1959), Psychoanalysis in groups: The role of values. *Amer. J. Psychoanal.*, 19:37–52.

——— ——— (1962), *Psychoanalysis in Groups*. New York: Grune & Stratton.

Wolfe, T. (1936), *The Story of a Novel*. New York: Charles Scribner's Sons.

Yablonsky, L. (1965), *The Tunnel Back: Synanon*. New York: Macmillan.

Yalom, I.D., & Lieberman, M.A. (1971), A study of encounter group casualties. *Arch. Gen. Psychiat*,. 25:16–30.

Part IV

Clinical Research

Chapter 11

Clinical Research in Adolescent Group Psychotherapy: Status, Guidelines, and Directions

FERN J. CRAMER AZIMA, PH.D.
KATHRYN R. DIES, PH.D.

There is an abundance of observational studies in the literature that report the beneficial use of group therapy with adolescents (Kraft, 1983). The marked importance of peer interaction and devaluation of the parent in this developmental phase makes group therapy most often a more viable option than individual therapy. Various authors have discussed the enabling effects for adolescents in group therapy to voice their rebelliousness and hostility toward authority figures (Azima, 1972, 1973; Singer, 1973), to deal with evoked feelings of anxiety toward the members of the opposite sex (Berkowitz, 1972; Singer, 1974), and to define the perception of the self in relation to others in a safe social testing ground (Ackerman, 1955; Azima, 1977, 1982).

As could be predicted, clinical research with resistant adolescents has lagged behind investigations of adults. The goals of this chapter are (1) to review and evaluate recent studies, (2) to present some guidelines for the choice of research methods and instruments, and (3) to suggest some future directions for clinicians who wish to carry out group research with adolescents.

From the onset there is the dilemma that clinicians are fearful of spoiling or contaminating therapeutic results by the inclusion of research approaches. Further, the members in a group may be apprehensive about the use of data and the forfeiting of their confidentiality. Adolescents, specifically, may be unmotivated and rebel against the authority's demand to complete "school-like forms" and to be observed. The fear of exposure of "secrets" related to feelings of inferiority, sexual inadequacy, use of drugs, alcohol, or delinquent acts may threaten the adolescent. Dies (in press) has suggested that research instruments completed by group members sensitize them to certain behaviors and generate a positive change process that is not completely related to the therapeutic process. Kazdin (1981) also feels confident that problems associated with testing are not likely to influence the therapeutic results if data are collected over a large number of occasions. In our opinion, the therapist must explain to the members that they are the immediate recipients of the findings of the research, and the nature of the resulting written publications will help other clinicians to improve their understanding and treatment of other adolescents, also treated in groups. The therapist must assure them that their identities will be kept anonymous as in any other area of scientific investigation. Under these conditions we have found that the adolescents show respect and enthusiasm in their participation in the serious treatment that is being studied and analyzed by a team of professionals. This age group is frequently sophisticated in the use of audiovisual and computer technology, and in fact may take for granted that these are acceptable observational techniques. We are in agreement with Pfeiffer, Heslin, and Jones (1973) and MacKenzie and Dies (1982) that utilizing research methods encourages patient involvement in the therapeutic process, clarifies treatment goals, increases objectivity of measuring patient change, sensitizes patients and therapists to the multifaceted nature of change, and improves communication between patients and therapist. Furthermore, in our view the therapist who concisely formulates his clinical and research goals in the early stages encourages both the cooperation of all members and intensifies the group psychotherapy process. In this way, the dual nature of clinical research is accomplished, namely, more effective patient care and contribution to the understanding of group dynamics and process, and in the present context perfecting group therapy techniques for adolescents.

RECENT RESEARCH STUDIES

A recent review of adolescent group psychotherapy research (Tramontana, 1980) confirms the dearth of sound empirical studies, especially when school-based reports are removed. Although the latter studies are important, they are not primarily psychotherapy oriented (Haynes and Avery, 1979; Silbergeld, Thune, and Manderscheid, 1979; Pentz, 1981; Avery, Rider, and Haynes-Clements, 1981; Sarason and Sarason, 1981; Rushton, 1982).

Of six clinical and thirteen experimental adolescent group psychotherapy investigations between 1967 and 1977 (Tramontana, 1980), only five are sufficiently well designed and rigorously executed to be considered as presenting evidence of this treatment modality's success (Persons, 1966, 1967; Redfering, 1972; Jesness, 1975). These studies were considered adequate as they incorporated a variety of instruments to measure outcome, and all included a follow-up component in their design, showing a significantly higher rate of positive outcome than control groups. Tramontana (1980) concludes that there is a need for a more valid picture of the adolescent's adjustment over time and across different settings. Bennis (1960), Dies (1983a), and Dies and Riester (1986) suggest a merger of clinical and research efforts, underscoring the importance of reciprocal interactions between clinicians and researchers.

The following selected studies since 1977 (Table 1) review outcome, process, and leadership utilizing the administration of standardized research tools, observer ratings, and structured interviews.

Lockwood (1981) conducted post hoc interviews with teachers, parents, and therapists to assess outcome for young adolescents who had completed activity group therapy, and found two common factors linked to a group improvement of 76 to 88 percent: (1) attendance at 25 or more sessions over a period of six months, and (2) family interest and involvement in therapy. Similar findings that detail the impact of attendance and parental support were also reported by Richmond and Gaines (1979) and Richmond, Gaines, and Fogt (1981) using a survey approach to measure outcome.

The process study of Fine, Knight-Webb, and Vernon (1977) evaluated the impact of placing volunteer members in therapy group to model appropriate group behaviors. Posttreatment telephone interviews revealed that group members perceived the volunteers to be useful in facilitating group process, showed increased rates of expressions of warmth, decreased verbalization of flight, and a greater sense of cohesion among members.

Bernfield, Clark, and Parker (1984) using observer ratings of

TABLE 1

Selected Studies of Adolescent Group Psychotherapy Research (1977–1984)

Investigators	Subjects (Groups)	Approach	Measurement	Findings
Fine, Knight-Webb, and Vernon (1977)	21 (1)	Volunteers to model behavior	Posttreatment telephone interviews	Volunteer models judged as facilitating group process.
Hurst, Stein, Korchin, and Soskin (1978)	96 (4)	Psychodynamic	Group cohesion (Lieberman et al., 1973) Leadership scale (Lieberman et al., 1973)	Leaders viewed as high on caring and self-expression enhanced the development of group cohesion.
Richmond and Gaines (1979)	254 (1 open-ended)	Psychodynamic, Interactional	Survey of clinic records	Male attendance higher; weekday attendance higher; overall attendance higher when referred by therapists leading groups, and when parents attended parallel group. 68% successful outcome for members whose parents attended vs. 48% for those who did not.
Richmond, Gaines, and Fogt (1981)	100 (1 open-ended)	Psychodynamic, Interactional	Survey of clinic records	
Silbergeld, Thune, and Manderscheid (1979)	45 (4)	Eclectic	HIM-G of audiotape	Leaders work style stable, fluctuations in content. Increase member interactions by reinforcement and modeling.
Weber (1980)	6 (1)	Videotape to stimulate feedback	Rater analysis	Videotaping increases expressions of warmth, decreases flight statements. Cohesiveness enhanced.

TABLE 1 *(continued)*

Investigators	Subjects (Groups)	Approach	Measurement	Findings
Corder, Whiteside, and Haizlip (1981)	16 (4)	Psychoanalytic	Q-Sort	Adolescents rank cohesion, universality, catharsis, and interpersonal learning as important curative factors. Least helpful—insight oriented interpretations.
Guyer and Matthews (1981)	20 (2)	Verbal vs. nonverbal exercises	Observer ratings of body posture Tennessee Self-Concept Scale, HIM	Nonverbal warm-up exercises enhance outcome.
Lockwood (1981)	25 (2)	Activity group therapy	Post hoc, structured interviews with parents, teachers, therapists	Ratings of improvement congruent across raters. Range from 76 to 88% improvement.
Bernfield, Clark, and Parker (1984)	22 (1 open-ended)	Psychodynamic	Observer rating of group member behaviors. Ratings of clinical functioning	Group roles increase, individual roles decrease, and task roles remain fairly constant over time.
Corder, Cornwall, and Whiteside (1984)	10 Sets of cotherapists	Eclectic	Cotherapist rating and critical incident form	Lowered anxiety level of cotherapists.
			Curative factors checklist	Rating differences related to problems in group. Improvement in planning, collaboration and supervision.

clinical functioning derived from Dimock's coding system (1971), indicated that individual roles gave way to group roles as therapy progressed. Individual roles were defined as responses that interfered with group process (i.e., resisting, withdrawing from discussion, digressing, or seeking recognition). Group roles were defined as maintaining the process of the group (i.e., coordinating, mediating, orienting, supporting, and following group rules). The progression toward the use of group roles was positively enhanced the longer the patient stayed in group therapy.

Corder, Whiteside, and Haizlip (1981) identified curative factors in the adolescent group process using a Q-Sort. These findings, quite similar to the adult group research, identified cohesion, universality, catharsis, and interpersonal learning to be the most important. Insight-oriented, direct interpretation was found to be least helpful. These authors suggest that "the high rankings attributed to opportunities for the cathartic expression of feelings indicate that training programs for therapists might focus research on techniques that allow expression, without developing the intolerable levels of group tension and anxiety often described in work with adolescents" (p. 354).

A posttreatment survey by Meyer and Zegans (1975) suggests some causal links between therapist characteristics and therapy outcome in adolescent groups, namely, that this age group admires clinicians who are supportive, interact emotionally, and are spontaneous, yet remain objective and insightful.

In a study of leadership style, Hurst, Stein, Korchin, and Soskin (1978) assessed adolescents' perceptions of and responses to leaders on the dimensions of self-expression, meaning attribution, caring and controlling, using the categories proposed by Lieberman, Yalom, and Miles (1973). Their findings indicated that adolescents are most likely to experience group cohesion when the therapist is viewed as particularly caring and, second, as self-expressing. This finding is at variance with Lieberman et al. (1973) whose college-age participants showed no significant relationship between caring and cohesion. As such, this study may reflect unique adolescent group member characteristics for this developmental stage.

In an investigation of leadership style, Silbergeld et al. (1979) find that therapists display similar styles across groups, but alter interactional content to meet group members' differing needs. In response to acting out, emotionally dependent, narcissistic adolescents, therapists tended to interact more frequently in the relationship mode, as well as model and sample group behaviors.

The study of Guyer and Matthews (1981) demonstrates the impact of pregroup verbal and nonverbal warm-up exercises in the promotion of cohesion and acceptance of adolescent group members. Utilizing the Tennessee Self-Concept Scale, the Hill Interaction Matrix, and observer ratings of body posture, their findings indicated that nonverbal warm-up exercises had a positive effect on treatment outcome, and observer ratings of group videotapes indicated a higher level of interaction among group members.

In an outcome study by Corder, Cornwall, and Whiteside (1984) techniques for increasing the effectiveness of cotherapists' functions in adolescent psychotherapy groups were explored. Ten sets of cotherapists over a two-year period completed a Rating of Critical Incidents and Issues Form. Prior to the onset of therapy (1) therapists met for a minimum of three sessions to develop common methods for scoring the "critical incidents" of the adolescent group; (2) therapists rated each other; (3) therapists rated the adolescent along a curative factor framework; and (4) observers rated therapists if there was a significant disagreement between them. The findings of the study revealed decreased anxiety levels for the cotherapists and increased collaboration, planning, and problem solving.

In summary, the use of common research criteria improved the effectiveness of the cotherapists in reaching agreement on how to treat the adolescents, and in the final analysis improved the quality of group therapy for the age group.

Omitted from this literature review were anecdotal studies that relied on subjective assessment of improvement or unidimensional measurement of outcome (Brown and Kingsley, 1975; Weber, 1980; Scott, 1980; Levin, 1983).

GUIDELINES FOR IMPROVING CLINICAL RESEARCH

The clinician who wishes to investigate either outcome or process dimensions must state achievable goals clearly, frame questions that can be meaningfully answered within the constraints of time, and choose relevant objective measures and methodology. It is usually crucial to obtain the services of a research consultant in the earliest planning stages to guarantee success of the project. It is rarely recommended that the group leader collect his own data in order not to prejudice his therapeutic position. In effect, the clinician is involved in two ongoing processes, namely, the patient group and the research group, and clearly the goals of the latter must serve the needs of the former.

Few therapeutic centers for adolescents have the personnel to carry out large-scale complex investigations unless they are in an academic setting where collaboration with statisticians and research associates can be assured. In fact, an overwhelming number of studies are evaluations of a single therapy group, and it is for this type of practical investigation that some guidelines are given to encourage clinical practitioners to integrate applied research strategies into their ongoing group therapy. It should be stressed, however, that a two-group design with matched controls, which shows the specific effects of a treatment modality, is a considerably stronger research investigation. These guidelines focus on the importance of (1) objective methods, (2) multiple assessment procedures, (3) outcome and follow-up measures, and (4) process measures.

Objective Methods

In the present context, objective methods refers to the systematic nonbiased quantification of the subjective evaluations of member and leader variables, as well as process and outcome variables that can be operationally defined, collected, and replicated by others in similar settings (Hartman, 1979; Kazdin, 1981).

In essence, the principle of objectivity allows the therapist to develop simple nonpretentious strategies of observation and data collection at the same time that therapy is ongoing. Proposing standard questions for group members and leaders at the beginning of treatment, and at defined intervals, provides a data base that is easily coded and quantifiable.

The tests or instruments chosen for the study should have reported reliability, validity, and norms applicable to the adolescent age group. For a general discussion of the statistical criteria relevant for group therapists, the reader is referred to Bennis (1960), Campbell and Stanley (1963), and Parloff and Dies (1978). Since there are few tests exclusively devised for adolescents, it may be possible at times to simply rephrase adult scales into more appropriate language (Reed, 1984). At other times suitable adolescent norms should be obtained from control subjects.

Selection procedures must be carefully considered when assessing therapeutic success or failure, and rarely is it possible in clinical research to randomize the selection of group therapy candidates. When the results of different studies are compared they should be matched for at least two or three variables (e.g., age, intelligence, education, diagnosis, sex).

Multiple Assessment Procedures

It is generally agreed that a varied battery of psychosocial tests decreases information variance, and the addition of multiple raters with high interrater reliability adds important significance to the criterion of external validity. Once again, the number of raters and the number of investigatory procedures must be parsimonious enough to test and analyze the relevant dimensions under investigation in an acceptable period of time. The battery of tests is usually administered before and after at specified time points during the group and at follow-up. MacKenzie and Dies (1982) recommend that an ideal battery be composed of

1. multiple measures, due to the complexity of therapeutic change,
2. objective and subjective viewpoints evaluating subjective impressions and behavioral observations,
3. a combination of individualized and standardized measurements,
4. assessment of various areas of functioning (e.g., self-esteem, interpersonal, and social role functioning),
5. measures from various sources of information including the therapist, client, and significant others (p. 14).

Reports of very successful outcomes frequently may be traced to the original selection and composition of very suitable group members. As yet there are inadequate criteria for inclusion and exclusion of group candidates (Berkowitz, 1972; Azima, 1973, 1983; Richmond, 1974, 1978; Sugar, 1975, 1979; Rachman, 1975; Brandes, 1977; Kraft, 1983; Rachman and Raubolt, 1983; Raubolt, 1983).

Both Singer (1974) and Brandes (1977) have cautioned that group therapy may not be indicated for all adolescents, for example, when they are developmentally immature, ego weak, or the diagnosis is too severe. In some cases prior intensive individual therapy is needed, while in others additional network therapies are necessary (Sugar, 1975).

Azima (1983) discusses selection criteria, indications and contraindications for group psychotherapy with personality disorder. For example, paranoid personalities require greater sensitivity to group composition and timing of introduction into the group, while dependent personalities benefit from the group members by both the gratification of dependent cravings and the confirmation of "overclinginess." Similar assessment of other diagnostic categories may offer some leads for testing selection criteria.

Psychotherapy research, in particular group research, has been faulted because of the lack of comparison with control groups. Gurman and Kniskern (1981) have stated that there is probably no such thing as a true control group, since those individuals who initially might be considered as "untreated" patients are often found to be seeking treatment from therapists outside the research protocol, a close friend, or the local bartender. These authors, as well as Budman, Demby, Feldstein, and Gold (1984), suggest that using patients on a waiting list who can avail themselves of "treatment on demand" (TOD) probably offers the closest "no treatment condition" in psychotherapy outcome research. Budman et al. further state that "although TOD probably reduces differences between treatment and control groups it is never really possible or ethically desirable to fully withhold therapeutic intervention from those in need" (p. 60).

In the absence of a control group, three alternatives may be considered as an effective way to evaluate differential treatment progress: (1) a contrast group with a different form of treatment (e.g., individual, family); (2) the aggregate of results from several groups; and (3) comparing individual members' progress with each other and with the group mean on outcome measures (Campbell and Stanley, 1963; Azima, 1970).

In addressing the issue of research of single case studies, Kazdin (1981) stated: "it is the anecdotal information that is the problem rather than the fact that an individual case is studied" (p. 185). McCullough (1984 a,b) urges clinicians to (1) view psychotherapy as an experimental test hypothesis using "time-series" methods of data collection of "target behaviors" that should be measured repeatedly and systematically through the process of case assessment, treatment implementation, termination, and follow-up; (2) treatment methodology should be carefully operationalized and standardized; (3) treatment subjects should be classified and matched according to symptom criteria; and (4) $N = 1$ studies should be suitably matched to controls and replicated, stressing external validity rather than exclusively internal validity. This shifting to the criterion of external validity and the inclusion of multiple raters outside of the patient group is of great importance for the judgment of change and provides indirect confirmation for the strength of therapeutic procedures. Additionally, external raters are able to provide evidence of important life events that may prejudice the results, for example, illness, loss of a friend, exam failure, and parental divorce. Doubtless, it remains a thorny problem to sift out developmental from therapeutic changes.

Although it may not be possible for certain therapists to carry out elaborate research designs, a certain minimum of planning can guarantee adequate measurement and analysis. Translating subjective or anecdotal material into behavioral and scorable referrants allows the clinician to add his own creativity to a battery of standardized tests. It must be cautioned, however, that overreliance on self-constructed, nonvalidated scales, "especially constructed for this study" limits the acceptability or replicability of the findings. At least four major criteria govern the following guidelines:

1. the statement of the clinical research goal(s)
2. the choice and combination of adequate process and outcome test measures
3. the selection of baseline, and time intervals for retest and follow-up
4. the selection of raters from varying perspectives of member, therapist, observer, parent, peer, or teacher

Difficulties inherent for adult group therapy research are magnified for adolescent research where there are few normed instruments, and there is an enmeshment of ongoing developmental changes. To deal with the latter dilemma, clinical changes should be correlated with ongoing life events, and ideally followed up over time to judge the maintenance of the improvement. Agreement among the raters and the test findings adds significantly to the acceptance of the results, as compared to the reliance on a single measure.

An added bonus to the use of a diverse multidimensional battery is the possibility of the construction of a global index of the level of improvement, health, and illness based on the integration and analysis of each member to assess separately the variation of treatment gains. Often, the direction of change in such areas as activity, anxiety, mood, and symptom differs. For example, a decrease in anxiety may be judged therapeutic for an obsessive adolescent, whereas an increase in anxiety may be judged equally therapeutic for an adolescent with sociopathic trends. Global scores may also be defined in terms of coping in the group therapy, with the family, peers, and school, and then matched with the presence or absence of pathological behaviors.

Outcome Measures

There is considerable controversy about the choice of adequate change measures within the field of group psychotherapy (Waskow and Parloff, 1975). The proponents of objectivity advocate overt behavioral measures, which are not completely satisfying for the therapist who is concerned with intrapsychic change. Lieberman (1983), in reviewing the problems of studying therapeutic mechanisms, states that the critical choice facing the investigator is between the use of external or internal frames of reference. The external perspective is reflected in observational measures that record frequency, intensity, and modification in verbal and nonverbal communication of each individual within the group context. The internal framework depends on the direct phenomenological inquiry about the members' personal report about ongoing events and his own idiosyncratic understanding. Lieberman et al. (1973) in their well-known encounter study opted for the self-report linkage to outcome, using two major sources of data. At the end of each the member was asked to reply to the question: "What was the most important event for you personally in the group today and why was it important." The second source of data was a final postgroup questionnaire of 14 different change mechanisms such as self disclosure, insight, hope, etc.

The choice of methodology depends on the goals of the investigator and the preciseness of the question he asks. Strupp and Hadley (1977) divide therapy outcome criteria into three categories: (1) the patient who is concerned with improvement in his subjective sense of well-being, (2) the society (family, authorities, employers) which focuses on the patient's behavioral adjustment, and (3) the therapist who concentrates on validation of theoretical constructs such as ego strength and self-esteem. Frequently, the patient may improve but there are discrepancies among the three areas. Adelstein, Gelso, Haws, Reed, and Spiegel (1983) in a study of the change process following time limited therapy, reported that the therapists assessed the therapeutic impact as substantially more negative then the patients both at the termination of therapy and at follow-up 18 months later. In small-scale research it is very difficult to obtain uniform, consistent patterns, and often the results are mixed or even contradictory. The clinical researcher is in the best position to study the total constellation of factors and to weight them in terms of positive, negative, or no change for each member. Present-day statistical design for small samples permits more reliable assessment, although it is also clear that therapy research must be more tolerant of deviations in methodological rigor (Oetting, 1976 a,b).

The CORE battery introduced by MacKenzie and Dies (1982) was an attempt to integrate a number of well-known outcome instruments for group therapy research. The battery consists of patient self-report, therapist, and "significant other" measures. Reed (1984) in a pilot study of 40 outpatient adolescents using the CORE battery reported success with the following measures:

1. *Self Report Symptom Inventory (SCL-90R).* This 90-item test developed by Derogatis (1977) yields scores on nine symptom dimensions (e.g., somatization, depression, anxiety) and three summary scores including a global severity index. The items are applicable to adolescents, easy to read, not overly difficult, and can be administered in 20 minutes.

2. *Social Adjustment Scale (SAS).* A self-report test developed by Weissman and Bothwell (1976) has been adapted by Reed (1984) for use with the adolescents' adjustment to leisure, family, and school.

3. *Multiple Affect Adjective Check List.* This test (Zuckerman and Lubin, 1965) was substituted for the Emotions Profile Index (Plutchik, 1980), which was not found useful with the teenage sample. This checklist identifies various emotions and their intensity, which can be reassessed at various intervals.

4. *Target Goals (Patient).* Based on Goal Attainment Scaling (Kiresuk and Sherman, 1968) and the Target Goals Procedure (Battle, Imber, Hoehn-Saric, Stone, Nash, and Frank, 1966) the subject is asked to make a list of the three most important goals he or she would like to work on during therapy. These goals are to be stated

in behavioral terms and are rerated on a seven-point scale from "worse" to "total improvement." This procedure allows the individual to decide on his unique problem areas and to assess his ability to overcome them.

5. *Target Goals (Therapist).* Similar to the above measure the therapist, after evaluating the member, sets three goals (in behavioral terms) and rerates them in terms of attainment at the end of therapy. The therapist is also responsible for recording the group composition, attendance, and diagnosis.

6. *Global Assessment Scale (GAS).* The Luborsky (1962) GAS consists of a 100-point continuum anchored by personality descriptions for every ten-point range. Case vignettes are given as guides to rate the appropriate degree of impairment in functioning. The therapist also completes a General Improvement Rating. The seven-point scale of Clinical Global Impressions and Global Improvement used in drug research are concise alternates (Guy, 1976).

7. *Measures of "Significant Others."* External evaluators are asked to complete the improvement ratings of the member on one or several of the above scales. Particularly useful are the Social Adjustment Scale and the GAS, which a relative or friend of the adolescent, or nurse or psychologist in the inpatient facility, can complete quickly, easily, and objectively.

Particularly useful in a battery for younger adolescents is the Achenbach Child Behavior Checklist (Achenbach and Edelbrock, 1979), which may be completed by parents, teachers, or other mental health professionals. This is a well-validated, reliable, normed instrument that holds good promise of confirming other outcome results.

In a controlled outcome study by Budman et al. (1984), the positive effects of short-term psychotherapy were judged by a battery which included target problems; the Derogatis Self Report Inventory; a personal assessment of interpersonal relations; a peer scale of learning and improvement by each group member of the other members; a therapist scale of the level of learning and improvement of group members; testimony ratings of the group experience, and attitudes toward the group therapy.

Each investigator will construct a battery with modifications and additions to measure the outcome on such variables as depression, anxiety, self-esteem, and acting out. A limited number of additional change instruments (outcome and process) are listed in Tables 2 and 3.

In reviewing the present outcome batteries, especially for adolescents, it is our view that there is insufficient emphasis placed on baseline measures such as intelligence, diagnosis, and personality evaluation. Positive improvement in therapy may be reflected in improved IQ scores, school performance, and ratings by teachers. Further, outcome batteries such as the CORE reveal individual change but lack information about group change or interaction (Coché, 1983).

Follow-up Measures

Most studies that offer follow-up measures do not usually extend beyond three-, six-, or twelve-month intervals. Longitudinal studies are particularly indicated for children and adolescents, for they assess the degree these changes persist and generalize, and in what stresses the problem behavior reoccurs (Azima, 1985). Are therapy improvements maintained from puberty to midadolescence to the onset of adulthood? Short-term outcome reratings are often possible by the clinical research team but for long-term follow-up of adaptive functioning external ratings of school success, juvenile offense records, recidivism, and hospitalization are necessary adjuncts (Persons, 1966; Taylor, 1967; Redfering, 1972; Jesness, 1975; Ro-Trock, Wellisch, and Schoolar, 1977). In longitudinal research the individual becomes his own control. Follow-up measures from clinics, inpatient, or private practice may include mailed forms, telephone surveys, and videoed structured interviews with the member himself. Instruments such as the Child Behavior Checklist can be used with parents, teachers, and specially constructed global improvement scales on identified parameters such as success–failure, interpersonal functioning, and symptom appearance are recommended (see Table 2).

A multidimensional, multiperspective approach for long-term follow-up would appear to reap the best rewards. A combination of repeated, self-report, behavioral questionnaires, structured interviews, normed tests, and confirmation by knowledgeable others would give a good evaluation of the member's functioning. It would be helpful in the global assessment follow-up to inquire about performance in group activities in school, sports, clubs, and with peers. After a period of time and distance from the actual therapy the

TABLE 2
Group Outcome Instruments

Outcome Instruments	Measurement	Investigator
Adjective Checklist	Perceptions of the self	Gough and Heilbrun (1965)
Anomie Scale	Feelings of social alienation	McClosky and Schaar (1965)
Beck Depression	Self-report of adult depression	Beck, Ward, Mendelson, Mock, and Erbaugh (1961)
Child Behavior Checklist	Significant others' objective evaluations of patient's behavioral change; for group members aged 6–16	Achenbach and Edelbrock (1979)
Clinical Global Impressions and Global Improvement Scale	Likert-type scales of global level of psychopathology and change	Guy (1976)
Emotions Profile Index	Self-report of affective states	Plutchik (1980)
Global Assessment Schedule (GAS)	A 100-point scale with anchors every 10 points; assesses global psychopathology using case vignettes	Luborsky (1962)
IPAT Anxiety Questionnaire (Self-Analysis Form)	Forty statements of anxiety-provoking situations rated by the group member	Cattell and Schier (1963)
Katz Adjustment Scale	Ratings of symptomatology and social behaviors	Katz and Lyerly (1963)

TABLE 2 *(continued)*

Outcome Instruments	Measurement	Investigator
Mach IV and Mach V	Likert-type and forced-choice instruments of Machiavellian/manipulative tendencies	Christie and Geis (1970)
Multiple Affect	A self-report of affective change	Zuckerman and Lubin (1965)
Psychiatric Status	Designed to improve the research value of clinical judgments of psychopathology and role functioning	Spitzer, Endicott, Fleiss, and Cohen (1970)
SCL-90R	Self-report symptom checklist normed for male and female adolescents	Derogatis (1977)
Self-Esteem Inventory	Patient level of self-esteem	Coopersmith (1967)
Semantic Differential	Self-perception and attitudes toward significant others	Snider and Osgood (1969)
Social Adjustment Scale	Self-report of social functioning in six major areas; applicable to adolescents with some modification	Weissman and Bothwell (1976)
Target goals for therapist and member	Assesses outcome vis-à-vis the evaluation of the achievement of stated goals	Battle, Imber, Hoehn-Saric, Stone, Nash, and Frank (1966)

TABLE 3
Group Process Instruments

Process Instruments	Measurement	Investigator
Acceptance versus Rejection of Others	Bipolar adjectives to describe group leader characteristics	Hurley and Rosenthal (1978)
Cotherapist Rating of Critical Incidents	Therapist rating of self and cotherapist on personality	Corder, Cornwall, and Whiteside (1984)
FIRO Scales	Focuses on interpersonal behaviors and feelings of member and leader	Schutz (1967)
Gross Cohesion Scale	Mutual stimulation and effect, commitment and compatibility of the group	Gross (1957)
Group Climate Questionnaire	Three dimensions of group climate (engagement, avoidance, and conflict)	MacKenzie (1981)
Group Environment Scale	Three dimensions of group environment (relationships, personal growth, and system maintenance)	Moos (1974)
Group Leader Self-Disclosure Scale	Leadership self-disclosure	Dies (1973, 1977)
Group Rating Scale	Five factors of group process (orientation, social climate, therapist involvement, therapist/client interaction, and cohesion)	Cooper (1977)

TABLE 3 *(continued)*

Process Instruments	Measurement	Investigator
Group Therapist Intervention Scale	Group leader behaviors	Nichols and Taylor (1975)
Hill Interaction Matrix	Content and style of interactions within groups	Hill (1977)
Interactional Process Analysis	Task and social–emotional behaviors; emphasizes problem solving strategies	Bales (1970)
Leadership Profile	Leadership behaviors from the perspectives of group members, therapists, and observers	Dies (1973)
Process Analysis Scoring System	Leader-member interactions	Gibbard and Hartman (1973)
Self-Report Change Mechanisms	Group cohesion: 14 curative factors; post-rating of critical group incidents	Lieberman, Yalom, and Miles (1973)
Social Information Processing Analysis (SIPA)	Verbal interactions from a communications perspective	Fisher, Drecksel, and Werbel (1979)

adolescents may be more willing and objective to talk about their group experience and what they felt about the process and leader.

Process Measures

Process measures provide the information of how the group functions and modifies and in what way individuals, including the leader, interact with each other, assume various roles, and develop a group atmosphere of cohesion, fear, and flight. Outcome measures indicate whether the individual has changed after the group, but rarely is it possible to relate the precise factors to the ongoing group interaction without process measures. A number of the instruments to be briefly discussed below may also be termed "outcome measures" as they follow the patient, the leader, and the group over time. Again the process instruments may be divided into self-report and observational schema. In addition to the self-report instruments dealt with in the outcome section, special scales or questions may be constructed that ask the members, at the end of each group session, to deal with such issues as cohesion (Gross, 1957; Piper, Marrache, Lacroix, Richardsen, and Jones, 1983), critical incidents in the group, and attitudes toward the leader (Dimock, 1971; Dies, 1983b), to list a few (see Table 3).

Excluded from most studies are detailed group interaction instruments such as those described in Bales (1950, 1970), Dimock (1971), and Hill (1977), which, although cumbersome, costly, and necessitate the training of skilled scorers, are the most detailed ways of recording group communication. The Bales allows recording of verbal and nonverbal communication in four major areas—questions, answers, positive emotions, and negative emotions (encompassing problem solving and emotional categories). It permits a social matrix of reciprocal interaction of member-to-member, member-to-leader, and to the group as a whole. Statistics of individual and group interaction over time are easy to compute.

Group interaction instruments have also been criticized in that they are cumulative, quantified measures that exclude the content and quality of the statement of behavior. However, present-day video techniques could allow the possibility of a parallel coding of content.

The Group Environment Scale (Moos, 1974), Group Atmosphere Scale (Silbergeld, Thune, and Manderscheid, 1979), and Group Climate Questionnaire (MacKenzie, 1981) are important process measures. The MacKenzie scale is a twelve-item measure that yields scores of engagement (cohesion), conflict, and avoidance. Modifications in the group climate over the various developmental phases of the group may be linked to therapeutic changes for the individual members. At the same time a knowledge of the group climate (e.g., threatening, cold) may help the therapist plan strategies to deal with these issues within the adolescent group.

Sociometric techniques have been used as a tool to measure both outcome and process. Livesley and MacKenzie (1983) have used this method to study the more participating members as compared to the silent ones, and those they describe as assuming "cautionary" roles. The latter they describe as members who may appear withdrawn and uninvolved yet in actuality are attentive to group events.

Application of sociometric techniques used in studies of children's sympathy and scapegoating in preschool groups (Cramer, 1949) would appear to be useful in adolescent groups to identify the roles of the popular, excluded, and powerful members.

The Osgood Semantic Differential (Osgood, 1952; Snider and Osgood, 1969) is a seven-point adjective rating of a concept in terms of evaluation, potency, and activity. In some ways it can be used as a sociometric technique since the results can be graphed in distances of the self, from the leader, other members, father, mother, and mental health (Azima, 1970).

The leadership profile (Dies, 1973, 1977) evaluates a variety of leadership behaviors and has recently been adapted for use with adolescents (Reed, 1984). The reader is referred to a detailed study by Dies (1983a) of the research on leadership in short-term groups. Assessment of the composite "ideal" therapist for an adolescent group was attempted by Meyer and Zegans (1975) who conducted interviews with former group members. Their description is of a positive, intuitive, spontaneous therapist who achieves "a charmed balance between supportive care and objective discernment . . . willingness to interact emotionally . . . and a respect for need for separateness and autonomy" (p. 22). Ricks's (1974) "supershrink" is an active, responsive, involved, but reality based therapist. Hurst et al. (1978) have suggested a correlation between leadership style and group cohesion in adolescent groups.

DIRECTIONS

The majority of research investigations have focused on evaluation and change, or prediction and outcome. Although process and outcome are intimately entwined, it has often seemed too great a challenge to conduct research on both simultaneously. It is because of the dynamic, ongoing time sequencing that it is difficult to hold the group process in focus. At the same time, there is a significant need for a detailed phenomenological description of the minutiae of process interaction, and also a need to evaluate what the effect and modifications are of therapy group processes on individual personalities. One can avoid confusing process with outcome if the research strategies and measuring instruments are chosen with both ends in mind and if care is taken in deciding which aspects of the process are of interest and which individual variables are being evaluated in psychotherapy. The direction for the clinical research is not merely a proof of positive outcome, but an analysis and explanation of how and what group processes and dynamics induce therapeutic change.

A multileveled study by Azima (1970) was designed to identify a methodology of interrelating outcome and process factors and to study the change in individual and group profiles of five women in short-term therapy. The methodology is easily adapted for adolescents and is an example of a direction for a complex combined outcome/process study. The procedure and methods consisted of the following:

1. Prior to therapy there was a pretesting of each member as regards intelligence and personality factors.
2. There was a two-week group therapy baseline during which the members became comfortable with the one-way screen setting and the clinical–research orientation.
3. A sociopsychological test battery was administered and scored by two research associates. The battery consisted of (a) a Self Esteem Inventory (Coopersmith, 1967); (b) the Osgood Semantic Differential (Osgood, 1952) (the list for adolescents can be modified to include such concepts as school, drugs, police, etc.); (c) the IPAT Anxiety Scale (Cattell and Schier, 1963); (d) the Machiavellian (Mach) Scale (Geis, Christie, and Nelson, 1963); and (e) the Anomie Scale (Srole, 1956).
4. Group process and interaction was recorded for all twelve

therapy sessions by a social psychologist using the Bales Interaction Process Analysis technique (1950). These data were computerized.

5. The therapist wrote brief personality sketches of each patient and made independent predictions of changes along each of the test variable (self-esteem, anxiety, and Machiavellianism), following the third session.
6. Posttherapy, the clinical and sociopsychological batteries were repeated and patient questionnaires completed. The latter included such items as benefit of the therapy to the member and to others, fulfillment of expectations, rating of helpful and nonhelpful members, and external assessment of change.

The data were analyzed for both individual and group portraits, and how the members interacted and modified over time. It was possible to identify successful candidates and high-risk candidates. Leader contributions to the matrix could be identified in relation to each member and to the group as a whole. With the greater accessibility of audiovisual and computer technology in most hospital and university settings, the organizing and analyzing of data are greatly facilitated. For a less complicated design the Interaction Process Analysis data can be recorded at baseline and subsequently at predetermined intervals during the therapy and at termination.

As has been suggested in the previous section, single case studies can be made more research oriented by following the rules of objectivity, the use of multiple measures, the inclusion of controls, or the aggregate of findings from small groups. Although it may be easier to design outcome studies, the omission of some process measures leaves one without the knowledge of what exactly transpired in the group and what effected the therapeutic changes. We would like to underline the value of baseline testing of intelligence, personality description, and diagnosis in order to determine more significantly the relationship of positive or negative outcome with these factors. Follow-up and longitudinal studies carry the advantage of external evaluators to determine the endurance of change at home, school, or work.

This review has stressed the importance of normed instruments, and it is hoped that newer measures will provide norms for younger as compared to older adolescents. There is considerable variability in development from ages 12 to 20. Analysis of peer interaction and relationship to authority for this age group may help define the appropriate theoretical, technical, and leader style to overcome these specific conflicts.

CONCLUSION

As a strategy for clinical research in group psychotherapy a combined outcome/process methodology appears to be the most satisfying approach. This is not to negate that outcome or process studies are also necessary. The following outline summarizes some trends and future directions for research, specifically with adolescents in the area of methodology, peer, therapist, and group variables.

I. *Methodology Variables*

1. The inclusion of baseline measures of intelligence, diagnosis, and personality variables.
2. The use and innovation of tests normed for adolescents.
3. Longitudinal follow-up by both the clinical research team and selected external raters from the family, school, work, and community.
4. Computerization of a battery of normed self-report and observational ratings, of live or televised sessions, that can be replicated by others.
5. Comparison with control or contrasts groups.

II. *Peer Variables*

1. Improvement of selection and composition criteria, varied according to age, sex, intelligence, and psychopathology.
2. Focus on the nature of peer bonding, relationship to the leader and to the group as a whole.
3. Auxiliary methods to foster conformity, self-reflection, positive group culture, group cohesion, and interpersonal learning (e.g., pretraining films, video playback, inclusion of well-functioning role models, psychodrama, projective art therapy, agenda and task-focused theme meetings, social outings).
4. Focus on clinical research of group treatments of adolescent depression, suicidal ideation, acting out, alienation, and gender identity problems.

III. *Therapist Variables*

1. Comparison of the efficacy of various types of therapeutic alliance and therapist intervention styles (e.g., empathy, confrontation, explanation, interpretation) with similar and contrasting adolescent groups.
2. Study of the self-disclosure patterns and qualities of leadership that influence the creation of a therapeutic group climate and effect positive change in the adolescent.
3. Analysis of the effects of therapist countertransference and error on individual members and the group process.
4. Comparison of the efficacy of single therapist- versus cotherapists-led groups.

IV. *Group Variables*

1. Comparison of "group only" versus combined approaches.
2. Comparison of inclusion and exclusion of parents in the treatment of younger and older adolescents.
3. Indications for and comparison of short-term versus long-term group approaches.

The twofold intent of this chapter has been to stimulate therapists to integrate research into their ongoing practice and to encourage the inclusion of a clinical–research module in the training programs for group therapists working with adolescents.

REFERENCES

Achenbach, T.M., & Edelbrock, C.S. (1979), The child behavior profile: II. Boys aged 12–16 and girls aged 6–11 and 12–16. *J. Consult. Clin. Psychol.*, 47:223–233.

Ackerman, N.W. (1955), Group psychotherapy with a mixed group of adolescents. *Internat. J. Group Psychother.*, 5:249–260.

Adelstein, D.M., Gelso, C.J., Haws, J.R., Reed, K.G., & Spiegel, S.B. (1983), The change process following time-limited therapy. In: *Explorations in Time-Limited Counseling and Psychotherapy,* eds. C.J. Gelso, & D.H. Johnson. New York: Teachers College, Columbia University, pp. 65–81.

Avery, A.W., Rider, K., & Haynes-Clements, L.A. (1981), Communication skills training for adolescents: A five month follow-up. *Adolescence,* 16:289–298.

Azima, F.J. Cramer (1970), A Multi-Levelled Explication of Projective Group Therapy. Unpublished doctoral dissertation. University of Montreal, Canada.

——— (1972), Transference–countertransference issues in group psychotherapy for adolescents. *Internat. J. Child Psychother.*, 4:51–70.

——— (1973), Transference–countertransference in adolescent group psychotherapy. In: *Group Therapy for the Adolescent*, eds. N.S. Brandes & M.L. Gardner. New York: Jason Aronson, pp. 101–126.

——— (1977), Effective communication in adolescent group therapy. In: *Psychotherapy—The Promised Land?*, eds. M. Berl & R. Vosberg. University, AL: University of Alabama Press, pp. 31–42.

——— (1982), Communication in adolescent group psychotherapy. In: *The Individual and the Group: Boundaries and Interrelations,* Vol. 2, eds. M. Pines & L. Rafelson. New York: Plenum Press, pp. 133–145.

——— (1983), Group psychotherapy with personality disorders. In: *Comprehensive Group Psychotherapy,* 2nd. ed., eds. H.I. Kaplan & B.J. Sadock. Baltimore: Williams & Wilkins, pp. 262–269.

——— (1985), Outpatient therapeutic servicing of children and adolescents: Review and preview. In: *Outpatient Psychiatry: Progress, Treatment, Prevention,* eds. R.E. Kogan & J.T. Salvendy. University, AL: University of Alabama Press, pp. 130–147.

Bales, R.F. (1950), *Interaction Process Analysis: A Method for the Study of Small Groups.* Cambridge, MA: Addison-Wesley.

——— (1970), *Personality and Interpersonal Behavior.* New York: Holt, Rinehart & Winston.

Battle, C., Imber, S., Hoehn-Saric, R., Stone, A., Nash, E., & Frank, J. (1966), Target complaints as criteria of improvement. *Amer. J. Psychother.*, 20:184–192.

Beck, A.T., Ward, C.H., Mendelson, N., Mock, J., & Erbaugh, J. (1961), An inventory for measuring depression. *Arch. Gen. Psychiat.*, 4:561–571.

Bennis, W.G. (1960), A critique of group therapy research. *Internat. J. Group Psychother.*, 10:63–77.

Berkowitz, I. (1972), *Adolescents Grow in Groups: Experience in Adolescent Group Psychotherapy.* New York: Brunner/Mazel.

Bernfield, G., Clark, L., & Parker, G. (1984), The process of adolescent group psychotherapy. *Internat. J. Group Psychother.*, 34:111–126.

Brandes, N.W. (1977), Group therapy is not for every adolescent: Two case illustrations. *Internat. J. Group Psychother.*, 27:507–510.

Brown, W., & Kingsley, R.F. (1975), The effect of individual contracting and guided group interaction upon behavior-disordered youth's self-concept. *J. School Health,* 45:399–401.

Budman, S., Demby, A., Feldstein, M., & Gold, M. (1984), Time-limited group psychotherapy. *Internat. J. Group Psychother.*, 34:587–603.

Campbell, D.T., & Stanley, J.C. (1963), *Experimental and Quasiexperimental Designs for Research.* Chicago: Rand-McNally.

Cattell, R.B., & Schier, I.H. (1963), *Handbook for the IPAT Anxiety Scale Questionnaire (Self-Analysis Form).* Champaign, IL: Institute for Personality and Ability Testing.

Christie, R., & Geis, F. (1970), *Studies in Machiavellianism.* New York: Academic Press.

Coché, E. (1983), Change measures and clinical practice in group psychotherapy. In: *Advances in Group Psychotherapy: Integrating Research and Practice,* eds. R.R. Dies & K.R. MacKenzie. New York: International Universities Press, pp. 79–101.

Cooper, C.L. (1977), Adverse and growthful effects of experiential learning groups: The role of the trainer, participant and group characteristics. *Hum. Rel.*, 30:1103–1129.

Coopersmith, S. (1967), *The Antecedents of Self-Esteem.* San Francisco: W.H. Freeman.

Corder, B.F., Whiteside, L., & Haizlip, T.M. (1981), A study of curative factors in group psychotherapy with adolescents. *Internat. J. Group Psychother.*, 31:345–354.

——— Cornwall, T., & Whiteside, R. (1984), Technique for increasing effectiveness of co-therapy functioning in adolescent psychotherapy groups. *Internat. J. Group Psychother.*, 34:643–654.

Cramer, F.J. (1949), The Study of Sympathetic Behavior Patterns in Pre-School Children. Unpublished master's thesis. Cornell University, Ithaca, New York.

Derogatis, L.R. (1977), *The SCL-90R, Administration, Scoring and Procedures Manual, I.* Baltimore: Clinical Psychometric Research.

Dies, R.R. (1973), Group therapist self-disclosure: Development and validation of a scale. *J. Consult. Clin. Psychol.*, 41:97–103.

——— (1977), Group leader disclosure scale. In: *The 1977 Annual Handbook for Group Facilitators,* eds. J.E. Jones & J.W. Pfeiffer. La Jolla, CA: University Associates.

——— (1983a), Bridging the gap between research and practice in group psychotherapy. In: *Advances in Group Psychotherapy: Integrating Research and Practice,* eds. R.R. Dies & R.K. MacKenzie. New York: International Universities Press, pp. 1–27.

——— (1983b), Clinical implications of research in leadership in short-term group psychotherapy. In: *Advances in Group Psychotherapy: Integrating Research and Practice*, eds. R.R. Dies & R.K. MacKenzie. New York: International Universities Press, pp. 27–78.

——— (in press), The multidimensional model of process research: Elaboration and critique. *Small Group Behav.*

——— Riester, A.E. (1986), Research on group therapy with children: Present status and future direction. In: *Child Group Psychotherapy: Future Tense,* eds. A.E. Riester & I. Kraft. Madison, CT: International Universities Press, pp. 173– 220.

Dimock, H.G. (1971), *How to Analyze and Evaluate Group Youth; Part I. How to Observe Your Group; Part II.* Leadership and Group Development Series. Montreal: Concordia University.

Fine, S., Knight-Webb, G., & Vernon, J. (1977), Selected volunteer adolescents in adolescent group therapy. *Adolescence,* 12:189–197.

Fisher, G.A., Drecksel, G.L., & Werbel, W.S. (1979), Social information processing analysis (SIPA): Coding ongoing human communication. *Small Group Behav.*, 10:3–21.

Geis, F., Christie, R., & Nelson, C. (1963), *In Search of the Machiavellians.* New York: Columbia University Press.

Gibbard, G.S., & Hartman, J.J. (1973), The oedipal paradigm in group development: A clinical and empirical study. *Small Group Behav.*, 4:305–354.

Gough, H.G., & Heilbrun, A.S., Jr. (1965), *The Adjective Checklist Manual.* Palo Alto, CA: Consulting Psychologists Press.

Gross, E.F. (1957), Empirical Study of the Concepts of Cohesiveness and Compatability. Unpublished honors thesis. Department of Social Relations, Harvard University, Cambridge, Mass.

Gurman, A.S., & Kniskern, D.P. (1981), Family therapy outcome research: Knowns and unknowns. In: *Handbook of Family Therapy,* eds. A.S. Gurman & D.P. Kniskern. New York: Brunner/Mazel, pp. 742–777.

Guy, W. (1976), *ECDEU Assessment Manual for Psychopharmocology.* Washington, DC: Department of Health, Education and Welfare.

Guyer II, C.G., & Matthews II, C.O. (1981) , Nonverbal warm-up exercises with adolescents: Effects on group counselling. *Small Group Behav.,* 12:55–67.

Hartman, J.J. (1979), Small group methods of personal change. *Ann. Rev. Psychol.,* 30:453–476.

Haynes, L.A., & Avery, A.W. (1979), Training adolescents in self disclosure and empathy skills. *J. Couns. Psychol.,* 26:526–530.

Hill, W.F. (1977), Hill interaction matrix (HIM): The conceptual framework, derived rating scales, and an updated bibliography. *Small Group Behav.,* 8:251–268.

Hurley, J.R., & Rosenthal, M. (1978), Interpersonal rating shifts during and after AGPA's institute groups. *Internat. J. Group Psychother.,* 28:115–121.

Hurst, A.G., Stein, K.B., Korchin, S.J., & Soskin, W.F. (1978), Leadership style determinants of cohesiveness in adolescent groups. *Internat. J. Group Psychother.,* 28:263–277.

Jesness, C.F. (1975), Comparative effectiveness of behavior modification and transactional analysis programs for delinquents. *J. Consult. Clin. Psychol.,* 43:758–779.

Katz, M.M., & Lyerly, S.B. (1963), Methods for measuring adjustment and social behavior in the community: I. Rationale, description, discriminative validity and scale development. *Psychol. Reports,* 13(2):503–535.

Kazdin, A.E. (1981), Drawing valid inferences from case studies. *J. Consult. Clin. Psychol.,* 49:183–192.

Kiresuk, T.J., & Sherman, R.E. (1968), Goal Attainment Scaling: A general method for evaluating comprehensive community mental programs. *Commun. Ment. Health J.,* 4:443–453.

Kraft, I.A. (1983), Child and adolescent group psychotherapy. In: *Comprehensive Group Psychotherapy,* 2nd ed., eds. H.I. Kaplan & B.J. Sadock. Baltimore: Williams & Wilkins, pp. 223–234.

Levin, S. (1983), The adolescent group as transitional object. *Internat. J. Group Psychother.,* 33:217–232.

Lieberman, M.A. (1983), Comparative analyses of change mechanisms in groups. In: *Advances in Group Psychotherapy: Integrating Research and Practice,* eds. R.R. Dies & K.R. MacKenzie. New York: International Universities Press, pp. 191–209.

——— Yalom I., & Miles, M. (1973), *Encounter Groups: First Facts.* New York: Basic Books.

Livesley, W.J., & MacKenzie, K.R. (1983), Social roles in psychotherapy groups. In: *Advances in Group Psychotherapy: Integrating Research and Practice,* eds. R.R. Dies & K.R. MacKenzie. New York: International Universities Press, pp. 117–137.

Lockwood, J.L. (1981), Treatment of disturbed children in verbal and experiential group psychotherapy. *Internat. J. Group Psychother.,* 31:355–366.

Luborsky, L. (1962), Clinicians' judgements of mental health. *Arch. Gen. Psychiat.*, 7:407–417.

MacKenzie, K.R. (1981), Measurement of group climate. *Internat. J. Group Psychother.*, 31:287–296.

——— (1983), The clinical application of a group climate measure. In: *Advances in Group Psychotherapy: Integrating Research and Practice,* eds. R.R. Dies & K.R. MacKenzie. New York: International Universities Press, pp. 159–171.

——— Dies, R.R. (1982), *The CORE Battery.* New York: American Group Psychotherapy Association.

McClosky, H., & Schaar, J.H. (1965), Psychological dimensions of anomie. *Amer. Sociol. Rev.*, 3:14–40.

McCullough, J.D. (1984a), Single case investigative research and its relevance for the nonoperant clinician. *Psychotherapy.*, 21(3):382–388.

——— (1984b), The need for new single-case design structure in applied cognitive psychology. *Psychotherapy*, 21(3):389–400.

Meyer, J.H., & Zegans, L.W. (1975), Adolescents perceive their psychotherapy. *Psychiatry,* 38:11–22.

Moos, R. (1974), *Evaluating Treatment Environments: A Social Ecological Approach.* New York: John Wiley.

Nichols, M.P., & Taylor, T.Y. (1975), Impact of therapist interventions on early sessions of group therapy. *J. Clin. Psychol.*, 31:726–729.

Oetting, E.R. (1976a), Evaluative research and orthodox science: Part 1. *Pers. Guid. J.*, 55:11–15.

——— (1976b), Planning and reporting evaluative research: Part 2. *Pers. Guid. J.*, 55:60–64.

Osgood, C.E. (1952), The nature and measurement of meaning. *Psychol. Bull.*, 49:197–237.

Parloff, M.B., & Dies, R.R. (1978), Group therapy outcome instrumentation: Guidelines for conducting research. *Small Group Behav.*, 9:243–286.

Pentz, M.A. (1981), The contribution of individual differences to assertion training outcome in adolescents. *J. Couns. Psychol.*, 28:529–532.

Persons, R. (1966), Psychological and behavioral change in delinquents following psychotherapy. *J. Clin. Psychol.*, 22:337–340.

——— (1967), Relationship between psychotherapy with institutionalized delinquent boys and subsequent community adjustment. *J. Consult. Psychol.*, 31:137–141.

Pfeiffer, J.W., Heslin, R., & Jones, J.E. (1973), *Instrumentation in Human Relations Training,* 2nd. ed. La Jolla, CA: University Associates.

Piper, W.E., Marrache, M., Lacroix, R., Richardsen, A.M., & Jones, B.D. (1983), Cohesion as a basic bond in groups. *Hum. Rel.*, 36(2):93–108.

Plutchik, R. (1980), *Emotions: A Psychoevolutionary Synthesis.* New York: Harper & Row.

Rachman, A. (1975), *Identity Group Psychotherapy with Adolescents.* Springfield, IL.: Charles C Thomas.

——— Raubolt, R.R. (1983), The pioneers of adolescent group psychotherapy. *Internat. J. Group Psychother.*, 34:387–413.

Raubolt, R.R. (1983), Brief, problem focused group psychotherapy with adolescents. *Amer. J. Orthopsychiat.*, 53:157–165.

Redfering, D.L. (1972), Group counseling with institutionalized delinquent females. *Amer. Corr. Ther. J.*, 26:160–163.

Reed, K.R. (1984), The applicability of the AGPA CORE Battery with adolescent psychotherapy groups. Paper presented at the 1984 Annual Conference of the American Group Psychotherapy Association, Dallas.
Richmond, L.H. (1974), Observations on private practice and community clinic adolescent psychotherapy groups. *Group Proc.,* 16:57–62
——— (1978), Some further observations on private practice and community clinic adolescent psychotherapy groups. *Correc. Soc. Psychiat.,* 24:57–61.
——— Gaines, T. (1979), Factors influencing with adolescents. *Adolescence,* 14:715–720.
——— ——— Fogt, M. (1981), The influence of parental participation on attendance and outcome of adolescent group psychotherapy. *J. Early Adol.,* 1:210–213.
Ricks, D.F. (1974), Supershrink: Methods of a therapist judged successful on the basis of adult outcomes of adolescent patients. In: *Life History Research in Psychopatholgy,* Vol. 3, eds. D.F. Ricks, A. Thomas, & M. Roff. Minneapolis: University of Minnesota Press, pp. 275–297.
Ro-Trock, G.K., Wellisch, D., & Schoolar, J.A. (1977), A family therapy outcome study in an inpatient setting. *Amer. J. Orthopsychiat.,* 47:514–522.
Rushton, A. (1982), Group work with adolescents in a girls' comprehensive school. *J. Adol.,* 5:267–284.
Sarason, I.G., & Sarason, B.R. (1981), Teaching cognitive and social skills to high school students. *J. Consult. Clin. Psychol.,* 49:908–918.
Schutz, W.C. (1967), *The FIRO Scales.* Palo Alto, CA: Consulting Psychologists Press.
Scott, E.M. (1980), The female delinquent narcissistic personality disorder: A case illustration. *Internat. J. Group Psychother.,* 30:503–508.
Silbergeld, S., Thune, E.S., & Manderscheid, R.W. (1979), The group therapist leadership role: Assessment in adolescent coping courses. *Small Group Behav.,* 10:176–199.
Singer, M. (1973), Durability of effects of group counseling with institutionalized delinquent females. *J. Abnorm. Psychol.,* 82:85–86.
——— (1974), Comments and caveats regarding adolescent groups in a combined approach. *Internat. J. Group Psychother.,* 24:429–438.
Snider, J.G., & Osgood, C.E. (1969), *Semantic Differential Technique.* Chicago: Aldine.
Spitzer, R.L., Endicott, J., Fleiss, J.L., & Cohen, J. (1970), The psychiatric status schedule. *Arch. Gen. Psychiat.,* 23:41–55.
Srole, L. (1956), Social integration and certain corrolaries: An explanatory study. *Amer. Sociol. Rev.,* 21:709–716.
Strupp, H.H., & Hadley, S.W. (1977), A tripartite model of mental health and therapy outcomes. *Amer. Psychol.,* 32:187–196.
Sugar, M. (1975), Office network therapy with adolescents. In: *The Adolescent in Group and Family Therapy,* ed. M. Sugar. New York: Brunner/Mazel.
——— (1979), Integration of therapeutic modalities in the treatment of an adolescent. *Internat. J. Group Psychother.,* 29:509–522.
Taylor, A. (1967), An evaluation of group psychotherapy in a girls' borstal. *Internat. J. Group Psychother.,* 17:168–177.
Tramontana, M.G. (1980), Critical review of research on psychotherapy outcome with adolescents: 1967–1977. *Psychol. Bull.,* 88:429–450.
Waskow, T.E., & Parloff, M.S., Eds. (1975), Psychotherapy Change Measures. Washington, DC: National Institute of Mental Health, U.S. Government Printing Office, Stock Number 1724-00397.

Weber, L.A. (1980), The effect of videotape and playback on an inpatient therapy group. *Internat. J. Group Psychother.*, 29:213–227.
Weissman, M.M., & Bothwell, S. (1976), Assessment of social adjustment by patient self report. *Arch. Gen. Psychiat.*, 33:1111–1115.
Zuckerman, M., & Lubin, B. (1965), *The Multiple Affect Adjective Checklist.* San Diego, CA: Educational and Industrial Testing Service.

Conclusion

FERN J. CRAMER AZIMA
LEWIS H. RICHMOND

The contributors to this book have demonstrated how they think and practice group psychotherapy with adolescents with different degrees of pathology and in various settings. Psychodynamic, psychoanalytic, existential, transactional, and behavioral theories and techniques are described in the treatment of inpatients, outpatients, the learning impaired, and addicted youth.

It has become increasingly clear that group therapy models for adolescents differ considerably from those practiced with children or adults (Cramer Azima, Rachman). Developmentally most adolescents have mastered verbal, symbolic, self-reflective, and interpretative thought but as yet have not adopted or integrated adult norms. Therapists working with adolescent groups differ in their own greater degree of activity, confrontation, spontaneity, and self disclosure. In addition, they are at greater ease with handling and working through the types of resistances and acting out of the teenager. They probably take themselves less seriously as authority figures and set boundaries more flexibly. They must be capable of empathizing both with the teen's conflicts as well as judiciously reflecting on the problems facing parents and society. In both dyadic and family therapies teenagers often withdraw, become silent, and rebel against parental authority and control. With their own peers they are more willing to listen and share problems more openly, with less mistrust or grievance. They are able to confront each other more honestly and admit their actual thoughts and feelings without fear of retribution or punishment. Over time they are able to internalize a code of values and behaviors that are acceptable both in and out of the therapy group. Additionally, the group modality offers the advantages of socialization, new learning, and mutual support.

Aside from these commonalities, the specificities of the treatment approaches are carefully delineated for the learning disabled, the problems encountered by teenagers and staff in school, and for those adolescents addicted to alcohol or drugs. One becomes increasingly aware of the extension and restriction of roles of the therapist working within the confines of school (Berkowitz), residence or hospital (Stein and Kymissis), or with forensic officers (Bratter, Raubolt). In some contexts parents or surrogates become part of the network treatment team, while in others they are vigorously excluded and the focus is on the developing autonomy of the teenager (Cramer Azima). Where parents pay for the therapy there is inevitably a need for the therapist to face this double loyalty. When cultural social systems (as for example in Canada) allow state payment and allow adolescents to seek treatment without parental consent after the age of sixteen, a different set of norms becomes operative. As a general rule the younger the patient, and the more severe the diagnosis, parents become part of the extended treatment (Richmond, Stein, and Kymissis; Coché and Fisher).

When there is the question of addiction, countertransference reactions to families, surrogates, and legal authorities add to the therapist's dilemma. Bratter and Raubolt detail their unique strategies in coping with these realities. Coché and Fisher, dealing with the learning disabled and retarded, demonstrate the effectiveness of an eclectic, theoretical approach within the confines of a residence that promotes change. Berkovitz's chapter deals with the consultative role in schools and the work in groups with teachers, principals, and counsellors. In this instance a training/supervision model is employed. In other settings group psychotherapy with students may be practiced within the school. The students with more severe problems are most often referred to more intensive treatment settings.

The final chapter on clinical research (Cramer Azima and Dies) has been prepared with the purpose of offering practical instruments and suitable methodologies to encourage research in the adolescent area, both in the areas of process and outcome studies. Clinicians have all too often been fearful of integrating research designs into their clinical practice.

It is hoped that a future monograph will update the technique of groups with adolescents who are chronically ill or suffer from AIDS, and those who have been abused and have been traumatized by difficult family divorce or loss. The role of preventive group therapy for young adolescents is an area of considerable importance to influence the inhibition of alcohol and drug consumption. Groups for runaways, homeless, and teens with gender disorders are gaining importance.

Lastly, the editors are hopeful that this monograph will make a helpful contribution to the training of professionals, in the group psychotherapy treatment and research of adolescents.

Name Index

Subject Index